India's sub-nationalisms come draped in discourses of culture but Pritam Singh's thesis is that the paramountcy of the project of Indian nation-building has forced individual states to play idiosyncratic roles – with profound consequences for the character of their sub-nationalisms. He illustrates this dramatically with the case of Punjab. Through flows of public finance the agricultural wealth of this culturally and geopolitically distinctive state has been harnessed nationally to the detriment of its balanced development. By 1991, Punjab was a curious paradox – a rich food bowl with a stunted industrial economy. Through his fine-grained research, Pritam Singh has made a significant contribution to our understanding of the politics of cultural aspiration and the political economy of federalism.

(Barbara Harriss-White, Professor of Development Studies and Director of the Department of International Development, Queen Elizabeth House, University of Oxford)

Dr Singh's book must be read by those interested in modern India. It deals with the central issue in Indian politics and planning at a pivotal stage in the nation's development.

(Ceri Peach, Professor of Social Geography, University of Oxford)

This book is a major contribution to the political economy of the Punjab, to the analysis of centre–state relations in the post-independence Indian union, and to the study of regional economic development in federally organised states. One of its strengths is its wide reach in terms of scholarship and analysis – it integrates knowledge from economic history, ethnic studies, geography and constitutional analysis.

(Colin Clarke, Emeritus Professor of Geography, University of Oxford, and Senior Research Fellow, Jesus College, Oxford)

FEDERALISM, NATIONALISM AND DEVELOPMENT

This book throws new light on the study of India's development through an exploration of the triangular relationship between federalism, nationalism and the development process. It focuses on one of the seemingly paradoxical cases of impressive development and sharp federal conflicts that have been witnessed in the state of Punjab. The book concentrates on the federal structure of the Indian polity and it examines the evolution of the relationship between the centre and the state of Punjab, taking into account the emergence of Punjabi Sikh nationalism and its conflict with Indian nationalism. Providing a template to analyse regional imbalances and tensions in national economies with federal structures and competing nationalisms, this book will not only be of interest to researchers on South Asian studies, but also to those working in the fields of politics, political economy, geography and development.

Pritam Singh is Senior Lecturer in Economics, Oxford Brookes University Business School, UK. His research focuses on radical political economy and development, secularism and religious revivalism; and nationalism, development and human rights. He is on the editorial board of several journals including *North East India Studies*, *Journal of Punjab Studies* and *International Journal of Green Economics*.

ROUTLEDGE CONTEMPORARY SOUTH ASIA SERIES

1 PAKISTAN
Social and cultural transformations in a Muslim nation
Mohammad A. Qadeer

2 LABOR, DEMOCRATIZATION AND DEVELOPMENT IN INDIA AND PAKISTAN
Workers and unions
Christopher Candland

3 CHINA–INDIA RELATIONS
Contemporary dynamics
Amardeep Athwal

4 MADRASAS IN SOUTH ASIA
Teaching terror?
Jamal Malik

5 LABOR, GLOBALIZATION AND THE STATE
Workers, women and migrants confront neoliberalism
Edited by Debdas Banerjee and Michael Goldfield

6 INDIAN LITERATURE AND POPULAR CINEMA
Recasting classics
Edited by Heidi R. M. Pauwels

7 ISLAMIST MILITANCY IN BANGLADESH
A complex web
Ali Riaz

8 REGIONALISM IN SOUTH ASIA
Negotiating co-operation, institutional structures
Kishore C. Dash

9 FEDERALISM, NATIONALISM AND DEVELOPMENT
India and the Punjab economy
Pritam Singh

FEDERALISM, NATIONALISM AND DEVELOPMENT

India and the Punjab economy

Pritam Singh

Routledge
Taylor & Francis Group
LONDON AND NEW YORK

First published 2008
by Routledge
2 Park Square, Milton Park, Abingdon, Oxon OX14 4RN

Simultaneously published in the USA and Canada
by Routledge
270 Madison Ave, New York, NY 10016

Routledge is an imprint of the Taylor & Francis Group, an informa business

Typeset in Times by Wearset Ltd, Boldon, Tyne and Wear
Printed and bound in Great Britain by TJI Digital, Padstow, Cornwall

British Library Cataloguing in Publication Data
A catalogue record for this book is available from the British Library

Library of Congress Cataloging in Publication Data
A catalog record for this book has been requested

ISBN10: 0-415-45666-5 (hbk)
ISBN10: 0-203-93020-7 (ebk)

ISBN13: 978-0-415-45666-1 (hbk)
ISBN13: 978-0-203-93020-5 (ebk)

IN THE MEMORY OF MY FATHER
SARDAR HUKAM SINGH GILL
(1917–2004)

CONTENTS

TABLES

PREFACE AND ACKNOWLEDGEMENTS

My intellectual interests in this area of study were triggered by a convergence of several forms of theoretical and political crises in the 1980s and 1990s. The disintegration of the Soviet Union and Yugoslavia raised several difficult questions about the relationship between Marxism, nationalism and strategies of planned development models. India witnessed traumatic events – the Indian army's storming of the Golden Temple in Punjab, the assassination of India's Prime Minister Indira Gandhi, unprecedented violence against the minority Sikh community, the eruption of secessionist movements in Punjab, Kashmir, Assam and its neighbouring north-eastern states. The crisis of federalism in India was accompanied by the crisis of its development model and the launch of a new regime of neo-liberal economic reforms. In the midst of these multiple forms of crises, my theoretical orientation towards Marxism inspired my search for internationalist perspectives while my family background simultaneously challenged me to think about Punjab. My co-edited book *Punjabi Identity in a Global Context* reflected this intellectual struggle to marry the global, regional and the personal (Singh and Thandi 1999). The Indian national state mediated and transformed this global–regional linkage. I was fascinated with the idea of exploring the process of global capital accumulation mediated through a nation state and operating at a regional, sub-national level in the tradition of political economy. Thus, in this book, I have focused on the mediation of the Indian nation state in shaping the regional development pattern in Punjab, and on exploring the politico-economic dimensions of the inter-relationship between the Indian central state and Indian nationalism. I pay particular attention to India's federal economic architecture both as a product of the politico-economic objectives of Indian nationalism as well as the vehicle to drive forward the project of Indian nationalism. Within this federal politico-economic structure, which specifies divisions of powers and responsibilities between the centre and the states, I have studied the role of central planning not only as an economic regulatory mechanism for India's development path but also as a political regulatory mechanism for nation-building.

It is commonly believed that the states in the Indian federation became organized as territorial units primarily on the basis of language. This study claims that each state also represented a sub-national community, and highlights the strategic role of the centre in constructing a unified Indian nationhood out of the diverse regional nationalisms located in the states. I put forward a new interpretation of centre–state relations in India as a dialectical interplay of the interests of Indian nationalism and several state-based regional nationalisms. By deploying this new interpretation, this study explores the political economy of the relations between the central government in India and Punjab, as an arena of contest between the project of Indian nationalism and the politico-economic aspirations of regional Punjabi nationalism.

This study has evolved over a long period of time during which I have benefited from a variety of interactions with a large number of persons. It started with a doctoral thesis at the University of Oxford. Barbara Harriss-White and David Harvey were most influential in shaping its direction at the earlier stage. They subjected my ideas and overall perspective to sharp critical scrutiny, and commented extensively on the earlier versions of Chapters 1, 3 and 4. David's comments encouraged me to think about larger theoretical issues regarding capital accumulation and formation of regions, and Barbara was meticulous in scrutinizing every line and formulation about India. I was sometimes overwhelmed with their criticisms from two apparently contradictory directions but eventually always felt enriched by the complementarity in their approaches towards my work. Gavin Williams commented extensively on the earlier versions of chapters 4 and 5, which deal with federal finance and the Green Revolution. I learnt a lot from his knowledge about peasant economies and federalism in Africa, in particular South Africa and Nigeria. Ceri Peach read most of the chapters in their more developed form. I am deeply indebted to him for his academic guidance and moral support in bringing this work to its completion. Colin Clarke's generous appreciation of my research and strong encouragement to publish was a powerful catalyst in getting this book out. My thanks also to Andrew Graham, Judith Heyer and Alan Montefiore for their general academic advice and support at different stages of this work.

During the last several years when this work has been in the making, I have benefited from discussions with many friends who included experienced academics and young researchers. I have had several chats with Meghnad Desai regarding my dissatisfaction about the inadequate development of the Marxian approach towards the study of centre–state relations. Too often his favourite and challenging reply was: if you are unhappy with the existing theory, develop one yourself. I thank him for the interest he always showed in my work. The late T. V. Sathyamurthy was one scholar with whose approach towards Indian federalism I felt great affinity. I have had many fruitful discussions with him. I felt his death personally, and it was a huge loss to the studies of federalism in India

In Oxford, I have shared my ideas on centralization and decentralization, development trends and competing nationalisms in India with many friends in several formal and informal ways. These people included Robin Archer, Rochana Bajpai, Jairus Banaji, Rohini Banaji, Judith Brown, Nandini Gooptu,

Yasmin Khan, Jesse Kharbanda, Iftikhar Malik, Tapan Raychaudhuri and Rajeswari Sunder Rajan. I have benefited also from discussions with Robert Cassen, the late Sanjay Lal, Neville Maxwell and Frances Stewart.

I have used the opportunity of visits to Oxford of several friends from India and Pakistan to discuss with them many of my ideas on the political economy and history of South Asia, India and Punjab. In particular, I must mention the names of Bina Agarwal, Imran Ali, Pritam Baruah, Bhupinder Brar, Satya Pal Gautam, Sucha Singh Gill, J. S. Grewal, Surinder Jhodka, Bhagwan Josh, Pramod Kumar, Ram Narayan Kumar, Harish Puri, Mahesh Rangarajan, Ahmad Salim, Arvinder Singh, Birinder Pal Singh, Iqbal Singh, Atul Sood, Mohammed Waseem and Yoginder Yadav.

On the dialectics of regional and national economic development in India, I have had some very fruitful exchanges of ideas with V. N. Balsubramanyam, G. S. Bhalla, Vijay Joshi and Ben Rogaly.

On many aspects of the history of Punjab and the Sikhs, I have gained from discussions and exchange of views with Jeevan Deol, Sewa Singh Kalsi, Hew Mcleod, Eleanor Nesbitt, Kanta Rhodes, Gurharpal Singh, Gurinder Mann, Nikki Guninder Kaur Singh and Pashaura Singh even when I have differed very seriously on some occasions.

I have enjoyed stimulating discussions on a range of economic and political issues concerning Punjab's place in India's federal structure with Ishtiaq Ahmed, the late Nirmal Azad, Gurdarshan Singh Dhillon, Virinder Kalra, Ajit Khaira, Baljit Malik, Harkishan Singh Mehta, Joyce Pettigrew, Tej Purewal, Ajit Singh, Bhupinder Singh, Gurbhagat Singh, Gurtej Singh, Patwant Singh, Pritam Singh PCS/IAS, Harjinder Shergill, Ian Talbot, Darshan Tatla, Dharam Vir and Paul Wallace.

I wish to thank Katharine Adeney, James Chiriyankandath and Emma Mawdsley for co-organizing panels with me on federalism and nationalism in South Asia at the European Conference on Modern South Asian Studies at Heidelberg (2002), Leiden (2006) and Edinburgh (2000), respectively, and Shinder Thandi for co-organizing panels on Punjab economy at the International Congress on Asian and African Studies (Hong Kong in 1993 and Budapest in 1997) and the European Conference on Modern South Asian Studies at Prague (1998) and Edinburgh (2000). These conference panel discussions were absolutely vital for me not only to test my ideas but also for further development of them. I also wish to thank all those who contributed papers to these panels.

In India, my friend Pramod Kumar's help in procuring the publications and documents of the Government of Punjab was absolutely vital. Some of the officials of the Punjab government who were especially helpful in Chandigarh in providing and arranging information on Punjab economy were B. R. Bajaj, R. N. Gupta, Rajan Kashyap, Amitabh Pandey, Amrik Singh Pooni and Harbhajan Singh. In Delhi, Pawan Chopra, Chitra Chopra, Surina Chetal and her husband Rajan, and Gurpreet Maini helped in obtaining the copies of the publications and documents of the Government of India. Pawan and Chitra Chopra also helped with acquiring the copies of the documents of the Government of Rajasthan. Similarly, Shanta Sinha helped with documents of the Government of Andhra Pradesh. The late Krishna Raj, the editor of *Economic and Political Weekly*, was also kind enough to send me some important official publications. Those who research on India know very well that without helpful friends it is very difficult, if not impossible, to get hold of government documents. My sincere thanks to all of them for providing this vital support.

Ranjit Singh, Ajmer Singh and my younger brother Hardeep Gill helped me by sending many cuttings from Indian newspapers relating to my work. I thank them warmly.

I am thankful to Oriel College and the Committee for Graduate Studies, University of Oxford, for two travel grants for covering some of the expenses for the field trips to India. I am grateful to the trustees of the Edward Boyle Memorial Trust and the Charles Wallace Trust for awarding me the Edward Boyle/Charles Wallace (India) Research Scholarship. University of Oxford also awarded me a research scholarship. I gratefully acknowledge this financial assistance.

Staff at the University of Oxford's various libraries, especially the Indian Institute Library, have been very helpful. At Oxford Brookes University, staff at the Wheatley Campus library and the inter-library loan section of the Gypsy Lane Campus library have been very generous in dealing with my requests for books and journals.

I am grateful to Oxford Brookes University Business School for giving me some relief from my teaching duties for doing research which has contributed to the writing of this book. All my colleagues at the Department of Economics and Strategy have been friendly and supportive. I take this opportunity to thank especially Andy Kilmister for his friendship and support during all these years. I wish to also thank Judith Piggott for being a very helpful colleague.

I must mention Punjab Research Group (UK) and the British Association for South Asian Studies for providing me the platform for sharing my ideas at the earlier stages of development of this project.

Sher Verick, Iqbal Sevea, Ludmilla Miteva, Boryana Bratanova, Daisy, Valia, Dani and Manvir Singh have helped me with typing, tabulation of data and cataloguing of my resources. My sincere thanks to all of them.

My daughter Tanya Singh and friend Bill MacKeith deserve special thanks. I thank Bill MacKeith for generously giving me his time, and the benefit of his wide experience, by reading earlier versions of some of my chapters. He tried to weed out as many of my English mistakes as he could, encouraging greater consistency and adherence to international practice. Tanya read all the chapters meticulously, was lovingly ruthless in demanding consistency and clarity, and made many suggestions for amendments. If after all this, there are still errors, I am entirely responsible.

We have been very fortunate to have a large group of very loving friends at Oxford though some of them have now moved away. In particular, I must mention the names of Robin Archer and Elisabeth Koegler, Mohammad and Nuzhat Abbas, Hanjo Glock and Gabi, Bill MacKeith and Liz Perez, Iftikhar and Nighat Malik, Ben Rogaly and Kirat Randhawa, and Shinderpal and Surinder. I take this opportunity to thank all of them for their love, friendship and support.

I especially thank my mother-in-law Sushila Dhanda for taking over my share of housework during her many visits and making time for me to concentrate on my writing. I must also thank my elder brother Balwinder Singh Gill for reading the whole draft of the book. With his experience in Indian banking, his feedback was very valuable in understanding the mechanism of financial flows in India's federal banking system. His emotional support at the last stage of the work had a calming influence during some difficult moments.

Dorothea Schaefter at Routledge deserves special thanks for the keen interest she has shown at every stage of this project. She was superb in providing much needed support and guidance whenever it was needed. Tom Bates was also very helpful. Thanks also to Susannah Wight, the copy-editor and Allie Waite the production editor, for their excellent support and cooperation.

I am thankful to Nigel James at the Bodleian Library Map Room, and Atul Sood and Kamlesh Poonia at Jawaharlal Nehru University, New Delhi for their suggestions and help regarding the map.

My wife Meena Dhanda has been an indispensable intellectual companion. I depended continuously on her philosophical expertise for testing the logical coherence and connections between different arguments. She and Tanya have been engaged with my research throughout, becoming deeply involved in its final stages. They spent many hours in helping me with almost every aspect of this work. I acknowledge their contribution with gratitude and love.

Pritam Singh
Oxford, 2008.

NOTE ON TERMINOLOGY

In the Indian literature on federalism, the usual practice is to capitalize many common nouns, such as centre, state, union, constitution, prime minister and government. I have chosen here to follow international standard practice on the whole, while retaining capitalization in the term 'Union territory' since it is used in a specific sense to refer to a territorial space that is directly controlled by the central government in Delhi.

Wherever the term 'state' is used in an abstract sense to refer to the government or a bureaucratic structure with an 'ideological state apparatus', it is either clear from the context or the specific use of the term has been mentioned.

Those Punjabi and Hindi words that have not been commonly absorbed into English have been italicized, and I have provided the brief meaning of the word e.g. *langar* (community cooking and eating of food). I have normally retained the use of 'crore' and 'lakh' to express the numerical value of some figures as used in the Indian literature. A crore is equal to ten millions and a lakh is equal to 100,000.

ABBREVIATIONS

BE	budget estimates
CMIE	Centre for Monitoring Indian Economy
CSO	Central Statistical Organisation
DWT	dead-weight tonnage
FC	Finance Commission
FCI	Food Corporation of India
GDP	gross domestic product
Govt	Government
GSDP	gross state domestic product
IDA	International Development Association
IDR Act	Industrial Development and Regulation Act
IMF	International Monetary Fund
LIC	Life Insurance Corporation
NDP	Net Domestic Product
NNP	Net National Product
OECD	Organisation for Economic Co-operation and Development
PC	Planning Commission
RBI	Reserve Bank of India
RE	revised estimates
SAP	Statistical Abstract of Punjab
SDP	state domestic product
SGPC	Shiromani Gurdwara Parbandhak Committee (Central Gurdwara Management Committee)
UT	Union territory

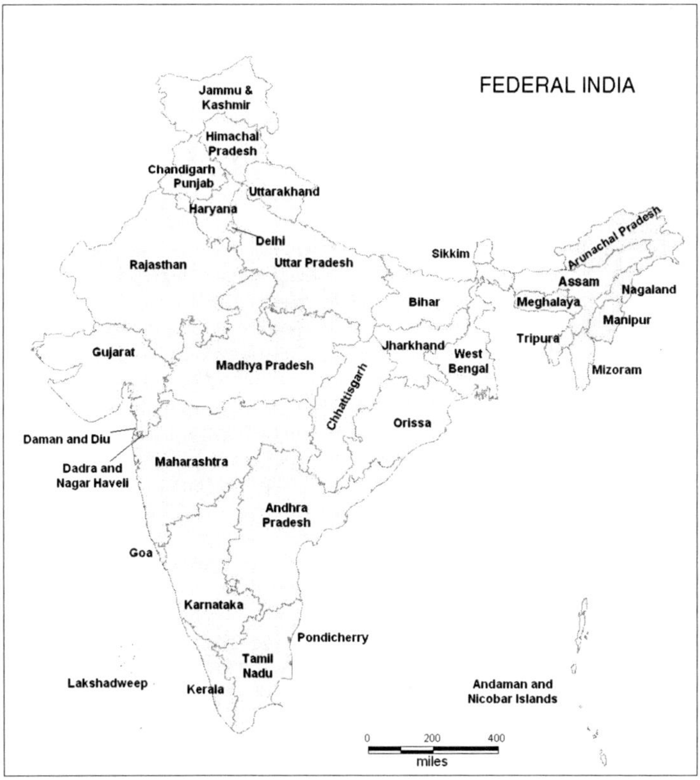

Figure 0.1 Map of Federal India (source: © 2007 Europa Technologies Ltd).

1

INTRODUCTION

The pattern of development of a region in a country with multiple nationalisms is different from that in a nationally homogenous country in one critical respect: the framework of negotiated relations between the region and the centre in a country with multiple nationalisms tends to become an influential institutional factor. Federalism, as a system of inter-governmental relations between the federal centre and the regions, provinces and states, developed out of the need to reconcile the goals of regional and national development in multi-national countries. Being a system of negotiated accommodation between the two parties – the centre on one hand and the states on the other – this arrangement is bound to be a dialectical mixture of harmony and conflict, satisfaction and dissatisfaction. To the extent that regional development is facilitated by the national pattern of development, it is likely to lead to a successful and strengthened federation; and to the extent that goals of national development entail neglecting the development of a region or demand sacrifices from a region for the sake of national development, it is likely to put the federation under strain. Neglect of a region or economic sacrifice from a region may follow either because of the necessity to centralize control over the utilization of resources or because of the necessity to transfer resources from one region to another (Schoenfeld 1960, Blough 1962, Svennilson 1962, Lakdawala 1967, Grewal 1975, Grewal 1986). Transfer of resources may take place due to the relatively weak bargaining power of the region being neglected vis-à-vis the centre or for the ostensible purpose of achieving balanced regional development. A federation may, therefore, come under stress due to either region–centre conflict (a vertical conflict) or a region–region conflict (a horizontal conflict), or a mixture of the two, with varying degrees of importance of these two forms of conflict.

As an area of study, federalism and development seems to attract more scholarly attention when federations fail or are in crisis than when they are successful (see Dikshit 1975, Hicks 1978, Davey 1983, Rath 1984, Hardy and Mihaljek 1992). Although only about 20 government systems out of the 150 or so territorial states can be considered as federal according to their constitutions, in terms of area, federations represent some of the largest national entities in the world: the United States of America (USA), Canada, Australia, Brazil, Argentina,

Venezuela, Mexico, Germany, India, Pakistan, Nigeria, Tanzania and South Africa. More than half of the inhabited space of the world lives under a federal form of government of one sort or another (Merkl 1975, Rath 1984). Federalism was a key issue in the negotiations between the Christian Democrats and the Social Democrats on the formation of a coalition government in Germany (Williamson 2005). The contestation on the dimensions of federalism in the Iraqi constitution and the growing power of Russia over its regions have also attracted serious media commentary on issues of federalism and governance (Anon 2005, 2005a).

The pre-Second World War federations such as the federations of the USA, Canada, Australia and Switzerland seem to be cases of successful federations, though Canada has faced a crisis in the Quebec region (Leslie 1988, Birch 1989). The former Union of Socialist Republics (USSR), the former Yugoslavia, Pakistan, the former Czechoslovakia and Ethiopia are some well-known examples where some of the units of these failed federations became independent nation states (Leff 1999). India and Sri Lanka in Asia (Phandis 1989), Nigeria and Sudan in Africa, and Spain in Europe are some of the cases which have witnessed a high level of tension in their federal political arrangements (Birch 1989). Cases of both lessening regional inequality and accentuating regional inequality have acted as catalysts for regions to feel dissatisfied with federal arrangements (Wheare 1962, Williamson 1965, Holland 1976, Davey 1983). If regional inequalities are accompanied by the conflicts of ethnicity and nationalism, the relationship of a region to the federal centre becomes even more conflict-ridden (Blaut 1987, Johnston *et al.* 1988, Keating 1988, Pritam Singh 1990, Sinha 2005).[1]

The most well-known cases of regional conflict with the federal centre are likely to be those where the region, because of its relative economic backwardness, feels dissatisfied with the prevailing structure of economic relations with the centre (Keating 1988, Birch 1989). North-eastern states (Assam, Nagaland and Mizoram) in India, the Kosovo region in the former Yugoslavia, Corsica in France, Sind in Pakistan and the Tamil region in Sri Lanka may be considered cases of this category (Blaut 1987, Keating 1988, Birch 1989, Phandis 1989, Rao and Singh 2005). The other, opposite, category of cases where a relatively developed region is in conflict with the centre may include the Basque region in Spain, Slovenia in former Yugoslavia, and the Baltic states (Lithuania, Estonia and Latvia) in the former USSR (Bookman 1991).

This study aims to capture the implications of Indian federal arrangements for Punjab's development pattern. My main thesis is that in order to overcome national food deficiency, the centre has exploited Punjab's agricultural resources to the detriment of Punjab's own need for all-round and diversified development.

In the mid-1960s, a national crisis of food scarcity led the Indian planning authorities to incorporate Punjab into the Green Revolution strategy, a strategy initiated for the maximization of national food output. This contributed to agricultural prosperity in Punjab in the 1960s and early 1970s. However, to sustain economic development, Punjab needed to diversify its economy by developing its industrial sector. Like all developing economies in their earlier stage of transition to industrialization, Punjab needed public sector investment for its industrialization. This crucial public sector investment was denied to Punjab by India's planning authorities for the sake of regional equalities and national integration. The diversification of Punjab's economy was thwarted. This created the material conditions for conflict between the aspirations of regional Punjabi nationalism and the needs of Indian nationalism articulated by the centre. This conflict further damaged Punjab's economic development.

Contextualizing Punjab

Punjab is one of the northern states of India. It is relatively small in terms of territory and population size but significant in terms of its economic, political and strategic importance in the Indian federation. The name Punjab derives from the Persian term *panj-ab* (five-waters), thus referring to a land of five rivers.[2] Punjab has a geographical unity distinct from neighbouring countries and the rest of India (Khushwant Singh 1999: 3). It was once dry desert land between the Khyber Pass and the Ganga basin, beyond the constricted passage between the Delhi Ridge and the Himalayan foothills. The rainfall from the south-west monsoon, which blows up the Ganges Valley from the Bay of Bengal, dies out as it reaches the Khyber. The semi-nomadic warriors inhabiting this dry Punjab, the entry-point to the wealth of India, contested this region with invaders from the north west. While attempting to control this region and block the external threat from the Khyber, the British developed an irrigation system based on the five rivers. Thus Punjab was transformed into an agricultural land of canal colonies in the nineteenth century, giving it a distinctive economic identity. Additionally, with the development of the Sikh religion, founded by Guru Nanak in the fifteenth century, Punjab came to be substantially occupied by a group with a distinctive religion, ethnicity and territorial identity.

The present Punjab acquired its distinct geographical and political identity as a Punjabi-speaking state in 1966. The focus of our study is on the period from 1966 to 1991, though the pre-1966 period is also taken into account to provide the historical context. I have also attempted to draw out the significance of the pre-1991 policy of economic development guided by central planning for the post-1991 period, when the Indian central government initiated a new policy regime of liberalization and structural adjustment in conformity with the World Bank and IMF perspective.

The planning policy regime operates within the framework of the Indian federal structure. The Indian constitution specifies the division of economic and political powers between the centre and the states. This study is, therefore, an exploration of the development experience of the state of Punjab as a part of the Indian federal state's experience of planned economic development.

Planning was viewed by the Indian federal state as a key political as well as economic tool with which to weld India into a strong unified nation. 'Jawaharlal Nehru [the first prime minister of independent India] thought of development planning as the new, strong and positive bond that would hold the country together' (Paranjape 1970: 34). The project of nation-making in India therefore included a process of framing the constitutional divisions of power between the centre and the states, setting up a planned development strategy, and then actually implementing constitutional provisions and the planning strategy.

Between 1966 and 1991 Punjab attracted the attention of academic scholars and policy planners predominantly for two reasons. In the 1960s and 1970s the success of the Green Revolution strategy in increasing food output was the most prominent issue concerning Punjab, while in the 1980s it was the rise of militant confrontation between the Punjabi/Sikh nationalists and the Indian federal state that attracted global attention.

Both the Green Revolution and Sikh militancy raised questions about the economic and political placing of Punjab in the federal structure of India's economic and political governance. The Green Revolution seemed to be a story of successful development, while the rise of Sikh militancy indicated some fault lines in the Indian state's federal political management.

Punjab: rich but not developed

Punjab between 1966 and 1991 seemed to present a mixed picture. By one criterion (per capita income), it was in the category of richer states in India.[3] By this criterion, Punjab may be more appropriately placed along with the second category of cases of regional conflict discussed earlier. However, judging by another criterion (degree of industrialization), Punjab appears in the category of less developed states in India. On the basis of the level of industrial production (aggregate net income generated in registered factory production, 1984–85), Punjab ranked 13th among the 25 Indian states and the Union territories (Govt of Punjab 1989: 370). In terms of per capita net income generated in the registered factory production sector, Punjab ranked 12th.[4] Based on the share of the secondary sector in state domestic product, Punjab had the lowest position among the 17 major states in India in 1990–91 (Bhattacharya and Sakthivel 2004). Agriculture, therefore, is the main contributor to Punjab's relatively higher per capita income level. Agriculture, as the mainstay of the economy, may be viewed as a sign of a weak structure for economic development and it may be argued that it belongs to the first category of cases of regional conflict mentioned above.

Two different indicators (per capita aggregate income, share of the secondary sector in the state domestic product) for comparing levels of economic performance may give two different perspectives on the contribution of centre–state economic relations to Punjab's economic development. One view, which may be described as the federal centre's view or the Indian nationalist view, can be put as follows:[5]

> The centre has pursued an agrarian policy in the constitutional framework of centre–state economic relations that has raised Punjab's per capita income to one of the highest levels among the Indian states. The centre's contribution has made Punjab the most developed agrarian region in the country. The classes/strata which have accumulated agrarian capital want the centre to pursue a similarly favourable industrial policy in order to help these strata to make transition to industrial capital. The centre cannot concede this demand because such an industrial policy will accentuate regional inequalities. The centre, in its role as nation-builder, has to follow a package of policies which lead to balanced regional development. The centre's inability to concede Punjab's demands has bred Punjab's dissatisfaction with the federal arrangement and has given birth to demands for state autonomy or secession. Such an approach on the part of those demanding autonomy or secession, apart from not being in the national interest, is short-sighted from the viewpoint of Punjab's interests also. Ultimately the federal centre's policy of balanced regional development will lead to a higher level of national development as a whole and this will be conducive to Punjab's development as well. Therefore, the existing pattern of centre–state economic relations is conducive, albeit in the long run, to Punjab's further economic development.

The opposite view, which may be considered the Punjabi nationalist view, can be summed up as follows:[6]

> Punjab, having been integrated into the federal centre's goal of national development through the network of centre–state economic relations, was forced to concentrate on agricultural development and that also on mainly two crops (wheat and paddy). According to the index number of agricultural production in Punjab (base: triennium ending 1969–70 = 100), the weight of food grain crops was 61.19 and that of the wheat–rice combination alone was 40.77 in 1969–70 (Govt of Punjab 1989: 172–173). This food grain oriented (mainly two-crop) agrarian economy hinders the diversification of agricultural development. Punjab's small-scale industrial structure does not have the potentiality of generating diversified and large-scale industrialization of the region. The federal centre, having contributed to Punjab's agricultural development in a specific way, chooses to concentrate public sector investment (crucial to industrialization in a less industrialized economy) in other states with the objective of attaining balanced regional development. The centre, through control of the licensing system in the existing structure of centre–state economic relations, has refused to grant licenses in adequate number either to the Punjab government or to Punjabi industrialists to set up industrial units in the public and private

> sector, respectively. Severe constraints are imposed even on expanding existing productive capacity. The structure of centre–state economic relations has, therefore, become an institutional fetter on Punjab's industrialization and further economic development. It is only through a fundamental restructuring of these economic relations and, failing that, through snapping ties with the federal centre that Punjab can move ahead on the path to autonomous, self-sustaining and internally articulated diversified agricultural and industrial development.

My study is situated in the context of these two competing contentions about the implications of centre–state economic relations for the Punjab economy.

The existing literature on centre–Punjab economic relations can be divided into two categories: journalistic and academic. The journalistic writings, some of which are of good quality, are either broad generalizations or on-the-spot quick impressions about some aspects of Punjab agriculture and industry.[7] The academic writings, very few in number, are in the form of chapters in edited books or journal articles.[8] So glaring is the absence of serious academic work on the subject that, so far, there is not even one book written on the subject.[9]

The forces and factors that determine the development of a state's economy in a federal structure may be classified into two categories: external and internal. Among the external factors, one may include historical and existing relations with the world economy and the national economy. Within the national economy, one can include the federal government and the other states in the federation. Among the internal factors, one may include: the endowment of resources (natural and human); the pattern of income/asset distribution in the industrial, agricultural and tertiary sectors; the consumption, savings and investment patterns; employer–employee relations; and the political, social and cultural institutions. The development process, in the end, can be viewed as the resultant effect of the interaction between the external and internal factors. The process of interaction, in turn, influences the behaviour of external and internal factors.

Of all these external and internal factors, the scope of my work is limited to focusing on an examination of the influence of only one of the external factors on the Punjab economy – that is, the federal centre–Punjab economic relations. To examine the implications of centre–state economic relations in India for Punjab's economy, I have focused on three aspects: state finances, agriculture and industry. To keep the present study within manageable limits, this study does not go into the implications of Punjab's horizontal economic relations with other states for the Punjab economy.

In studies on centre–state relations in India, the overwhelming emphasis has been on centre–state financial relations. The study of centre–state relations in the fields of agriculture and industry has largely been neglected. The main reasons for this lopsided emphasis on financial relations can be identified as follows:

1 These relations (financial) directly affect the revenue and expenditure accounts of the annual budgets of the central and state governments. The bargaining over respective shares is, therefore, clearly visible and has immediate consequences.
2 Relatively speaking, there are more clearly defined constitutional provisions and institutional arrangements for regulating centre–state financial relations than for regulating centre–state relations in agriculture and industry. For example, in comparison with the Finance Commission (appointed every five years or less often), there is no one institution to regulate centre–state relations in agriculture and industry.

I have identified four approaches used in the substantial literature on centre–state financial relations: compensatory criterion vs redistributive criterion; resource position vs expenditure responsibilities; constitutionalist; and centralization vs decentralization. The meagre literature on centre–state relations in agriculture and industry can be classified under two approaches: constitutionalist and issue-oriented.

The main approaches to the study of centre–state financial relations

The main approaches to the study of centre–state financial relations are to consider the compensatory criterion vs the redistributive criterion, the resource position vs expenditure responsibilities, the constitutionalist approach and centralization vs decentralization.

Compensatory criterion vs redistributive criterion (or relative weighting of the two)

The compensatory criterion examines a state's contribution to the total taxable revenue and the compensation to the state in terms of transfers to it from this central pool. The redistributive criterion examines whether the pattern of transfers from the centre reduces or increases regional inequalities in the resource position of different states. Relatively rich states advocate the compensatory criterion and justify this on grounds of efficiency, while the relatively poor ones support the redistributive criterion on the grounds of equity. Various formulae for resource transfers from the centre to the states tend to mediate between these extreme positions and these mediations reflect the bargaining power of the richer vis-à-vis poorer states and the policy objectives of the central government in a given context. Studies aimed at examining the implications of centre–state financial relations either for regional inequalities or for increasing the total quantum of resources have adopted this approach (see Parkash 1983, Prasad 1983, Ansari 1987, Gulati and George 1987, Nanjundappa and Rao 1987, Rao 1987, Vithal 1987, Gupta and Kalra 2005).

Resource position vs expenditure responsibilities

This approach has been adopted in studies aimed at finding out if the pattern of centre–state financial relations enables each level of government to have the resources to fulfil its constitutionally given expenditure responsibilities (see Grewal 1975, Datta 1987, Gulati 1987a).

Constitutionalist approach

A slightly different version of the second approach is adopted by those studies that adhere to a strict constitutionalist perspective. Such studies look on the prevailing system of centre–state financial relations to assess whether these are in accordance with the constitutional provisions or not (see George 1986, Gulati 1987, Jhaveri 1987, Khatkhate and Bhatt 1987). Studies adopting this approach are critical of the increasing role of the Planning Commission (PC) and the central ministries in resource transfers mainly because the transfers through the PC and the ministries are not considered to be sanctified by the constitution.

This approach differs from the second approach because it does not concern itself with the question of whether or not a system of centre–state financial relations leads to compatibility of resource position with expenditure responsibility for a given level of government. It deals merely with the formalistic adherence of a system of centre–state financial relations to the constitution.

Centralization vs decentralization

Some studies examine the trend towards centralization vs decentralization irrespective of the considerations mentioned in the three approaches above (see Mitra 1983, Mitra 1987, S. Ali 1989, Johar and Rana 1990). This approach, also called the vertical balance vs imbalance approach, tries to examine the politico-economic implications of centralization (economies/diseconomies of scale, authoritarianism/bureaucratization) and decentralization (targeting/responsibility, democratization). Advocates of centralization claim it to be a more efficient managerial control system and advocate it on the grounds of its compatibility with national developmental goals.[10] Their view is that moves towards decentralization may make it unmanageable, chaotic and therefore inefficient. Supporters of decentralization claim that it introduces greater accountability and, therefore, efficiency while centralization accelerates unaccountable bureaucratic control and impedes efficiency in resource mobilization and expenditure utilization (Mitra 1983, 1987).

The main approaches to the study of centre–state relations in agriculture

Although there has been increasing evidence of conflict between the central government and state governments almost since independence in the sphere of agricultural policy and development, and although the scholarly work on Indian agriculture has been of outstanding quality, the area of centre–state relations in agriculture in an explicit sense has, by and large, remained unexamined. On the basis of the limited literature on the subject, two approaches can be identified: the constitutionalist approach and the issue-oriented approach.

Constitutionalist approach

This approach emphasizes that, according to the constitution, agriculture and related activities are in the states' jurisdiction, and that the centre has been encroaching on the states' sphere by extending its control over agriculture through the use of the constitutional provision that, where matters of 'national interest' are involved, the centre can overrule the states.[11] The centre's definition of 'national' and 'public' interest has been questioned.[12] This approach, extending its domain to the question of centralization–decentralization in agriculture, is mainly aimed at examining the degree of states' autonomy in agriculture vis-à-vis centre's control.

Issue-oriented approach

This approach has tended to identify specific issues where centre–state relations are involved. Major issues identified can be listed as: centrally sponsored schemes, pricing of agricultural items, input supply, credit supply and agricultural research (see Srinivasan 1972, Sims 1988, Fadia and Menaria 1990).

The main approaches to the study of centre–state relations in industry

The limited number of studies on the subject can be classified into two categories in terms of their approaches: the constitutionalist approach and the issue-oriented approach.

Constitutionalist approach

The major concern of this approach has been to highlight that the constitutional provisions regarding the power of the central government to take control of any industry 'in the public interest' has led to an unfettered expansion of the centre's domain in determining and shaping the pattern of industrial development of any state.[13] Critics of this trend towards centralization and erosion of state autonomy have drawn attention to the fact that the centre had extended its control even over such items as bicycles, razor-blades, pressure cookers and hurricane lanterns (see Fadia and Menaria 1990).[14] Such critics cite these examples as evidence of the centre's excessive and widespread control over industry. Some commentators have attributed this expanding role of the centre to the lobbying power of the big industrial bourgeoisie at the centre.[15]

Issue-oriented approach

This approach has focused on what can be called the key issues of centre–state relations in industry, namely licensing policy, location of central public sector projects, freight equalization policy (raised only by the Assam government), policy towards small-scale industries and policy on the development of backward industrial areas (see Fadia and Menaria 1990).[16]

Methodology: qualitative and quantitative dimensions in centre–state relations

Centre–state economic relations in India can influence the state finances, agriculture and industry of a state in two ways: first, in shaping the *pattern* of state finances, industrial and agricultural development – this can be called 'qualitative influence'; second, in effecting the *quantitative level* of state finances, industrial and agricultural development – this can be called 'quantitative influence'.

From the methodological point of view, for the purpose of specifying the implications of centre–state relations for any state's economy, the finances of a state on one side, and its agriculture and industry together on the other, fall into two different categories. For the state finances, the implications of centre–state relations can be specified in terms of both its pattern and the quantitative levels of revenue and expenditure. But for agriculture and industry, the implications are more likely to be identified for the pattern of development and less strongly for the quantitative level of agricultural and industrial development. This difference in the state finances on one hand and agriculture and industry taken together on the other, in terms of implications for the quantitative level of state finances, agriculture and industry, can be attributed to two interrelated aspects: the nature of data available on state finances, agriculture and industry, and the institutional arrangement for regulating centre–state relations in finance, agriculture and industry.

The data on state finances can directly tell us about the share of a state and the centre in the state's revenue resources and expenditure. For industry and agriculture, there are no existing data from which the centre and a state's direct contribution to total agricultural and industrial production can be separately identified. As regards institutional arrangements, there exists a clearly defined institutional arrangement of a Finance Commission for the sharing of financial resources between the centre and the states. Even for those resources that are not shared through the Finance Commission, there exists a clearly defined institutional arrangement of a Planning Commission and central ministries to effect those transfers. One of the reasons for better availability of data on financial relations is the existence of these institutional arrangements.

For agriculture and industry, there is no comparable institutional arrangement to regulate centre–state relations. In view of these methodological dimensions of assessing the implications of centre–state relations for a state's finances, agriculture and industry, my work examines mainly the *qualitative* implications for Punjab's state finances, agriculture and industry. The quantitative data have been used to build a picture of qualitative dimensions such as patterns and trends in state finances, agriculture and industry, and not to make any claims specifically on particular facts, data and figures. I elaborate my approach below, first for studying financial relations and then for agriculture and industry. I call this the reconfigured centralization–decentralization (RCD) approach.

Each of the four main approaches I identified above is relevant and useful depending on the objective of a study. The compensatory criterion vs redistributive criterion approach would be relevant for assessing the objectives of efficiency vs regional equity; the resource position vs expenditure responsibility approach would be relevant for assessing the functional utility of the existing financial relations; the constitutionalist approach would be relevant and useful to assess the adherence or otherwise of the existing financial relations to constitutional provisions; and the centralization vs decentralization approach would be crucial to examine the trends towards vertical fiscal dependence vs state fiscal autonomy.

Since my objective is to examine the implications of the existing structure of centre–state financial relations for Punjab's state finances, none of these approaches in isolation is wholly relevant for me. All three approaches aim at macroeconomic analysis of India's centre–state financial relations to assess macroeconomic objectives. My study requires examination of the macro-trends to the extent these trends have implications for a micro-unit (the state of Punjab). The need for a new integrated approach is evident from consideration of the following points:

1 A study of the compensatory vs redistributive trends has direct implications for Punjab's state finances. Since Punjab is a state with relatively higher tax effort, a greater emphasis on the compensatory principle will strengthen Punjab's state finances while emphasizing the redistributive principle will weaken them.[17] I have, therefore, tried to show in my chapter on finance how the centre's objective of balanced regional development, which follows from the centralist state's need to act as the architect of Indian nationalism, is tilted in favour of the redistributive criterion. This structural dimension of the role of the centre in the context of Indian federalism implies that Punjab becomes a donor state. Punjab's state finances are consequently adversely affected. This highlights the contradiction inherent in the strategy of the centre's role as the mediator and arbiter between the states.
2 An examination of the resource position vs expenditure responsibilities reveals that the state governments' expenditure responsibilities are expanding as a result of their increasing role in socio-economic development and the resource position is shrinking because of the narrow taxation base of the states. This hiatus between expanding expenditure responsibilities and shrinking resource position is the logical outcome of the structure of the

constitutional division of responsibilities and financial powers between the centre and the states. The subjects under the jurisdiction of the states, such as irrigation, education, health and social welfare, demand massive infrastructural expenditure responsibilities and generate very low returns. On the resource side, the domain of states' taxation power is very limited. This approach also helps us to trace out the structural roots of states' indebtedness to the centre, and has special significance for Punjab because, apart from the normal developmental expenditure, in the 1980s the Punjab government had to incur a huge non-developmental expenditure on security forces engaged in meeting the Sikh militant challenge to the authority of the Indian state. The Ninth Finance Commission noted that special loans of the value of Rs.2,300 crores (Rs.23 billion) had been given to Punjab during 1984–1989 to meet the extra expenditure needs of the Punjab government arising out of the need for 'combating terrorism' (Govt of India 1989: 39).

3 The constitutionalist approach sheds light on the increasing importance of extra-constitutional discretionary transfers through the Planning Commission and central ministries. By highlighting the increasing importance of discretionary transfers, this approach highlights the financial vulnerability of the state governments to the central government control. I have used this approach to examine the relative weighting of statutory, planned and central ministries' transfers in the total transfers from the centre to Punjab and the implications of this for the vulnerability of Punjab's state finances to the discretionary power of the central government administration.

4 The centralization–decentralization approach helps to reveal the vertical imbalance in the financial relations between the centre and the states. I have used this approach to highlight two aspects of this trend towards centralization: First, the existing constitutional provisions are themselves oriented towards centralization because the more revenue-generating sources are in the centre's domain. Second, the trend towards centralization has been accelerated because the centre has used its constitutionally given power to amend the constitution (states do not have this power) to corner more elastic sources of tax revenue. Corporation tax, surcharge on income tax and additional excise duties are examples of this kind. The implication of this increasing trend towards centralization for Punjab's state finances is that the Punjab government's taxation base is narrowing down, which, in turn, weakens Punjab's state finances.

Applying the RCD approach to the study of centre–state financial relations

The trend towards greater emphasis on the redistributive criterion eventually results in a more interventionist role for the centre; the increasing revenue–expenditure gap is both a reflection of the centralist bias inherent in the constitution as well as a catalyst for increasing the trend towards centralization, and finally the constitutional amendments are again both the manifestation of the centre's unilateral power to amend the constitution and a pointer towards increasing centralization.

The use of the RCD approach is especially fruitful because it helps to generate a theoretical framework to examine the implications of macro-trends (all India) for micro-units (states). For example, the two key aspects of the implications of centre–state financial relations for the finances of any state (including Punjab) that get highlighted through the use of the centralization–decentralization approach are first, the loss or otherwise of state autonomy (increasing centralization indicating loss of state autonomy and increasing decentralization suggesting gain for state autonomy); and, second, adverse or favourable impact on the finances of a state due to loss or gain in state autonomy.

The loss (or decrease) in state autonomy because of some aspects of centralization (e.g. greater weighting to the redistributive criterion) may have a favourable consequence for the finances of one state (a poorer one like Bihar or Orissa) and unfavourable consequences for another state (a richer one like Punjab or Maharashtra). Another aspect of centralization (e.g. the narrow tax base for the states) leading to diminution of state autonomy may have uniformly adverse consequences for the finances of all the states.

Applying the RCD approach to the study of centre–state relations in agriculture

The two main approaches to the study of centre–state relations in agriculture mentioned earlier (the constitutional approach and the issue-oriented approach) can be incorporated in my RCD approach. My objective is to study the macro-trends in centre–state relations in agriculture in so far as they have implications for Punjab agriculture. The alleged centralist bias inherent in the constitution because of the centre's overriding powers to legislate and its role in each of the issues mentioned earlier can be studied to reveal the trends towards centralization–decentralization in the sphere of agriculture. Keeping the specific context of Punjab agriculture in mind, I will focus on an examination of the incorporation of Punjab agriculture in the Indian federal state's strategy of Green Revolution to increase agricultural production in general and food production in particular.

Applying the RCD approach to the study of centre–state relations in industry

The two main approaches to the study of centre–state relations in industry mentioned earlier (the constitutional approach and the issue-oriented approach) are useful to study either the macro-trends or a specific issue in the industry. Since my objective is to examine the implications of both macro-level changes and specific issues in centre–state relations in industry for Punjab industry, my RCD approach can take account of both the general and the specific changes. This approach will be helpful in examining the impact of the trends in centralization or decentralization on the autonomy of the states in fashioning their pattern of industrial development. Within the specific context of Punjab industry, I will focus on examining the preponderance of the small-scale industrial sector in Punjab.

Sources and use of data

The major sources of data for my study are the official publications of the Government of India and the Government of Punjab. Reports of independent commissions and enquiries, though appointed by the government, were also used. Data presented by professionally competent and well-known non-governmental organizations such as the Centre of Monitoring Indian Economy, Bombay, were also used.

To supplement the information available from official and non-official sources, I conducted two field trips to Delhi and Punjab in 1989 and in 1991 to interview key individuals who had been involved in the decision-making process regarding centre–state relations. I was fortunate to get two former chief ministers of Punjab to give me valuable interviews in Chandigarh to share their first-hand experiences of centre–state relations. Sardar Parkash Singh Badal and Sardar Surjit Singh Barnala gave me their time very generously. I was impressed with the detailed knowledge that both of them, especially Barnala, had of the subject. It was under Barnala's chief ministership (1985–1987) that the Punjab government had prepared the memorandum that was submitted to the Commission on Centre–State Relations appointed by the Indian government in 1983.[18] I was also fortunate to have a very long and detailed interview in Delhi with Dr Karam Singh Gill, a development economist, a former chairman of the Punjab Planning Board, who had written the Punjab government memorandum submitted to the Commission on Centre–State Relations in 1987. The interviews with Badal and Barnala gave me valuable political insights into the institutional and contestable dimensions of centre–state relations and the interview with Gill was very useful for understanding the economic and political dimensions of the states' viewpoint on centre–state relations. Dr Gill was an intellectually powerful critic of what he called the trend towards growing power of the centre. All three also contributed to my understanding of Punjab's perspective on different aspects of centre–state relations. In understanding Punjab's perspective, I benefited also from interviews with several civil servants of the Punjab government. Some of them wanted to remain anonymous while others were happy to be quoted.

I wanted to get first-hand knowledge of Punjab industry and agriculture in order to understand the problems and prospects of these two sectors. For an understanding of the issues concerning industry, I interviewed several industrialists in Ludhiana, the hub of small-scale industry in Punjab, and visited several factory sites. I must especially mention the names of two individuals who were brilliant in understanding the needs of my project and who not only gave several interviews but helped to arrange more interviews, procure reports on Punjab industry and arrange visits to factory sites. One was Satish Dhanda and the other Sunil Munjal. They are not only leading industrialists of Punjab but also industry representatives on a number of high-ranking committees of Indian government and industry. They helped me to arrange interviews with officials of the Punjab and Haryana Chamber of Commerce and Industry at Delhi. Both of them have visited me in the UK and have continued to help me with my demands for more documents and reports relating to industry in India and Punjab.

To understand firsthand the issues concerning Punjab agriculture, I met and interviewed several farmers in the villages belonging to the districts of Ferozepur, Faridkot, Moga, Muktsar and Sangrur at different times in the last several years. I also interviewed the vice-chancellor of Ludhiana's Punjab Agricultural University (PAU), the dean of research at the university and several faculty members of the Department of Economics and Sociology, including its head of department. I was able to get most valuable publications of the university dealing with several aspects of Punjab agriculture which were of interest to me. I also met Dr Sukhdev Singh, a former vice-chancellor of the university. Another key individual whom I interviewed regarding Punjab agriculture was Dr Sardara Singh Johl. A leading academic expert on Punjab agriculture, he has been a leading educational administrator and economic policy-maker in Punjab and Indian agriculture. He has held the posts of head of the economics and sociology department at PAU; vice-chancellor of PAU and of Punjabi University, Patiala; chairman of the Punjab government's Planning Board; chairman of the Government of India's Commission on Agriculture Costs and Prices; and chairman of the Punjab government's Committee on Diversification of Crops in Agriculture. I interviewed him twice on one of his visits to the UK.[19]

In Delhi, I was lucky to get interviews with two key individuals who had had perhaps the best opportunity available to anyone to understand the functioning of centre–state relations in India. One was Justice Ranjit Singh Sarkaria, a former judge of the Supreme Court of India, who was appointed as chairman of the Commission on Centre–State Relations in India by the Government of India in 1983; the other was Professor Raja Chelliah, the only person to be a member of both of the Ninth Finance Commission and the Seventh Planning Commission. The report of the Ninth Finance Commission was submitted in two parts, in 1988 and 1989. Both men spent many hours answering my questions and sharing their knowledge, expertise and experience with me. While I was interviewing Professor Chelliah, an interesting development took place. Two very high officials of the Congress Party in India (Madhav Rao Scindia and Mani Shankar Aiyar)[20] turned up at the Professor's house to seek his advice, I was told, on some urgent economic issues. Professor Chelliah had to interrupt the interview with me but he introduced me to them and asked them if I could join their discussion. They did not object. As it turned out, they had come to seek clarification regarding some issues on the recommendations of the Ninth Finance Commission. This unexpected interruption proved very useful to me in adding to my understanding of the Congress Party's perspective on centre–state relations.

Justice Sarkaria was kind enough to give me signed copies of the two-volume report on centre–state relations in India prepared under his chairmanship and submitted to the Government of India in 1987 and 1988. He showed such keen interest in my project that he gave me several key documents and materials which were not publicly available. I was deeply touched by the trust and confidence he reposed in me. He was so kind that he agreed to give me a follow-up interview later on, despite the fact that he was not in good health. In his death on 12 October 2007 India has lost one of the best constitutional experts on Indian federalism.

The interviews with Professor Chelliah and Justice Sarkaria proved valuable to me in two different ways. The interview with Professor Chelliah enriched my understanding of the centre's perspective on centre–state relations, while the interview with Justice Sarkaria gave me an insight into a jurist's way of understanding the contestations over centre–state relations.

Structure of the book

The book is divided into seven chapters. Chapter 1, the introduction, provides a broad indication of the thrust of my work. Chapters 2 and 3 deal with two fairly distinct issues but the aim is that the two chapters together in combination provide an historical background to the study of Punjab–centre relations in the post-1966 period. Chapter 2 deals with Punjab and Sikh history, and Chapter 3 deals with the history of centre–state relations in India.

Chapter 2 is an attempt to provide an overview of the geographical and political history of Punjab and the Sikhs. A fresh perspective on reading Punjab and Sikh history has been attempted in this chapter by delineating the rise of the Sikh religion as also the rise of region-based Punjabi nationalism. Key historical turning points in Punjab and Sikh history – the founding of the Sikh faith, its transformation from a pacifist faith to a militant religio-political movement trying to demarcate its own territorial space for self-rule, and eventually the rise of the Sikhs to political power in Punjab in 1799 – are studied as evolutionary steps in the rise of Punjabi and Sikh nationalism. This re-reading of Punjab and Sikh history is then made the basis for an interpretation of the recurring phenomenon of harmony and conflict between Punjab-based nationalism and Delhi-based central powers. The relationship between three Delhi-based central powers – the Mughal monarchical state, the British colonial state and the Indian national state – and Punjab-based regional nationalism is examined within this framework. This framework is then employed to explain the dialectics of the tension-ridden relationship between the post-1966 Sikh-majority Punjab and the Hindu-majority, though formally secular, federal Indian state.

The emergence of the Punjabi-speaking state in 1966 as the territorial space in which the Sikhs for the first time became a majority and came to control political power, albeit within the limitations of Indian federal structure, is interpreted as a significant historical event in the rise of Punjabi and Sikh nationalism. The inner contradictions of competing nationalisms based on language and religion are briefly explored to capture the complexity of Punjab-centre relations. The rise of the Sikh movement for autonomy and eventually for secession from India in the 1980s, and its suppression by the Indian federal state, are examined to chronicle the vicissitudes of Punjab–centre relations. This chapter also aims at providing a background to our subsequent argument that centre–state relations must be understood in the context of the political economy of nation-building by the Indian federal state. This is to underline the larger point that federal conflicts in a nation state, characterized by the existence of multiple nationalities, are conflicts about control over economic resources as well as nationalist conflicts about control over political power.

Chapter 3 provides an historical overview of the evolution of centre–state relations in India. A brief exposition of the nature of centre–state relations during British rule over India is provided to highlight the link between the arrangements during the British period and the shaping of the Indian constitution in the post-1947 period. I also refer to the partition of India and the adoption of the planned development strategy by the Indian political leadership as playing critical roles in giving a centralist bias to the Indian constitution. I then interpret various articles of the constitution to substantiate the argument that it has a strong centralist bias. Having provided this historical background in Chapters 2 and 3, I move on to Chapters 4, 5 and 6 dealing with the three key areas of this work: the implications of centre–state relations for the state finances, agriculture and industry of Punjab. In all three chapters, the *reconfigured centralization–decentralization* approach has been employed to monitor the trends in these sectors.

Chapter 4 examines centre–state financial relations and their implications for Punjab's state finances during our study period. A major part of the chapter is devoted to an examination of the constitutional provisions relating to centre–state financial relations and to an identification of the trends in centre–state financial relations during this period. I have dealt at some length with the evolution of the vertical imbalance that had taken place between the centre on one hand and all the states on the other regarding the revenue powers and expenditure responsibilities of the centre versus the states'. I have demonstrated that the centre had taken control over major sources of revenue and the states had been left with rather inelastic sources of revenue. On the other hand, the expenditure responsibilities of the states have expanded disproportionately more than those of the centre. The chapter examines this big hiatus between the revenue powers and the expenditure responsibilities of the states and highlights the indebtedness of the states to the centre.

Having drawn this overall picture of the nature of the centre's overwhelming power vis-à-vis the states, the implications of this are drawn out for Punjab's state finances. The political economy of the Indian nation-building project is brought into the picture to explain the relatively low share of central resources transferred to Punjab. The politico-economic project of reducing regional inequalities is used to explain the phenomenon of disproportionately low central transfers to a relatively high per capita income state like Punjab.

Chapter 5 takes up the examination of centre–state relations in agriculture and their implications for Punjab agriculture. The first part of the chapter examines closely the Indian constitutional provisions regarding centre–state relations in agriculture and explains the seemingly paradoxical phenomenon that though in the Indian constitution agriculture is a state subject, the centre had taken an overwhelming control in directing the path of agricultural development in the country.

The introduction of the Green Revolution strategy in Punjab to raise food output is examined in the context of the centrally directed development strategy in the agriculture sector. The reasons why Punjab was chosen to introduce this strategy are examined by providing the background of Punjab's agricultural advancement, especially its irrigation network, during the period of British rule in India. I have also explained that the resort to central planning in the Indian nationalist state's development strategy was responsible for further strengthening the role of the centre in agricultural development. The idea of the centre as the self-conscious defender of Indian national interests is put forward and elaborated. Particular emphasis is placed on explaining how the political economy of Indian nationalism in making India self-reliant in food availability was the driving force behind the centre's introduction of the Green Revolution strategy in Punjab. The chapter then goes on to examine the implications of the introduction of the Green Revolution strategy for Punjab agriculture. In particular, the issues of cropping pattern, the rise in agricultural productivity, the limitations of this strategy and the signs of a saturation crisis in Punjab agriculture are explored.

Chapter 6 is devoted to examining centre–state relations in industry and the implications of these for Punjab industry. Having examined the rise in per capita income in Punjab as a result of the introduction of the Green Revolution, this chapter highlights the industrial backwardness of Punjab. It starts by examining the constitutional provisions regarding the roles and powers of the centre and the states in the field of industry and shows that despite industry having been formally put in the state list, the overall centralist provisions of the constitution have enabled the centre to assume commanding control in shaping the direction of industrial development in the country. The importance attached to central planning in the development strategy further facilitated the growing power of the centre in the field of industry. This chapter further takes up the aspect of the politico-economic project of Indian nation building in explaining the role assigned to central planning in reducing inter-state inequalities. The location of central public-sector investment for the industrialization of different states is especially considered from this perspective of reducing inter-state inequalities. The argument that disproportionately low central public-sector investment in Punjab was a major contributor to Punjab's industrial backwardness is developed. The chapter situates this disproportionately low public-sector investment in Punjab in the context of the political economy of Indian nationalism, which demanded that instead of Punjab, which had acquired high per capita income status as a result of agrarian advancement, it was states with relatively low per capita income that deserved the allocation of central public-sector plants. It provides evidence to demonstrate that Indian policy-makers attached such high importance to the role of central public-sector investment in reducing inter-state inequalities that they sometimes sacrificed the criterion of efficient returns in deciding the location of a central public-sector plant.

The chapter then devotes considerable space to highlight that Punjab's industrial sector is characterized by a preponderance of small-scale industry and the glaring absence of large-scale industry. This industrial backwardness of Punjab is explained in the light of the very low public-sector investment in Punjab which was needed to set the pace for industrialization. The cumulative effect of Punjab's industrial backwardness is highlighted by providing evidence that by 1990–91, Punjab ranked lowest among the 17 major states of India in terms of the share of the secondary sector in the state's domestic product.

Finally, Chapter 7 sums up the argument of this study and highlights the main conclusions.

2

THE GEOGRAPHY AND THE POLITICAL ECONOMY OF PUNJAB

An historical overview of Punjab–centre relations

The current geographical boundary of Punjab was drawn on 1 November 1966 when Punjab was reconstituted as a Punjabi-speaking state. Although this study focuses on this post-1966 Punjab as a geographical entity, the historical background to the creation of the present Punjab is of vital importance in understanding the politico-economic, religious and demographic dynamics in Punjab and Indian society that have resulted in its creation. These processes have a significant bearing on the modes of relationship between today's Punjab and the Indian central state.

One aspect of Punjab, which distinguishes it from all the other states in India, is that it is the homeland of the Sikh people. Punjab is the only state in India where the Sikhs are in a majority. According to the 1991 census, the Sikhs were only 2 per cent of India's population but about 63 per cent of that of Punjab. 78.6 per cent of India's total Sikh population was settled in Punjab.[1] Majority status for the Sikhs in Punjab is a relatively recent phenomenon – they became the majority religious community only after the territorial reorganization of 1 November 1966. This duality of the Sikh location – a minority in India but a majority in Punjab – is a continuing source of political conflict and tension between Sikh majority Punjab and Hindu majority India. In this chapter, I will try to examine and elaborate some of these interlinked processes: the history of the birth and growth of the Sikhs as a religious–political community, the links between the Sikhs and the Punjabi language, the emergence of the Punjabi-speaking state, and the fluctuating relationship of harmony and conflict between Punjab and the Sikhs on one hand and the Indian central state and the Hindus on the other.

The birth of Sikhism and its early guru period (1469–1708)

The Sikh religion was founded by Guru Nanak (1469–1539). Nanak was born in a village, Talwandi Rai Bhoe, now called Nankana Sahib, about 40 miles from Lahore (Khushwant Singh 1999: 29–30). His was an upper caste Khatri Hindu family and his father an administrative official in the office of a local Muslim chieftain. Nanak showed signs of early childhood rebellion against religious orthodoxy, hypocrisy and the Hindu caste hierarchy. In his youth, he used the medium of music, poetry, song and speech to preach the love of God and to attack the politically oppressive policies of the Muslim Mughal regime and the socially oppressive practices of the orthodox Brahminical Hindu religion. He also attacked the wealthy for their greed and spoke in favour of an equitable social status for women (Nikky-Guninder Kaur Singh 1993, Dhillon 2006). He used the language of the masses, the Punjabi language, to preach his ideas.

This practice was in sharp contrast with that of the Hindu priests and the Muslim clergy, who used Sanskrit and Arabic, respectively. Sanskrit and Arabic were inaccessible to the mass of the population; the traditional priestly classes used the old classical languages to exercise their intellectual hegemony. They believed that by using a language the masses could not understand, they could display their superiority of learning and develop a mystique around them. Guru Nanak seems to have made a conscious break with this tradition. Rejecting Sanksrit (which used to be called *dev bhasha*, the language of the gods), he used Punjabi (*lok bhasha*, people's language) to communicate his egalitarian teachings. He attracted a following among the lower castes, mainly Hindus but some converts to Islam.

His followers came to be known as Sikhs; *sikh*, a Punjabi word, means a learner or a disciple. It is a variant of the Sanskrit word *shishya*, which means pupil (Harbans Singh 1994: 1). Some of his followers came from his own Khatri caste. The Khatris, though an upper caste, were one step lower than the highest Hindu caste, the Brahmins. The Khatris felt that in Sikhism they had found a religion in which they did not have to feel inferior to the Brahmins and, ironically, they had the satisfaction of feeling that they enjoyed the status of the highest caste in the new religion. The Khatris, therefore, felt that this was their own religion and this sense of ownership became a powerful source of attraction for them to become Sikhs. However, for the large mass of Punjabis who were attracted to Guru Nanak's teachings, it was the content of his teachings (equality), the medium of his communication (the Punjabi language) and the form of his communication (poetry, song and music), which attracted them to Sikhism. He can therefore be legitimately characterized as the founder and articulator of a truly Punjabi religion. Roger Ballard, a Punjab studies scholar, in his attempt to conceptualize a Punjabi religion, pays particular attention to the Punjabi dimension of Nanak's teachings. He calls Punjab 'the home base of Guru Nanak' (Ballard 1999: 14) and imagines Nanak to be calling all Punjabis to rise above all religious divisions among them:

> After all if Nanak were still with us to comment on current developments, it is far from unreasonable to suggest that he would wish to add

> the phrase *koi na Sikh* [no one is a Sikh] to his celebrated epigram *koi na Hindu, koi na Musulman* [no one is a Hindu, no one is a Muslim].
>
> (Ballard 1999: 16, translation added)

Khushwant Singh, the most celebrated scholar of Sikh history, interprets the emergence of Guru Nanak as being a Punjabi nationalist response to the historical changes taking place in Punjab in the fifteenth century (Khushwant Singh 1999: 13–16). He writes:

> The Punjab, being the main gateway into India, was fated to be the perpetual field of battle and the first home of all the conquerors. Few invaders, if any, brought wives with them, and most of those who settled in their conquered domains acquired local women. Thus the blood of many conquering races came to mingle, and many alien languages – Arabic, Persian, Pushto, and Turkish – came to be spoken in the land. Thus, too, was the animism of the aboriginal subjected to the Vedantic, Jain, and Buddhist religions of the Aryans, and to the Islamic faith of the Arabs, Turks, Mongols, Persians, and Afghans. Out of this mixture of blood and speech were born the Punjabi people and their language. *There also grew a sense of expectancy that out of the many faiths of their ancestors would be born a new faith for the people of the Punjab.* [...] By the end of the 15th century, the different races that had come together in the Punjab had lost the nostalgic memories of the lands of their birth and begun to develop an attachment to the land of their adoption. *The chief factor in the growth of Punjabi consciousness was the evolution of one common tongue from a babel of languages.* [...] Although the Punjabis were sharply divided into Muslims and Hindus, attempts had been made to bring about a rapprochement between the two faiths and a certain desire to live and let live had grown among the people. *It was left to Guru Nanak and his nine successors to harness the spirit of tolerance and give it a positive content in the shape of Punjabi nationalism.*
>
> (Khushwant Singh 1999: 13–14, italics added)

After Guru Nanak, there were nine other gurus who provided spiritual and political leadership to the Sikh community. Guru Nanak's immediate successor, Guru Angad (1504–1552,[2] guru 1539–1552), developed the Gurmukhi script for the Punjabi language. The third guru, Guru Amar Das (1479–1574, guru 1552–1574), introduced the practice of *sangat* (community congregation), *langar* (community cooking and eating of food) and *pangat* (that all members of the community, irrespective of caste, gender and social status, sit in a row to partake in the community-cooked food). The fourth guru, Guru Ram Das (1534–1581, guru 1574–1581), founded Amritsar as the centre of activities for the emerging community. The fifth guru, Guru Arjan Dev (1563–1606, guru

1581–1606), compiled the Sikh holy book, the Adi Granth (later known as the Guru Granth Sahib). In compiling the Adi Granth, Guru Arjan showed a remarkable commitment to pluralism, including in it not only the teachings and writings of all the five Sikh gurus but also the contributions made between the twelfth and sixteenth centuries by many Hindu *bhaktas* (devotees of God) and Muslim Sufi saints.[3]

Guru Arjan's other major contribution to the consolidation of self-identity among the Sikhs as a community was the construction of the Harimandar Sahib (later known more popularly as the Golden Temple) in Amritsar.[4] To project the pluralism and the openness of the holiest Sikh shrine, Guru Arjan invited a revered Muslim Sufi saint Mian Mir to lay the foundation stone of the Golden Temple, and created four gates of entry to the shrine to symbolize its openness to the members of all the four *varnas* (the hierarchical caste system) into which the Hindu society was divided. Ultimately, Guru Arjan came into conflict with the Mughal emperor Jehangir in Delhi after giving blessings to a rebel of the Mughal court who had come to him seeking his blessings. This was the first conflict in the subsequent long history of the Punjab-based Sikhs' conflict with the centre in Delhi. It ended in tragedy. Guru Arjan was tortured to death in 1606 by the Mughal emperor. Guru Arjan became the first martyr of the Sikhs (Vohra 1978: 80–82, Pashaura Singh 2005, 2006).[5]

His son Hargobind (1595–1644) became the sixth guru (1606–1644). Guru Hargobind made a break with the so far pacifist tradition of the Sikh community. He gave a call to his followers to procure arms and horses with the purpose of building an army to wage a war against the Mughal rulers. He built a small fortress, Lohgarh (the castle of steel), in Amritsar. Across from the Harimandar, he built the Akal Takhat (the throne of the Timeless God), where he sat on a throne like an emperor and held court (Khushwant Singh 1999: 63). He girded two swords, one symbolizing his spiritual authority and the other his temporal power (Grewal 1998: 64).

By this time, the social base of the Sikh community had expanded. The geographical location of the work of all the five gurus after Guru Nanak was the Majha area of Punjab around Amritsar, the heartland of the Jat peasant community. This Jat caste peasant community had a long-standing tradition of social egalitarianism. The egalitarian teachings of the Sikh gurus attracted the Jats into the fold of Sikhism (Habib 1976: 95–98). The large-scale conversion of the Majha Jat peasantry to Sikhism contributed significantly towards transforming the character of the Sikh community from a purely religious-spiritual community to a community that was also concerned with worldly and material affairs (McLeod 1996: 9–13).[6] The gurus' town and gurdwaraִ building projects also played a pioneering role in giving a boost to the emergence of the pilgrimage centres as centres also of trade and commerce. Their growth expanded the influence of Sikhism among the trading communities of Punjab and, to some extent, even outside Punjab (Grewal 1998: 66). The Sikh gurus can, therefore, be called the harbingers of the emergence of the indigenous trading bourgeoisie in Punjab.

The growth of an indigenous bourgeoisie is always crucial to the emergence of nationhood.

After the first experience of armed resistance to Mughal rule during Guru Hargobind's time, the period of guruship of the seventh guru, Guru Har Rai (1630–1661, guru 1644–1661), and that of the eighth, Guru Har Krishan (1656–1664, guru 1661–1664), was one of quiet organization of the Sikh community. The ninth guru, Guru Tegh Bahadur (1621–1675, guru 1664–1675), came into conflict with the Mughal emperor because he defended the religious rights of the Brahmin community, which was being targeted for persecution by the Mughal ruler Aurangzeb. The Guru was tortured to death along with his three associates in Delhi on 11 November 1675 (Khushwant Singh 1999: 73–74, Grewal 1998: 72).[7] His son Gobind Singh (1666–1708) became the tenth and the last living guru (guruship 1675–1708) of the Sikhs.

History now repeated itself. In the same way that the killing of the fifth guru by the Mughal rulers in Delhi had led his son, the sixth guru, to give a call to his Punjab-based followers for an armed rebellion, the killing of the ninth guru led his son and the tenth guru to impart a military reorientation to the Sikh community. Guru Gobind Singh called on his followers to become a community of 'saint-soldiers', of people who were inspired by a moral-religious vision of righteousness to take up arms against oppressive rulers. At a historic gathering of his followers on the Vaisakhi day (13 April) of 1699 at Anandpur Sahib, a hill town which had become his headquarters, he made a dramatic announcement about the transformation – symbolic, physical, ideological and political – of the community. Aimed at symbolically representing the abolition of the hierarchical caste system in which a surname identified the caste of the person, all Sikh males were called on to have the same surname 'Singh' (lion) and all female members to have the same surname 'Kaur' (lioness or princess). By requiring all members of the community to wear the symbolic 'five Ks' – *kesh* (unshorn hair), *kirpan* (sword), *kara* (iron bracelet), *kachha* (underwear) and *kangha* (comb) – a distinct physical appearance of the community was created (Uberoi 1980: 131–146). The waging of an armed struggle to capture state power and thus ensure righteous conduct became a moral religious duty. A new community of the Khalsa (*khalsa* meaning pure), a community of *sant-sipahis* (saint-soldiers), was created.

In the history of the evolution of the distinct identity of the Sikhs, the creation of the Khalsa in 1699 remains the most defining moment. The Sikhs had acquired by then an almost complete package of elements making up their distinct identity – a holy book (the Guru Granth Sahib), a holy city (Amritsar), a holy religious centre (the Harimandar or Golden Temple), a centre for taking political decisions (the Akal Takhat at Amritsar) and a distinctive physical appearance with uncut hair. The only element missing in this package was the control of state power, which they were to acquire later in 1799.

The armed guerrilla bands under the leadership of the tenth Sikh guru Gobind Singh engaged in battles with Mughal forces at many places in the central districts of Punjab where the Jat peasants had converted en masse to Sikhism. The Sikhs lost many men in these battles. Two of the guru's four sons were killed and the younger two, aged nine and seven, were captured by the Mughals and put to death by being walled up alive. The guru's mother committed suicide on hearing the news of the death of her two younger grandsons. The guru himself suffered a terrible personal loss in the process of expanding and consolidating the social and political base of the Sikh community in Punjab. The guru's defiance of Mughal rule even at such enormous personal cost has left forever a powerful impact on the Sikhs' self-image and collective memory as a community of valiant fighters against repressive rulers. Before his death in 1708, Guru Gobind Singh made three important decisions regarding the Sikh community: first, that there would be no living guru after him; second, that the holy book Guru Granth Sahib would be considered as the guru for spiritual guidance while the Sikh congregations would continue to enjoy the power to take decisions regarding political and temporal issues regarding the Sikh community; third, his disciple Banda Singh Bahadur (*bahadur* meaning brave) would lead the community's political and armed campaign against the Mughals.

The rise of the Sikhs to political power (1708–1799)

Banda Singh Bahadur (1670–1716) proved to be an effective political and military successor to Guru Gobind Singh. He combined a social programme, of land redistribution after expropriating feudal estates, with a military campaign to demolish the fort of the Nawab of Sirhind who had ordered the death of the two younger sons of Guru Gobind Singh. His visible success in razing the Sirhind fort in May 1710 contributed to increasing popularity among the peasant masses and to the further spread of Sikhism. He became the virtual master of the territories between the rivers Jumna and Sutlej, which yielded 'an annual revenue of thirty-six lacs of rupees' (Khushwant Singh 1999: 106). A large number of Hindu and Muslim peasants converted to Sikhism from conviction, fear, economic motives, or a combination of the three (Khushwant Singh 1999: 106; Ganda Singh 1935: 73). Banda Singh Bahadur assumed the style of royalty and introduced a new calendar dating from his capture of Sirhind. He made the old fort of Mukhlisgarh, in the safety of the Himalayas, his capital headquarters, and renamed it Lohgarh. He had coins struck in the name of Guru Nanak and Guru Gobind Singh (Ganda Singh 1992: 274, Grewal 1998: 83, Khushwant Singh 1999: 106–107, Saran Singh n.d.: 12–13). Though the successes of Banda were impressive, the superior military might of the Mughal rulers in Delhi eventually prevailed. He was defeated, captured, tortured and killed along with 700 of his associates and his four-year-old son in Delhi on 9 June 1716 (Ganda Singh 1992: 275).[8]

Banda Singh's rule was short-lived, but it nonetheless shook 'one of the most powerful empires in the world to its very foundations with such violence that it was never again able to re-establish its authority' (Khushwant Singh 1999:

117–118). In the seven stormy years (1710–1716) of the campaign, which Khushwant Singh rightly characterized as an 'agrarian uprising', Banda Bahadur changed the class structure of land holdings in the southern half of Punjab by liquidating many of the big Muslim *zamindar* (land-owning) families. The large feudal estates controlled by these families were broken up into smaller holdings and the proprietary rights on these holdings were transferred to the Hindu and Sikh peasants cultivating them. With the rise of Sikh power later on, these holdings were once again grouped together to form large estates in the hands of Sikh chieftains (Khushwant Singh 1999: 118, Ganda Singh 1992: 274). Banda Singh Bahadur can, therefore, be called the historical midwife for the rise of the Sikh feudal aristocracy in the late eighteenth century.

Though Banda's campaign was primarily an agrarian revolt, the fact that the main losers to his movement were Muslim landlords and the main beneficiaries were the Hindu and Sikh peasants resulted in the sharpening of sectarian communal divisions in Punjabi society. Banda also lacked the moral stature of the Sikh gurus who, despite their confrontations with the Mughal rulers, were able to evoke respect and following among the ordinary Muslim masses. The savagery of his campaign 'hardened the hearts of the Muslim peasants and made them as anti-Sikh as their government' (Khushwant Singh 1999: 119). The Sikh movement, which had shown encouraging potential under the gurus' leadership to emerge as the movement of Punjabi nationalism, 'received a setback with Banda' (Khushwant Singh 1999: 118).

The death of Banda left the Sikhs leaderless and disorganized. Between 1716 and 1799, the Sikhs fought a long drawn-out guerrilla struggle against the Mughal empire through a number of decentralized bands. These bands were loosely grouped together as an organization called Dal Khalsa (*dal* meaning collective). During this turbulent period of Sikh history, the ordinary Sikh men and women faced the wrath of the Delhi rulers without the guidance of a centralized command. Twice during this period, large massacres of Sikhs occurred. The first took place in May 1746 when about 10,000 Sikh men and women were killed (Ganda Singh 1956: 33) and the second in February 1762 when about 30,000 Sikhs were killed (Khushwant Singh 1999: 154).[9] The Sikhs regrouped themselves after these crushing defeats and reorganized themselves into 12 clearly organized bands called *misls*. Each *misl* had a chosen leader with a clearly defined geographical area of operations. These *misls* came together under the command of the Dal Khalsa when the need arose to repel or launch an attack and then dispersed again.

By the end of eighteenth century, the Sikhs had become virtual rulers of Punjab. The Sikh struggle of this period brought into prominence several men of remarkable competence who not only 'built up the Khalsa Commonwealth but also won back the confidence of the Muslim peasantry' (Khushwant Singh 1999: 183). The spirit of Punjabi nationalism, which had almost been destroyed by Banda Singh Bahadur's campaigns, was resurrected. Sikh resistance against the Persian and Afghan invaders and their Mughal collaborators 'built up (perhaps unconsciously) the notion that the Punjab would be better off if it were ruled by Punjabis rather than remain a part of the kingdom of Kabul or the Mughal Empire' (Khushwant Singh 1999: 183). An English traveller, George Forster, writing in 1783, observed:

> The discordant interests which agitate the Sicque [*sic*] nation, and the constitutional genius of the people, must incapacitate them, during the existence of these causes, from becoming a formidable offensive power [...] Should any future cause call forth the combined efforts of the Sicques [*sic*] to maintain the existence of empire and religion, we may see some ambitious chief led on by his genius and success, and absorbing the power of his associates, display, from the ruins of their Commonwealth, the standards of monarchy[.]
>
> (Forster 1798 quoted by Gupta 1992: 495–496)

This prophetic observation became true 16 years later when Maharaja Ranjit Singh occupied Lahore.

The Sikh Empire (1799–1849)

In 1799, Ranjit Singh (1780–1839) the chief of the Sukerchakia *misl* emerged as the supreme political and military leader among the competing *misls*, captured Lahore and became the first and only Sikh emperor of Punjab. Punjab existed as a sovereign state for 50 years (1799–1849) before it was annexed by the British in 1849 and merged with the rest of India under colonial rule. Though Ranjit Singh's Punjab was a Muslim-majority country and the administrators were chosen on merit not only from the main religious communities – Muslims, Hindus and Sikhs – but also from European Christian visitors, the fact that the ruler was a powerful Sikh maharaja remains embedded in the consciousness of both the Sikh elites and the masses that the Sikhs were once rulers of an independent sovereign state of Punjab.[10] The importance of this historical memory among the Sikhs can be gauged from the historical and literary narratives by the Sikhs which portray Maharaja Ranjit Singh as the most important Sikh so far after the ten gurus. He is referred to as the 'Lion of the Punjab' (Khushwant Singh 1997).

Ranjit Singh's legacy remains a contested terrain. On one hand, he represents the realization of the Sikh dream of statehood and political sovereignty, and, on the other, he is a symbol of composite Punjabi identity and is celebrated as a secular Punjabi ruler.[11] His death on 27 June 1839 resulted in a bloody succession war and eventually in the British annexation of Punjab after the almost leaderless Sikh army was defeated in two bitterly fought Anglo-Sikh wars (Hasrat 1992, 1992a). Ranjit Singh's last surviving son, Dalip Singh (1838–1893), was converted to Christianity in 1853, and brought to England in 1854 where he was given a feudal estate at Elveden to afford the luxury lifestyle of a prince. When he grew up, he reconverted to Sikhism but was not allowed to go to Punjab for fear of becoming a rallying point for the Sikhs to demand the return of their lost kingdom. Bitter, disappointed and lonely, he died in a humble hotel room in Paris on 22 October 1893 (Wylam 1992).

Punjab under British rule (1849–1947)

The British annexation of Punjab in 1849 after the defeat of the Sikh army had three significant consequences. First, the conquering British generals, impressed by the bravery of the defeated Sikh soldiers and generals, decided to incorporate them with honour into the British army in India. This resulted in a strategic, though temporary, success in turning the Sikhs into allies of the British rule in India. Second, the defeated Sikhs nurtured a grievance against the Indians who had enlisted themselves in the British army that had defeated the Sikhs. Third, the British used this Sikh grievance against the Indians in enlisting Sikh support against the Sepoy Mutiny of 1857 in India (Omissi 1994, Pritam Singh 2007d). A combination of all these three consequences resulted in a long-term troubled relationship of distrust between the Punjabi Sikhs and the rest of India.

After 1857, the Sikhs' relationship with the colonial rulers reflected two conflicting moods in the community. One was a mood of anger and revenge against the Raj for having annexed their kingdom, the other of demoralization, resignation and adaptation to the historic reality of the power of the British Empire. A section of the religious minded Sikhs and ex-soldiers of Ranjit Singh's army gave expression to the mood of revenge by indulging in acts of violent and non-violent defiance of British rule. Large numbers of Sikh peasants and soldiers sympathized silently with these acts of defiance but were also tempted by the lure of a career in the British army. The colonial rulers dealt very harshly with the small defiant section of the community and offered generous and seemingly honourable opportunities to the accomodationist section. A large number of Sikhs were recruited into the British army and their religious practices were respected with great care (Omissi 1994). The respect shown to the religious practices of the Sikh soldiers seemed to be the result of two considerations: first, it was an attempt at correcting the damage the British rulers had suffered in 1857 as a result of the real and rumoured disrespect shown to the religious practices of the Hindu and Muslim soldiers; second, the British had understood that Sikh soldiers true to the *sant-sipahi* tradition of Guru Gobind Singh were likely to be a better and more motivated fighting force than the non-Khalsa tradition (Omissi 1994).

Soldiers retiring from the army were given attractive economic rewards in the form of land grants in areas of west Punjab where irrigation facilities for agriculture were made available by building a network of canals. These areas came to be known as canal colonies (Ali 1999). The development of the irrigation networks and canal colonies was one of the most impressive projects the British empire had undertaken in India. Three interlocking goals seemed to be behind this massive project: first, to increase agricultural output in order to maximize land revenue returns; second, to facilitate military recruitment from the peasantry by making military service an economically attractive route to land acquirement; third, to create a loyal political base in the countryside for British rule (Ali 1989). This politico-economic development strategy generated long-term favourable conditions for an agriculturally oriented pattern of development in Punjab (Pritam Singh 1994). The implications of this British strategy become clearer if we compare this strategy with that adopted in some of the coastal provinces like the Bombay Presidency (the present Maharashtra, Gujarat region), the Madras Presidency (the present Tamil Nadu region) and the Calcutta Presidency (the present Bengal region), which favoured some degree of industrialization (Bharadwaj 1982). This was also a fine example of an externally governed politico-economic strategy having a crucial impact on changing the internal development pattern of a region (Ali 1989, Pritam Singh 1994).

The strategy did provide economic, political and military dividends to the British rule for a limited period of time in the late nineteenth century. However, two other developments were taking place simultaneously, which were undermining political support for the British rule among the Punjabis in general and the Sikhs in particular. One was the growing indebtedness of the peasantry as a combined result of the land revenue burden and the necessity for investment expenditure to modernize agricultural practices (Darling 1947, Sukhwant Singh 1980, 1982). The other was the opposition of the religious establishments of Punjabi Hindus, Muslims and Sikhs to the Christian missionaries supported by the Raj to spread Christianity among the Punjabis, and especially among the poorer sections (Webster 1976).

The indebtedness of the peasantry was forcing them to mortgage their land or sell it to money lenders (Sohal 1983). The peasants were predominantly Sikhs and Muslims, though in eastern Punjab (now constituting Haryana) they were Hindus – while the money lenders were everywhere predominantly Hindus (Sukhwant Singh 1983). This contributed not only to sharpening internal religious divisions among the Punjabis but also to growing grievances among them against British rule, though for different reasons. The British government was worried that the unrest among Sikh and Muslim peasants could spread to the army and, therefore, passed the Land Alienation Act of 1900 which prohibited land sale to what the Act classified as 'non-agricultural castes'. The Punjabi Hindus perceived this Act as a discriminatory policy aimed against them and therefore became more active supporters of the Indian nationalist movement led by the Indian National Congress party (Robinson 1987). All three main religious communities of Punjab harboured economic resentment, though not for the same reasons, against the policies of the British rule.

Along with this economic resentment came cultural and religious resentment against the Christian missionaries. Each of the three main religious communities perceived Christianity as a threat to its identity and survival. This gave birth to religious reform movements within each community to oppose the spread of

Christianity.[12] In the process of defining their religious principles and practices in opposition to Christianity, these reform movements sharpened also the differences between the three communities – Muslims, Hindus and Sikhs.[13] In particular, the sharpening of Sikh identity as distinct from the Hindus was further accelerated by this process of drawing religious boundaries (Oberoi 1994).[14]

The Sikh movement for the control and self-management of their gurdwaras, the religious institutions, put the Sikhs in opposition to both the Hindu community (especially within Punjab) and the British government (Kapur 1986). The control of many of these gurdwaras had fallen into the hands of a pacifist Sikh sect, the Udasi, in the eighteenth century while the Sikh community had been engaged in armed combat against the Mughal rulers for the mere survival of the community. The Mughal rulers had tolerated this pacifist sect as a tactic against the armed guerrilla bands of the Sikh resistance. Initially, the broader Sikh community was also respectful to the Udasi sect since its founder Sri Chand was one of the sons of the first Sikh guru, Guru Nanak (Sulakhan Singh 1980). However, the sect had over a period of time become Hinduized in its religious practices (Sulakhan Singh 1983). For example, it had installed the pictures of Hindu gods within the gurdwara buildings and had started the practice of idol worship, which was against Sikh religious principles. Some members of the sect were also misappropriating the income of the gurdwaras generated by the offerings of the Sikh devotees.[15]

When the Sikhs launched a movement in the 1920s to regain democratic control of these gurdwaras, the existing managers used private militias to attack the Sikh groups seeking control. The British government supported these managers because of the wider anti-establishment implications of the Sikh demand. Some Hindu leaders of Punjab also supported the existing management because they suspected a Sikh impulse for separate identity behind the Sikh opposition to Hindu religious practices in the gurdwaras. Mahatma Gandhi and some leaders of the Indian national movement, however, supported the Sikh demand because of its opposition to the British-supported gurdwara management and its potential for becoming a part of the wider national movement for India's independence (Mohinder Singh 1978 and 1988).

The turning point in this increasingly bitter dispute between the Sikhs and the Udasi gurdwara management came on 20 February 1921 when 130 Sikhs were killed by the private militiamen employed by the manager of the Nankana Sahib Gurdwara, the birthplace of Guru Nanak (Kapur 1986: 109). The British government reversed its policy and agreed to give control to a democratically elected committee of the Sikhs.[16] The culmination of the Sikh success came when the Shiromani Gurdwara Parbandhak Committee (SGPC) won control of the Golden Temple at Amritsar in January 1922. Mahatma Gandhi put an Indian nationalist spin on this victory of the Sikhs by characterizing it in a telegram to the Sikh leader Baba Kharak Singh as: 'FIRST BATTLE FOR INDIA'S INDEPENDENCE WON. CONGRATULATIONS'.[17] Kapur, whose study is the most rigorous on this subject, argues that though the Sikh politicians 'collaborated with the largely Hindu politicians in the Punjab, their participation in the nationalist campaign stemmed from a desire to promote their separate existence in what they saw as a hostile world' (1986: xiv). The birth of the SGPC contributed very significantly to the institutionalization of the separate Sikh identity. With its 120 members elected by the entire adult Sikh population in Punjab, the SGPC rightfully came to be recognized as the 'mini-Parliament' of the Sikhs.[18]

As the movement for India's independence grew, despite many downswings, the scenarios for the future shape of the Indian polity started emerging, including those for Punjab as part of India's future. Two diametrically opposite scenarios were taking shape in Punjab. One was represented by the Unionist Party, which was a party of the landed elites of the Hindus, Muslims and Sikhs. This party was the most resourceful and powerful in Punjab. Its influence eclipsed even that of the Indian National Congress. The party had managed to put together a coalition government in Punjab, which represented the landed interests of all three main communities of Punjab. In the midst of competing scenarios for the future India, the Unionist Party made an unsuccessful bid to argue that Punjab be carved out as an independent multi-community country (Talbot 1994, Tiwana 1999). The opposite scenario was represented by groups and parties advocating separate interests of each of the three communities. The Muslim League claimed to represent the Muslims (Malik 1995, 1998, 1999), the Akali Dal claimed to represent the Sikhs (Grewal 1996) and the Indian National Congress represented mainly the Hindus, though its ideological position was one of Indian nationalism (Jaffrelot 1994).[19]

As it became more likely in the 1940s that India would be partitioned between a Muslim majority, Pakistan, and a Hindu majority (though formally secular), India, the position of the Sikhs became more precarious. The Sikhs did not want the division of the country but if the division became inevitable, they wanted a separate Sikh-dominated 'Khalistan' (Yong 1994, Riar 1999). However, the Sikh population was scattered throughout Punjab and, with only 13 per cent of the total Punjab population, they were in a majority only in two *tehsil* (sub-district) areas of Moga and Taran Taran (Riar 1999: 242).[20] Many of the British administrators, while sympathetic, expressed their inability to accept the Sikh demand due to demographic and geographic constraints. Jinnah, the Muslim League leader, tried to win over the Sikh leadership by offering various concessions to the Sikhs in Pakistan's future political set-up if the Sikhs and the whole of Punjab were to come over to Pakistan.[21] Gandhi and Nehru promised significant autonomy to the Sikhs if they were to throw their lot with India.[22] Weighing all the options, the Sikh leadership decided to repose confidence in the promises made by Gandhi and Nehru. The Sikhs opted for India. Punjab was partitioned along with Bengal (Spate 1947). About 4.5 million Sikhs and Hindus migrated from West Punjab to India's East Punjab and approximately 5.5 million Muslims migrated from East Punjab to Pakistan's West Punjab. Around 500,000 people were killed in the brutal sectarian violence that accompanied the partition (Hansen 2002: 1).

The partition of Punjab was extremely painful for the Sikhs due to the large number of deaths in sectarian violence and the loss of some of their most sacred gurdwaras, including the birthplace of Guru Nanak, which were left in Pakistan.[23] However, the Sikhs became politically more powerful because of the new geographical concentration of the Sikh population in the new Punjab in India as a result of the Sikh migration from West Punjab and the out migration of the Muslims. For the first time in their history, the Sikhs became a majority in many districts of Punjab. Overall, though, they were still a minority in Punjab. In 1951, the Sikhs were 35 per cent of the total population of the state (Brass 1974: 301).[24]

The struggle for a Punjabi-speaking state (1947–1966)

Linguistically, the new Indian Punjab was not a pure Punjabi-speaking state. Some southern districts were Hindi-speaking areas and the population in a few north-eastern districts spoke Pahari, which is a mixed dialect of Punjabi and Hindi but closer to Punjabi. The Indian government had accepted the principle of reorganizing the Indian states on the basis of language. Encouraged by this, the Shiromani Akali Dal (referred to as Akali Dal henceforth), the main Sikh party, launched a movement in the early 1950s to demand the creation of a Punjabi-speaking state. This demand was no different from the demand of other linguistic groups asking for the creation of states for their respective languages. However, in Punjab some distinctive features added to the complexity of the situation. The movement in Punjab for a Punjabi-speaking state, led by the Sikh party Akali Dal, had a mode of articulation of the demand that made it appear as a Sikh demand. The Indian political leadership interpreted this as a thinly disguised demand for a Sikh majority state. The fact of Punjab being geographically located on the Indian border with Pakistan further raised fears in the mind of the Indian political leadership that, if a Punjabi-speaking state with Sikh majority was created, it could give impetus later on to a demand for secession from the Hindu majority India. The severity of the opposition of the Indian political leadership led by Jawaharlal Nehru to the demand for the creation of a Punjabi-speaking state – in contrast with its conciliatory attitude towards the demands for a creation of other linguistic states – was interpreted by the Sikh political leadership led by Master Tara Singh as an instance of discrimination against the Sikhs, Punjabi language and Punjab. There was a situation of mutual mistrust (Gill 1998, 1999).

It was only after Nehru died in 1964 and Tara Singh was replaced as a leader of the Akali Sikh party by Sant Fateh Singh, who focused on the linguistic aspect of the demand, that a new political milieu was created for resolving this most contentious political conflict in Punjab after India's independence in 1947. Lal Bahadur Shastri, who succeeded Nehru as India's prime minister agreed to the demand for carving a Punjabi-speaking state out of the existing multi-lingual Punjab. The process started by Shastri could not be reversed by Indira Gandhi who became the Prime Minister on 20 January 1966 after Shastri's death in Tashkent on 11 January. On 1 November, the Punjabi-speaking areas of the united Punjab were grouped together to create a new Punjabi-speaking state. The Hindi-speaking areas were merged together to create a new state of Haryana[25] and the Pahari-speaking areas were merged with the already existing hill state of Himachal Pradesh (Grewal 1998: 181–204).

Punjab–centre conflict (1966–1991)

In this newly demarcated post-1966 Punjab, the Sikhs for the fist time in their history had a state in which they were a majority. The 1971 census showed that Sikhs were 60.22 per cent of the total population of Punjab (Census of India data, cited by Robinson 1987: 313). Even during Ranjit Singh's regime (1799–1849), which is the only time when Punjab was ruled by a sovereign Sikh ruler, the Sikhs were in a minority. The data for 1868 show that the Sikhs were then only 6.5 per cent of Punjab's population while the Muslims were 53 per cent and the Hindus were 34.8 per cent (Robinson 1987: 82). The birth of a Punjabi-speaking state was a historic moment in the evolution of the Punjabi language, and the emergence of a Sikh majority in a state was a historic moment in the evolution of the Sikh community.[26] This seemed close to a sense of achieving national independence. The jubilation was marred, however, by a few unsatisfactory aspects of the reorganization of the state. Chandigarh, the capital of Punjab, was not given to Punjab. The city was overwhelmingly Punjabi-speaking yet it was not transferred to Punjab because the majority of its inhabitants were Hindus. The linguistic criterion was over-ridden by a religious criterion. The city was made a joint capital of Punjab and Haryana and put under the administrative control of the central government as a Union territory. A few other Punjabi-speaking areas with a Hindu majority on the border between the two states of Punjab and Haryana were given to Haryana. The control of Beas and Bhakhra Dam hydro-electric projects was transferred to the central government, which had adverse implications regarding Punjab's control over its river waters and electricity resources. The faulty structure of the reorganization regarding the territory, the capital city and the water resources left a bitter taste among the Sikh leadership with regard to the central government. The long-held feeling among the Sikhs that they were viewed with suspicion by the national leadership, and treated in a biased and discriminatory fashion, was partly allayed by the central government's decision to create a Punjabi-speaking state and partly reignited by the faulty reorganization. An historic opportunity to build a relationship of trust between the centre and the Punjabi Sikhs was lost.[27]

After the creation of the new Punjabi-speaking state, the first election held to the Punjab state assembly in 1967 witnessed the defeat of the Indian National Congress, which had ruled at the centre and in Punjab since independence.[28] The Indian National Congress represented the centre and Indian nationalism in the popular imagination. The defeat of the Congress in Punjab was a reflection of the dominant anti-centre political sentiment among the Punjabis in general and the Sikhs in particular. Similar anti-Congress and, to some extent, anti-centre trends were visible in a number of other states in India where regional or left-wing parties defeated the Congress party in the 1967 assembly elections held there (Weiner 1968). In Punjab, the Akali Dal, the party which represented an ambiguous mix of Punjabi and Sikh nationalism, emerged as the main party heading the non-Congress United Front of parties that formed the governing coalition in Punjab after the 1967 elections (Narang 1983: 180).

At the centre, however, the Congress party was still in power. It had not adjusted to the idea that it could lose power anywhere. It soon started various manoeuvres against the non-Congress governments in several states. In Punjab, the eight-month-old Akali Dal-led United Front government was ousted on 22 November 1967 by Congress-supported defections in the Akali Dal. An Akali defector, Lachhman Singh Gill, formed a minority government with Congress support. This government fell in August 1968 when the Congress party withdrew its support. Central rule through the governor was imposed on Punjab on 23 August 1968 (Govt of India 1988: 188). However, the Congress aim of coming back to power was defeated when in the elections held to the Punjab state assembly in 1969, the Akali Dal-led coalition returned to power (Brass 1974: 314). This government was also brought down through Congress manoeuvres and the President's Rule was imposed on 15 June 1971 (Govt of India 1988: 188).

Mrs Indira Gandhi, the Congress prime minister, sensed a national mood in favour of the Congress party after the Indian government's success in dismembering Pakistan and the creation of Bangladesh. From the viewpoint of Congress prospects in Punjab, the fact that a Sikh army general, Lieutenant General Jagjit Singh Arora, had led the Indian army in its success against Pakistan was subtly used to woo Sikh voters to Indian nationalism and the Congress party. In the general elections held in March 1972 a few months after the December 1971 victory over Pakistan, the Congress party achieved a convincing victory in the Punjab state assembly. The overwhelming wave of pro-Indian nationalism helped Indira Gandhi's Congress party to also win a majority of Punjab's seats to India's central parliament.

The bringing down of two Akali Dal-led governments in Punjab by the Congress-led central government and the re-installation of Congress into power in Punjab made the Akali Sikh leadership feel that unless there was a fundamental restructuring of centre–state relations in favour of the states, they (the Akali Sikhs) could not hope to achieve sustainable power in Punjab. The Akali Dal formed a committee consisting of top political leaders of the party and a few Sikh intellectuals on 11 December 1972 to prepare a policy paper outlining the long-term perspective of the Akali Dal on the two interrelated questions: the place of the Sikhs in India and the power of the states in India's federal system. A position paper prepared by this committee was adopted by the Working Committee of the Akali Dal on 16–17 October 1973 at Anandpur Sahib, the town where the tenth Sikh guru had given the Khalsa orientation to the Sikh community in 1699. This position paper came to be known as the Anandpur Sahib Resolution. It was endorsed in the form of a succession of resolutions at the eighteenth All India Akali Conference of the Shiromani Akali Dal at Ludhiana on 28–29 October 1978 (Amarinder Singh 1992: 133–141, Giani Ajmer Singh 1977).

The core of the Anandpur Sahib Resolution is an elaboration of two propositions: that the Sikhs are a nation and that the Indian political system needs to be restructured by devolving power from the centre to the states in all areas except defence, foreign affairs, currency and communications. These two core aspects do not appear to be reconcilable if one accepts the position that every nation has to have its own sovereign state. That position would entail the establishment of a sovereign Sikh state and the aspect of devolution of power to the provinces within an Indian federal structure would then be redundant. However, the two aspects are reconcilable if it is accepted that there could be multi-nation sovereign countries. A further debatable point within that position would be whether the criterion for nationhood is language or religion. The language criterion would justify the claim of a Punjabi nation and the religious criterion that of a Sikh nation. A more layered and complex perspective of a multi-national country would make the three claims of a Sikh nationhood, a Punjabi nationhood and an Indian nationhood compatible with each other (Pritam Singh 1999).

The competing interpretations and the possible implications of the Anandpur Sahib Resolution did not attract much attention until the 1980s, when the political stakes on these interpretations and implications were raised very high. As we shall see later on, in 1984, Rajiv Gandhi, the Indian prime minister, made the separatist and secessionist interpretation of the Resolution a key election plank to mobilize Indian and Hindu nationalist sentiment against the Sikhs in his Congress party's campaign in the general election of December 1984. This sectarian campaign produced an unparalleled election success for the Congress party. But before we are able to examine the implications of this success for Punjab's relations with the centre, we need to look back at a set of critical developments that took place in the 1970s.

In 1975, Mrs Indira Gandhi, then Indian prime minister, imposed a national emergency in the country to deal with the rising opposition threat to her political power. A large number of Akali leaders and activists were arrested as a part of the national swoop against all anti-emergency political currents in the country. The Akali leaders and activists who managed to escape arrest organized the most active and persistent segment of the non-violent countrywide opposition to emergency rule. Every day during the entire 19 months of emergency rule, a group of Akali volunteers would pray at the Golden Temple and would come out and shout slogans against the emergency. The group would then be arrested for violating the prohibitory orders. Over 40,000 Akali workers were arrested for their participation in the anti-emergency campaign (Narang 1983: 192). The Akalis' organizational skill in arranging this sustainable movement attracted

Mrs Gandhi's attention because almost all the rest of India had submitted to the power of the central state. Only small groups of socialist and Maoist activists organized sporadic acts of violent defiance. Mrs Gandhi offered the Akalis the rule of Punjab if, in turn, they offered their support to her rule at the centre. She was visualizing a repeat of the Tamil Nadu formula in which a Tamil regionalist party had reached a similar agreement with her. The Akali leadership rejected Mrs Gandhi's offer (Narang 1983: 192). This rejection embittered her against the Akalis and contributed to complicating the resolution of many subsequent issues relating to the centre's relations with Punjab and the Sikhs during the early 1980s. After Mrs Gandhi lifted the emergency, the Akalis joined the Janata Party-led national opposition, which defeated her in the general election of 1977. The Akali Dal joined the Janata Party-led coalition government at the centre (Narang 1983: 193). One of the Akali nominees in the coalition government was made the minister for agriculture in recognition of Akali Dal's agrarian electoral base and that of Punjab as an agrarian state. The coming to power of a non-Congress government at the centre was a new development in Indian politics and the Akali Dal becoming a partner in government at the centre was a new development in Punjab politics. However, this proved to be a short-lived interregnum. The Janata Party-led coalition government fell because of internal squabbles and Mrs Gandhi returned back to power in the 1980 general election.

Parallel with these political developments in the 1970s was another set of socio-cultural developments taking place in Punjab, which were to cast a deep shadow on the centre's conflict with Punjab and the Sikhs in the 1980s.

The Green Revolution strategy of agricultural development in the 1960s led to the extension and deepening of the capitalist mode of production in Punjab agriculture. The commodification of social life as a consequence of increasing capitalist modernization in Punjab's rural society resulted in several forms of fissures in social practices and cultural norms. Two diametrically opposite ideological currents emerged as a response to this socio-cultural crisis: one a radical Marxism-inspired vision of an alternative collectivist socialist life, the other a religious revivalist vision of a pure Sikh way of life (Pritam Singh 1987). The radical vision became especially popular with Sikh students in the universities and the professional medical and engineering colleges. Many of these students were the first generation of their rural families to enter higher education. The radicalization of student and youth movements all over the world in the late 1960s also contributed to the spread of Marxist ideas among the educated Punjabi rural youth. The specific form this Marxist influence in Punjab took was the emergence of the Maoist Naxalite movement in Punjab from the late 1960s and early/mid-1970s.[29] The Maoist emphasis on 'armed struggle' jelled very well with the Sikh tradition and contributed further to the valorization of Sikh identity. While the Maoist movement was crushed through brutal state terror by the mid-1970s (Judge 1992), its intellectual and political legacy did leave some impact on Punjab's political culture.

The egalitarianism derived from the Marxist tradition coexisted with that of the Sikh tradition. Some isolated intellectual attempts were made towards a critical synthesis of the two traditions but the dominant practice remained one of uncritical coexistence. This coexistence on one hand radicalized the intellectual vocabulary of the Punjabi Sikh intelligentsia and on the other contributed to strengthening Sikh identity. Maoist internationalism, by weakening the ideological appeal of Indian nationalism among the Punjabi Sikh intelligentsia, made its own indirect contribution to the strengthening of separate Sikh identity. It is not surprising, therefore, that later on some activists from the Naxalite tradition either joined or aligned with a section of the Sikh militants who campaigned for a separate Sikh homeland of Khalistan.[30]

The collapse of the Naxalite movement in the early/mid-1970s was followed by the emergence of religious revivalist currents, though there is no direct causal link between the two. The indirect link, however, can be imagined. The political vacuum created by the defeat of the Naxalite movement did contribute to creating a fertile ground for the emergence of alternative visions and the Sikh religious vision which had remained dormant in the previous decade seemed to acquire added attraction in the new context. A number of Sikh revivalist groups started preaching the superiority of a simple Sikh ethical way of life over the decadent consumerist style of life penetrating the rural society of Punjab as a result of the degenerative forms of capitalist modernization. 'This degenerative form of modernization expressed itself in the menacing spread of alcoholism, smoking, drug-addiction, pornographic literature, lewd music and vulgar cinema' (Pritam Singh 1987: 169). The religious revivalist groups found a responsive audience among the rural Sikh population when they launched a moral and ideological crusade against this degenerative form of capitalist modernization.

Though many organizations and individuals played a crucial role in the Sikh revivalist movement, it was Sant Jarnail Singh Bhindranwale who, after becoming the head of the Sikh 'orthodox' organization Damdami Taksal in 1977 came to occupy the central role and eventually to symbolize the Sikh revivalist movement. His movement went through a number of phases: first, a moral, humanist and egalitarian phase when he focused on preaching against vulgar consumerism and casteism (Pritam Singh 1987: 170–171); second, a Sikh 'orthodoxy' phase during which he collided with a 'heterodox' sect called the Nirankaris in 1978 in Amritsar when over a dozen Sikhs were killed in a Sikh–Nirankari clash (Dhillon 1992: 143, Grewal 1998: 216); third, an anti-Hindu phase when he directed his tirade against a Hindu press baron, Jagat Narain, who had supported the Nirankari campaign against the Sikhs (Deol 2000, chapter 6) and finally his insistence that the central government must accept the provisions of the Anandpur Sahib Resolution (Sandhu 1999: 476–477). It was in the last two stages that he started to become portrayed in the Indian media as anti-Hindu and anti-centre.

The moderate and constitutionalist Akali party was eventually sucked into the confrontation between Bhindranwale and the centre (Pritam Singh 1982). After losing power to the Congress party in 1980, the Akalis started to build a movement on secular demands against what they perceived as the centre's discrimination against Punjab. They started with a *nehar roko morcha* (struggle to stop the canal) in alliance with the Communist Party of India (Marxist) on 24 April 1982 to stop the construction of the Satluj–Yamuna Link (SYL) Canal, which was planned by the centre to divert some of the river water resources of Punjab to the neighbouring states of Haryana and Rajasthan. For the water-dependent agrarian economy of Punjab, the matter of utilization of its river water resources was of critical importance. Equally important was the question of the method of resolving the competing claims of the centre ('for national development') and different states (for their respective 'regional development') over river water resources.

The dispute had a history of its own.[31] According to the Indus Water Treaty of 1955, the water needs of Punjab were roughly estimated to be 7.20 million acre feet (*maf*),[32] Rajasthan was supposed to need eight *maf*, while Jammu and Kashmir were supposed to require 0.65 *maf*. The Punjab Reorganization Act of 1966, which stipulated the division of territory and the various resources between the newly demarcated states of Punjab and Haryana, provided for the waters of the Punjab rivers to be divided between Punjab and Haryana through mutual agreement but did not provide for any claims of Punjab on the waters of the Yamuna river from which Punjab until then had been drawing water for irrigation. It was also stipulated that if the two states of Punjab and Haryana failed to reach an agreement on sharing the waters of the Punjab rivers, the central government was to decide their shares. Indira Gandhi had decided during the emergency in 1976 that out of the 7.20 *maf* of the Punjab share, 0.20 *maf* be given to Delhi for drinking purposes and the remaining seven *maf* be equally divided between Punjab and Haryana. This decision was blatantly unjust on two grounds. First, the water for Delhi was being taken out of the total pool without any justifiable and legal grounds; second, the 50:50 division of the remaining pool between Punjab and Haryana was discriminatory against Punjab because the general formula used for division of resources had been agreed as a 60:40 division based on the bigger population and territory of Punjab. Even the Congress chief minister of Punjab, Giani Zail Singh, was reported to have expressed his displeasure at the blatant injustice done to his state. However, the threatening prospect of losing his chief ministership if he did not accept Indira Gandhi's verdict, kept him quiet (Nayar and Singh 1984: 47).

When the Akalis came back into power in the wake of the anti-emergency movement against Indira Gandhi, they took up the issue with the Janata Party prime minister, Morarji Desai. He agreed that Rajasthan had little to do with Punjab rivers but was not prepared to reopen the decision of 1955. He was prepared to give his own verdict on the shares of Punjab and Haryana but only on condition that his verdict would be final. When the Akalis suggested that they could take the issue to the Supreme Court, Desai raised no objection. A suit was then filed by the Akali Government of Punjab and the case was pending in the Supreme Court when in 1980 the Janata government fell and Congress again came to power both at the centre and in Punjab. The new Congress chief minister of Punjab, Darbara Singh, was forced to withdraw the Punjab government's case from the Supreme Court. Indira Gandhi seemed to be keen on getting the SYL Canal dug for Haryana in view of the impending state assembly elections in Haryana.

The Akali Dal was thus pushed into launching its *nehar roko morcha*. Though the support given by the Communist Party of India (Marxist) added to the moral basis of the campaign, the agitation failed to mobilize the peasantry in large numbers. On 26 July 1982 the Akalis decided at last to launch their *dharam yudh morcha* (righteous war/struggle) with effect from 4 August from the precincts of the holiest Sikh shrine, the Golden Temple of Amritsar. The Communist Party disagreed with the Akali decision to move the headquarters of the agitation to the Golden Temple and to the presentation of the agitation in religious overtones. It therefore dissociated itself from the agitation. The Akalis, however, gained another ally. Sant Jarnail Singh Bhindranwale, who had been organizing another agitation from the Golden Temple against the arrest of some of his associates, joined the *dharam yudh morcha* under the leadership of the Akali Dal president, Sant Harchand Singh Longowal.

The *dharam yudh morcha* started on 4 August 1982 with the top Akali leader Parkash Singh Badal, who had twice been chief minister of Punjab, courting arrest with over 5,000 other volunteers. The *dharam yudh morcha* for the political, economic, cultural and religious demands of Punjab and the Sikhs was hugely successful in mobilizing public support from all sections of the Sikhs. Within two months of the *morcha*, the government found it difficult to find room for the protesting volunteers in the existing jails. After the *Punjabi suba morcha* (struggle for a Punjabi-speaking state) of the 1950s and early 1960s for the creation of a Punjabi-speaking state, this was turning out to be potentially the bitterest conflict between Punjab and the Sikhs on one side and the Congress government at the centre on the other.

Of the various mediations that were attempted to resolve the conflict, the most serious and potentially hopeful was the one made by Swaran Singh, who had held several senior positions as a cabinet minister in the central governments led by Nehru, Shastri and Indira Gandhi. He was trusted by the Akalis and was respected by the Congress leadership. Indira Gandhi had authorized him on her behalf to reach a negotiated settlement with the Akali leadership. He hammered out a mutually acceptable formula on several important issues, like river waters, Chandigarh and centre–state relations. A cabinet sub-committee appointed by Indira Gandhi to consider the formula, accepted it. On that basis, Swaran Singh told the Akali leaders that the government had approved the formula.

However, the statement placed before the parliament turned out to be materially different from what had been agreed (Nayar and Singh 1984: 62–63). It seemed that Indira Gandhi had herself sabotaged the negotiated settlement. She appeared to have other plans. She was sensing a Hindu communal backlash building in the rest of the country and especially in north India. She seemed to want to cash in on this backlash for the forthcoming elections by appearing to be tough with the Akalis and the Sikhs (Bhambri 1985, Sheth and Narang 1985). Her political designs weakened the moderate and constitutionalist Akali tendency represented by Sant Harchand Singh Longowal and Parkash Singh Badal.

Sant Jarnail Singh Bhindranwale seemed to be gathering more support among the Sikh masses for advocating that the use of violence was more likely to lead to the *morcha* victory than the path of peaceful agitation promoted by the moderate tendency. He was especially adamant regarding the acceptance of the Anandpur Sahib Resolution as a part of the negotiated settlement (Sandhu 1999: 476–477). The acceptance of the positions in the Anandpur Sahib Resolution required a significant restructuring of centre–state relations and Indira Gandhi feared that she would lose the support of the majority Hindu electorate if she were seen to be yielding to an Akali–Sikh demand for devolution of power to the states. The moderate Akalis felt in danger of being marginalized by the competing intransigence of Bhindranwale and Indira Gandhi. Bhindranwale ridiculed the Akalis as 'weak' and 'cowards' in negotiating with the centre while Indira Gandhi's government and Congress party criticized the Akalis for not standing up to Bhindranwale's extremism. Some of Bhindranwale's followers were killed in police custody and were reported by the police to have been killed in encounters. Such 'encounters', which came to be known in the media as 'fake encounters', increased in number.

Bhindranwale's followers and other Sikh extremist groups stepped up their violent attacks on police, government officials, Nirankaris and politicians. There were also bank robberies and attacks on central government property, such as the burning of railway stations and the cutting of telegraph wires. A new dimension was added to this escalating violent confrontation when on 5–6 October 1983, a group of innocent Hindu passengers were pulled out of a Delhi-bound bus near Dhilwan village in Kapurthala district and shot dead. The government blamed the extremists, while Sikh politicians suspected the involvement of the government's secret intelligence agencies. The killers were never found and even the identity of the killed was never made public. Indira Gandhi acted very swiftly and dismissed the Punjab government headed by her own party man Darbara Singh.

Punjab was brought under direct central rule by imposing President's Rule on 6 October 1983. On 7 October, Punjab was declared to be a 'disturbed area', allowing the security forces extra powers of operation. These measures, however, did not succeed in controlling violence. The activities of some Hindu extremist organizations in Punjab and the neighbouring states contributed further to the worsening violent atmosphere. A gurdwara at Charu in Rajasthan was burnt down on 26–27 November 1983. On 14 February 1984, an extremist Hindu organization called the Hindu Suraksha Samiti (Hindu Protection Organization) organized a *bandh* (closure of all public and private sector activities) in Punjab in which 11 persons died. During the *bandh*, according to the government's *White Paper on the Punjab Agitation*, '[some] members of extremist

Hindu organizations committed the sacrilege of damaging the model of the Golden Temple and a picture of Guru Ram Das at the Amritsar Railway Station' (Govt of India 1984: 30).[33] From 15 to 20 February 1984, there was mob violence in Haryana against the Sikhs, 'generally believed to have been engineered by its Chief Minister on the insistence of the leader of a powerful lobby in Delhi' (Grewal 1998: 224). On 19 February, eight Sikhs were killed on the Grand Trunk Road in Panipat within sight of the Haryana police. Thirty-five Hindus were killed in Punjab in the following five days (Grewal 1998: 224).

The Akalis tried to seize the initiative in this hopelessly violence-ridden atmosphere by organizing a Punjab *bandh* on 8 February 1984 to demonstrate their strength and commitment to non-violent modes of protest. The *bandh* was a success. Despite increasing frustration at the reluctance of Indira Gandhi's government to reach a negotiated settlement, the Akalis agreed after persuasion by some opposition leaders to participate in a tripartite meeting in Delhi on 14 and 15 February as a last-ditch effort to arrive at a negotiated political settlement. This tripartite meeting was attended by four cabinet ministers and five secretaries, five of the Akali leaders and 15 leaders from the opposition parties (Govt of India 1984: 97). It came close to a successful settlement.

It was at this juncture that anti-Sikh violence was orchestrated in Haryana to frustrate settlement. Indira Gandhi's government seemed to be playing a diabolical game. On the one hand, it was keeping face with the national opposition by still holding meetings and parleys to discuss the possibility of a negotiated settlement; on the other, it was giving free reign to those elements in the government and the Congress party who were stepping up confrontation with the Sikhs and to the mobilization of Hindu communal sentiments against the Sikhs.

The Akali leadership was being pushed against the wall. The increasing tempo of Hindu-Sikh polarization forced the Akalis to highlight the danger to Sikh identity in a predominantly Hindu country. On 27 February the Akali leaders carried out their decision to burn the pages of the constitution of India which contained Article 25 (2) (b) stipulating that certain religious, social and legal practices applicable to the Hindus meant that they were applicable to the Sikhs also along with the Jains and the Buddhists. The increasing religious sectarian polarization meant that the Akalis were shifting their focus from secular demands like water and territory to a religious one of protecting the separate identity of the Sikhs (Pritam Singh 1984a: 195–196). One concession that Indira Gandhi had made in June 1983, though in the right direction, was made in a calculated fashion to make it appear not as a concession to the Akalis. She made a unilateral decision to appoint a Supreme Court judge Justice Ranjit Singh Sarkaria, a Sikh, to head a commission to inquire into centre–state relations (Govt of India 1984: 17, Govt of India 1988: iii). This was partly in response to suggestions made by opposition leaders and some other public figures that the Akalis' demand for the examination of centre–state relations was a justified one and shared by many other regional parties in the country. Had this demand been conceded as a part of a comprehensive package in a negotiated settlement, the

Akalis could have claimed the victory of their *dharma yudh morcha* and would have marginalized the extremist Bhindranwale. In making a unilateral announcement on this vital issue, Indira Gandhi wanted to appear generous without seeming to yield to the Akalis. This posture was in tune with keeping intact her Hindu electorate base while pacifying some of her non-Akali critics in the opposition. In moments of intense bargaining and game play, the form, sometimes, acquires as much importance as the content. The manner in which central government formally stated its position regarding the Akali demand for restructuring centre–state relations was indicative of the political strategy of the Congress party as I have outlined above. Its position was as follows:

> Recognizing the importance of the subject, the Government set up in June 1983, a Commission under the chairmanship of Shri Justice Ranjit Singh Sarkaria to examine and review the work of the existing arrangements between the Union and the States in regard to powers, functions and responsibilities in all spheres and recommend such changes or other measures as may be appropriate. *The Commission was to keep in view the scheme and framework of the Constitution designed to ensure the unity and integrity of the country.* The Government's decision to initiate such a comprehensive review of Centre–State relations should have satisfied the Akali Dal, as it did other opposition parties which had also raised this issue. But *the Akali Dal was adamant* that Government should make specific mention of the Anandpur Sahib Resolution while referring the matter to the Sarkaria Commission.... The position of the Government has been stated unambiguously ... The propositions contained in Anandpur Sahib Resolution on Centre–State relations are at total variance with the basic concept of the unity and integrity of the nation as expressed in our Constitution. These cannot be accepted even as a basis for discussion. *The people of India do not accept the proposition that India is a multi-national society. The Indian people constitute one nation.... The affirmation of India's nationhood ... does not brook any challenge.*
>
> (Govt of India 1984: 17, italics added)

Indira Gandhi's tactics convinced the Akali leadership that unless the full weight of their mobilizational strength was brought to bear on the central government, Mrs Gandhi would not feel the urgency to reach a negotiated settlement with them. With this calculation in mind, Sant Harchand Singh Longowal, president of Akali Dal, issued a call on 23 May 1984 for non-co-operation with the centre with effect from 3 June 1984. Longowal, who had been ridiculed by Bhindranwale as Gandhi because of his commitment to non-violence, wanted to invoke the spirit of Mahatma Gandhi's non-co-operation movement against the British rule in India. Through this, he wanted to win the hearts and minds of his countrymen and women in the rest of the country. However, the proposed non-co-operation movement's threat to stop the transport of wheat from Punjab to the rest of India put a sting in his otherwise peaceful sounding initiative.

The Indira Gandhi government, meanwhile, had been contemplating a military take-over of Punjab. The question of army action in Punjab was first discussed in December 1983 and in these discussions 'the idea figured that army action would consolidate Hindu vote in favour of the Congress' (Grewal 1998: 226). Indira Gandhi finally decided in favour of army action in April 1984 (Grewal 1998: 226).[34] Before the Akalis could start their non-co-operation movement on 3 June, Mrs Gandhi in her broadcast to the nation on 2 June 1984 announced the army take-over of Punjab.[35] This army operation was named Operation Blue Star. At the operational level, the central aim was twofold: to take control of the Golden Temple at Amritsar and other key gurdwaras from Bhindranwale's armed supporters and Akali activists, and to facilitate the transport of wheat from Punjab to the rest of the country and thus defeat the Akalis' threatened disruption of this wheat transport. However, there was another larger underlying political motive behind the operation as a sub-text of the message. This was to convey to the majority Hindu population that Indira Gandhi was the saviour of the nation from the disruptive Sikhs. She was hailed in 1971 as the Hindu goddess Durga who had defeated Muslim Pakistan's army and had dismembered the 'enemy' Pakistan by creating Bangladesh out of it. She wanted her Durga goddess image to re-emerge by 'slaying' the Sikh 'enemy' this time. She had swept the polls after the 1971 victory and she wanted a repeat performance now. Victory was assured. A few hundred armed supporters of Bhindranwale, however well entrenched in the protective location of the Golden Temple complex, were no match for the military might of the Indian state. Both the combatants inside the Golden Temple complex and the planners of the attack from outside knew this. Both had their game plans. The combatants inside wanted to die fighting as martyrs. They hoped to lay the foundation for Khalistan through their martyrdom. The planners of the attack from outside wanted to demonstrate Hindu supremacy by 'slaying the evil enemy' inside. Khalistan was the aim of the one and 'the unity and integrity of India' was the aim of the other. Sikh assertion was the aim of the one and Hindu domination was the aim of the other. Both succeeded at least temporarily.

Never before in their history had Sikhs been so alienated from the Hindus and India as they were after Operation Blue Star. Never before had anti-Sikh sentiment among the Hindus been unleashed as powerfully as it was after 1984.[36] The level and intensity of the military confrontation between the Sikh combatants and the Indian state had no parallel in post-independent India. This operation was the first of its kind in India in which seven divisions of the army were deployed and the three wings of the armed forces – the army, the navy and the air force (though the latter two on a lesser scale) – were brought to suppress an internal rebellion.[37] As many as 13 tanks were used in the attack (Dhillon 1992: 221). Estimates of persons killed vary from 493, according to the Government of India (Govt of India 1984: 169) to over 8,000, according to another estimate

(Dhillon 1992: 226). The most reliable, and the most recent, is an estimate by Khushwant Singh, who writes that 'in the cross-fire upwards of 5,000 people, a majority of them pilgrims, including women and children lost their lives'.[38] The Akal Takhat was very severely damaged in the operation.[39]

For the Sikhs, it was a tragedy that none of the living generation of the Sikhs had seen in their lives. For India and the overwhelming majority of the Hindus, especially in Hindi-speaking north India, it was an unprecedented victory for the Indian and Hindu nation. The government media actively pandered to Hindu prejudices (Pritam Singh 1984, 1985, 1985a). The Sikhs mourned and protested, and also hailed their 'martyrs'. They mourned the destruction of the Akal Takhat and the sacrilege committed at the Harimandar; they protested, literally everywhere in the world where they had settled in small or large numbers, against the army action; and they hailed the sacrifice of the Sikh fighters who resisted the army's entry into the Golden Temple. The dead Bhindranwale eclipsed every living Sikh leader in terms of popularity among the Sikhs. His defiance and sacrifice was hailed as resembling those of the great Sikh martyrs of the eighteenth century. The large numbers of deaths of the Sikhs at the Golden Temple complex were called a *ghallughara* (holocaust). This term had previously been used only twice in Sikh history – *chotta ghallughara* (the small holocaust) referred to the massacre of Sikhs in 1746 and *vadha ghallughara* (the big holocaust) referred to the large-scale massacre of the Sikh men, women and children in 1762.

The feeling of mourning soon turned into a desire for revenge against all those who had planned and executed Operation Blue Star. The main target was Indira Gandhi. History was invoked. References were made to previous episodes in Sikh history when anyone who had attacked the Golden Temple had been subsequently killed. An expatriate Sikh activist in London, Jagjit Singh Chauhan, outraged the Indian authorities by publicly echoing the dominant Sikh sentiment that Indira Gandhi would be punished soon and he clearly hinted at the possibility of her assassination.[40] Indira Gandhi, meanwhile, had risen in stature in the eyes of the majority Hindu population. She openly donned the mantle of a Hindu goddess Durga and that of a saviour of the Hindu nation. She openly stated that 'Hindu dharma [faith] was under attack from the Sikhs' (Bose 1998: 123). She appeared to recapture the political glory that she had reached in 1971 after defeating the Pakistan army. Events were moving to another tragic collision.

On 31 October 1984, two of Indira Gandhi's Sikh bodyguards pumped several bullets into her body. She died on the way to hospital. Within hours of the news of her death, minor and stray incidents of attacks on the Sikhs in Delhi began to be reported. The government media (television and radio), helped by a majority of the non-government media, actively contributed to building anti-Sikh sentiments among the Hindus (Pritam Singh 1985, 1985a). On 1 November, reports started emerging of large-scale killings of Sikhs and the burning of their gurdwaras and businesses not only in Delhi but in many other towns of north India. 'In Delhi and nearabouts it is believed that 4,000–5,000 Sikhs were killed. Out of them, 5–10 percent were burnt alive' (Amrik Singh 1985: 317). '50,000–60,000 people [Sikhs] ... had been rendered homeless and subjected to unspeakable humiliation and torture' (Amrik Singh 1985: 321). Several top leaders of the Congress party's Delhi unit were named for organizing and participating in this anti-Sikh genocidal violence in well-documented reports by three human rights organizations (Noorani 1985). These reports called for the arrest and trial of the suspected individuals. This call for justice seemed to be the desperate cry for sanity of a small group of Delhi-based activists and intellectuals who felt silenced in the deafening chorus of hatred and revenge against the Sikhs.

The Congress party leadership was aware of the electoral windfall for it from this massive polarization of the majority Hindu electorate against a tiny 2 per cent Sikh population in the country. A tidal wave of sympathy for the murdered Indira Gandhi's Congress party seemed to sweep the country (Sheth and Narang 1985: 134). Her son, Rajiv Gandhi, was appointed prime minister though he was not even a member of parliament. Soon after he took over, he publicly justified, in a speech at the Delhi Boat Club rally on 19 November, the massacre of the Sikhs in the wake of his mother's murder by saying that when a big tree falls, the earth shakes (Noorani 1985: 274). He ordered elections to the parliament to legitimize his appointment and to seek mandate for his Congress party. In the election campaign, he chose to focus on the Anandpur Sahib Resolution as the sole issue. He characterized the Resolution as secessionist and asked for a vote for him and his party to preserve 'the unity and integrity' of India.

In a professionally organized media campaign in which the government-controlled television and radio were systematically used for the benefit of the Congress party, the message conveyed to the voters was that the choice before them was: the Sikhs, the Anandpur Sahib Resolution and secessionism vs the Hindus, the constitution of India and the territorial integrity of the country (Pritam Singh 1985a: 183). As expected, Rajiv Gandhi scored a massive election victory that even his grandfather, Jawaharlal Nehru, never had scored. The elections were not held in Punjab. If the elections had been held there, it would not have quantitatively changed the overall electoral verdict because Punjab's share is just 13 seats out of 542 but the expected victory of Sikh candidates opposed to Congress could have qualitatively diminished the significance of Congress's overall victory by revealing it to be the product of a sectarian manipulation of the Hindu vote in the rest of the country. An influential functionary of the Hindu nationalist Bharatiya Janata Party (Indian Peoples' Party), which won only two seats, commented very perceptively, that 'organizationally, the Congress has won but ideologically, the BJP has won'.[41]

Having achieved such a massive victory on a patently anti-Sikh platform, Rajiv Gandhi did not want to risk an adverse reaction from his Hindu electoral base by showing any sign of reconciliation with the Sikhs. He rejected the demand for an enquiry into the anti-Sikh carnage in November 1984. However, the continuing Punjab crisis was the major political challenge facing his administration. Punjab had been under President's Rule since October 1983 and the constitution of India had been amended several times since then to overcome the constitutional legal hurdle that a state cannot be under President's Rule for more than six months between a dissolved state assembly and a newly constituted one. His leadership skills at resolving this national crisis were at stake.

By mid-1985, he initiated some moves to test Hindu opinion in the country on resolving the Punjab crisis. He appointed Arjan Singh as the new governor of Punjab. A former Congress chief minister of the central Indian state of Madhya Pradesh, Arjan Singh was considered very close to the Nehru-Gandhi family and as one of the key advisers of Rajiv Gandhi.[42] The Hindu Rajput community he came from was generally viewed as favourably inclined towards the Sikhs because the Rajputs and the Sikhs viewed each other, and were viewed by others, as 'martial races' (Dhillon 2007). Both the communities were recruited heavily into the armed forces during the colonial rule and were well represented in the post-colonial India army. The appointment of Arjan Singh was, therefore, a clear signal of a change of track in the policy of dealing with the Sikhs and the Punjab crisis. It was a change from an earlier confrontationist and 'law and order solution' approach to a conciliatory and 'political solution' approach. Rajiv Gandhi made another significant conciliatory move. He ordered the release of the top Akali leaders including Sant Harchand Singh Longowal, the president of the Akali Dal, from the jail where they had been incarcerated since the June 1984 army operation at the Golden Temple (Grewal 1996: 159).

Arjan Singh developed a good rapport with Sant Longowal and had played a crucial role in persuading Rajiv Gandhi to release him and the other Akali leaders from the jail. The government media was used extensively to build up an acceptable image of Sant Longowal, i.e. acceptable to the Hindu population which until recently had been fed on a diet of anti-Akali and anti-Sikh propaganda. The government faced another difficulty from the Sikh side in getting Sant Longowal to come to the negotiating table. Two Akali leaders, Parkash Singh Badal and Gurcharan Singh Tohra who were next to Sant Longowal in the Akali leadership hierarchy, were opposed to talking to the Rajiv Gandhi government because of its recent record of anti-Sikh actions (Nayar 1985: 394). Arjan Singh in his eagerness to get some settlement with the Sikhs, succeeded in persuading two other Akali leaders, Surjit Singh Barnala and Balwant Singh, who were lower in the Akali hierarchy than Badal and Tohra, to accompany Sant Longowal in negotiating with Rajiv Gandhi (Grewal 1996: 159).

The settlement, called the Punjab Accord or Rajiv Longowal Accord, was reached very quickly. It was signed by Rajiv Gandhi on behalf of the Government of India and Sant Longowal on behalf of the Akali Dal on 24 July 1985 (Amrik Singh 1985: 381). The Punjab Accord was, in most respects, a serious gesture of conciliation with the Sikhs. It stipulated, among other things, the holding of fresh state assembly elections in Punjab, the handover of Chandigarh to Punjab by 26 January 1986, rehabilitation of Sikh soldiers who had deserted the army in protest against Operation Blue Star, compensation to victims of 1984 anti-Sikh violence in Delhi and some other towns, an appointment of a commission of inquiry into the 1984 violence against the Sikhs, the release of imprisoned Sikh activists who did not have any serious charge against them and the examination of centre–state relations in the light of the Anandpur Sahib Resolution (Noorani 1985a: 383–389).

Two clauses of the Accord, however, weakened its overall generous promise. One related to the identification and transfer of Hindi-speaking areas from Punjab to Haryana in lieu of the exclusive control of Chandigarh to be transferred to Punjab. The other related to the diversion of river waters of Punjab to Haryana. The government media hailed the Punjab Accord as a great success of Rajiv Gandhi's skills of political management. It was interpreted as a peaceful way of defeating the threat in Punjab to India's 'unity and integrity'. The fact that the Sikhs had been militarily defeated and the government was seen as talking from a position of strength made the Accord seem acceptable to the majority Hindu population as victor's generosity to the defeated. The government dipped into this sentiment of the Hindu community by using the language of 'healing the wounds'. In order to make the settlement with Sant Longowal acceptable to the Hindu majority, the government media, helped by the non-government media, built the image of the Sant as a 'messiah of peace'. Some even called him the second Mahatma Gandhi (Dhillon 1992: 351).

The government was successful in getting the majority Hindu population to accept the Accord. On the Sikh side, however, there were problems. The Accord had been reached without any attempt having been made to let a consensus develop among the Akali leaders. Fearing opposition from Badal and Tohra, it was reached in a clandestine fashion by excluding them and by offering, it was rumoured, different sorts of prospects and incentives to Sant Longowal and the relatively junior leaders Surjit Singh Barnala and Balwant Singh. It appears that Sant Longowal was persuaded by the general prospect of peace in Punjab in the wake of the Accord. Barnala and Balwant Singh were lured by the incentive of leading the new government in Punjab which was expected to be formed after the promised state assembly elections (Dhillon 1992: 350). The initial reaction of Badal and Tohra to the Accord was to denounce it as a 'sell-out'. Their denunciation was partly a response to their having been personally sidelined in the Accord-reaching process and partly an articulation of the oppositionist sentiment in the Sikh community.

The oppositionist stance taken more strongly by hard-line militant groups pointed to the glaring omission in the Accord of the need for an apology from the Congress government for the Operation Blue Star action. The militant groups also wanted complete amnesty for the mutinous Sikh soldiers, unconditional handover of Chandigarh to Punjab, stoppage of the SYL Canal aimed at diverting Punjab river waters to the other states, and acceptance of the provision of Anandpur Sahib Resolution relating to centre–state relations. They did not doubt Sant Longowal's moral integrity but suspected that Balwant Singh, the only well-known Akali leader who was not imprisoned after Operation Blue Star due to his political and financial collaboration with the central government, had manipulated Longowal by projecting the Accord as the only viable solution to the troubles facing the Sikhs (Nayar 1985: 395). Barnala, who was generally respected by all sections of opinion in and outside Punjab as a moderate with an unblemished political record (Jeffrey 1994: 208), was rumoured to have been lured into the alliance by the prospect of becoming the chief minister of Punjab in a situation where his senior Badal had been excluded from the credit of reaching the Accord.

However, Badal and Tohra did not persist in opposing the Accord and eventually gave grudging support to Sant Longowal. This left the leadership of the anti-Accord tendencies in the hands of hardcore militant groups (Gobinder Singh 1987: 342). Sant Longowal was assassinated by a previously unknown group of Sikh militants on 20 August 1985. His assassins represented the raw sentiments of the most bitter and militant sections of the Sikh community which considered his act of reaching the Accord as surrender to the Delhi government.[43] His death left the Sikh community shocked and bewildered. The vast majority of the Sikhs felt sad at his death even if some of them were opposed to the Accord.[44] The fear of being left leaderless at this critical juncture in the history of the Sikh community in post-independent India made the overwhelming majority of the Sikhs rally behind Barnala, who was considered as the most trusted associate of Longowal.

In the elections held to the Punjab state assembly on 25 September barely a month after the assassination of Longowal, the Akali Dal under the leadership of Barnala won a resounding victory. If after Mrs Gandhi's assassination the consolidation of the Hindu vote behind the Congress party gave that party an unprecedented victory in the 1984 parliamentary election, the death of Sant Longowal contributed to the consolidation of the Sikh vote in Punjab behind Akali Dal to give the Dal an unprecedented victory in the Punjab assembly elections in September 1985. A section of the Hindu voters had also voted for the Akali Dal because of the fear that its defeat might strengthen the militant Sikh groups.[45] The militant groups, which had called for a boycott of the elections, did not get much response beyond a few isolated villages. These militants had not understood the dominant mood of the Sikh community, which was to vote heavily in favour of the Akali Dal in order to prevent the return to power of the hated Congress party (Dhillon 1992: 362–363). The Congress party itself had conducted a low-key election campaign to ensure that Barnala came to power so that the Punjab Accord could be implemented.[46] Rajiv Gandhi's positive reaction to the Akali Dal victory and his party's defeat in Punjab reflected his government's unusual attitude to this election verdict. In a statesman-like comment, which appeared to rephrase a Hindu ideologue's reaction to the Congress victory in December 1984 parliamentary elections, he said: 'Though our party has lost, the nation has won.'

In keeping with the sub-text of the Accord, Surjit Singh Barnala was sworn in as the chief minister of Punjab on 29 September 1985. His ally Balwant Singh became the finance minister and number two in the cabinet (Dhillon 1992: 363). The end of the President's Rule and the installation of a democratically elected government in Punjab allowed the militant dissidents also to operate more freely and openly. Two pro-militant organizations became prominent during this period: Damdami Taksal, a religiously orthodox Sikh seminary, which was headed before 1984 by Bhindranwale; and the All India Sikh Students Federation (AISSF), which was headed before 1984 by Bhindranwale's close associate Amrik Singh, who had also died resisting the Indian army's entry into the Golden Temple in June 1984. The two organizations had an uneasy alliance with a newly formed Akali Dal which named itself as United Akali Dal. The United Akali Dal was headed by Baba Joginder Singh, the father of Bhindranwale.

All three organizations had widespread but diffused support among the Sikhs in Punjab. Some militants released from jail at the recommendation of the Justice Bains Committee appointed by the Barnala government lent support to these organizations and some of them even became activists in them. These organizations had very organized and widespread support among the diaspora Sikh population and financial assistance provided by the diaspora Sikhs further added to the groups' political weight (Helweg 1989, Tatla 1999).

The Barnala government and the militant organizations competed with each other in securing support from the Sikh community. The key to their respective strength depended on what the central government was going to do regarding the implementation of the Punjab Accord. The Barnala government was hoping to demonstrate to the Sikh community that the strategy of adopting moderate and constitutional means was more powerful in getting the demands of the Sikh community and the Punjab state accepted than the strategy of militant confrontation advocated by the troika of Damdami Taksal-AISSF and United Akali Dal. The government's hopes of demonstrating the superiority of its political strategy rested, in the immediate future, on securing Chandigarh for Punjab by 26 January 1986 as provided for in the Punjab Accord. However, the change in the political priorities of the Rajiv Gandhi government since the signing of the Punjab Accord indicated that Barnala government was heading towards humiliation.

Getting a democratically elected government in Punjab to secure peace was the top political priority of the Rajiv Gandhi government around the time of signing the Accord in August 1985. This changed when the securing of election victory in the coming state assembly elections in the neighbouring Haryana state, which was in dispute with Punjab over the Chandigarh issue, became the Congress party's top-most political priority by the time the crucial date of 26 January 1986 approached. Rajiv's Congress party was worried that if Chandigarh was transferred to Punjab on 26 January 1986 as per the Accord, the anti-Congress parties in Haryana would portray this as an anti-Haryana measure and would, therefore, succeed in mobilizing public opinion in Haryana to defeat the Congress party in the state assembly election scheduled to be held in 1986. A bigger worry for the Congress party was that defeat in Haryana might herald a series of further defeats in the other neighbouring Hindi-speaking states. A clause in the Punjab Accord, which stipulated that in return for Chandigarh's transfer to Punjab some Hindi-speaking areas will be identified in Punjab to be transferred to Haryana, came in handy for Rajiv's government to fulfil its immediate political objectives. A commission appointed to identify Hindi-speaking areas in Punjab for transfer to Haryana failed to identify such areas.

Chandigarh was, therefore, not transferred to Punjab on 26 January 1986 (Grewal 1996: 160). The party political interests of the Congress party had taken precedence over the national needs of resolving the Punjab crisis. The logic of holding on to power at the centre had again forced the ruling party at the centre to act in a way that reinforced the Sikhs' mistrust of the centre. It signalled the death knell of the Punjab Accord. It was a blow to the Barnala government and to the moderate tendency in Akali politics, but a shot in the arm for the militant tendency. The Sikh militant groups had called for a congregation in the Golden Temple complex on 26 January 1986 and it attracted a massive gathering.[47] Emboldened by this response, they announced the formation of a five-member Panthic Committee as the supreme organization to lead the Sikh struggle against the central government. All five members of the Panthic Committee were close associates of the dead Bhindranwale.[48] They also announced their take-over of the most important religious centres of the Sikh community including that of the Golden Temple. They announced the dismissal of the existing head priests of these religious centres whom they viewed as moderate and appointed pro-militant head priests as their replacements. The resolution passed at the congregation called for stepping up the struggle against the central government in Delhi and mentioned the need to use all forms of struggle to achieve their objectives. They used radical Marxist-sounding language to articulate their cultural, religious and secular aspirations:

> This congregation declares with full determination that the struggle of the Sikhs for achieving their rights is on and they will fight by seeking co-operation and support of all those people in India and the entire world who are struggling for free expression of their voice of conscience. The Sikhs will give full assistance to such struggling people. This congregation wishes to make it clear that the Sikhs have no conflict with any religion, community, caste, race or the population of any region, but they will retaliate with full determination against the repression by those tyrants who have snatched away their rights [...] This congregation requests the entire Sikh world (*Sarbat Khalsa*) that not only among the Sikhs but also in the whole of India and the entire world, in every activity and organization of society, they should ceaselessly fight for the hegemony of morality and especially so in the realm of politics. It is only by following the path of truth and righteousness that the destructive forces of the world can be checkmated and their tendency to squander away the wealth of society created by the sweat

> of human labour can be stopped and the world peace can be established.[49]

Alarmed by this upsurge of support for the militants, the central government started pressing the Barnala government to take action against them. Politically weakened, the Barnala government resorted to repressive police measures against the militants under pressure from the central government. This further boosted the popularity of the militants. They held another impressive congregation at Amritsar on 13 April 1986 and finally, on 29 April 1986, they announced from a room in the Golden Temple complex that their goal was to achieve a sovereign Khalistan, a Sikh republic (Grewal 1996: 160). They also announced the launch of armed struggle under the command of their self-appointed Khalistan Commando Force to achieve their goal of Khalistan. The Barnala government, under the threat of dismissal by the centre if it did not take action against the Khalistani activists, sent police into the Golden Temple complex to arrest these activists. They had already escaped by the time the police arrived. The entry of the police into the Golden Temple at the order of the Barnala government caused a split in his government and his party, the Akali Dal. Badal and Tohra condemned the action, resigned from the Akali Dal headed by Barnala, and announced the formation of a new Badal-led Akali Dal. Several ministers resigned from the Barnala cabinet and joined the Badal-led Akali Dal. The Barnala government thus became politically even weaker.

The violent confrontations between the armed Sikh guerrilla groups and the police increased every month (Pettigrew 1995). The central government dismissed the Barnala government on 12 May 1987 and re-imposed direct central rule over Punjab (Grewal 1996: 162). The Punjab Accord was dead. The moderate Akali project collapsed, at least for the time being. Punjab became a battleground between Indian security forces including the army and the Sikh guerrilla organizations (Dhillon 1998, P. Kumar 1998, Birinder Pal Singh 1998, 2002a). A large number of Sikh youths joined these organizations, which got considerable financial support from a large pool of their supporters among the Sikh diaspora (Helweg 1989, Tatla 1999). The Government of Pakistan, a traditional geo-political rival of India, also provided logistical support to these organizations.[50] Punjab remained under direct central rule via its governor until February 1992. Large-scale violations of human rights took place during the Indian security forces' operation against the Sikh guerrillas and their supporters (Pettigrew 1995, Pritam Singh 1998, R. N. Kumar 2000, 2002, R. N. Kumar *et al.* 2003). The Sikh guerrillas' retaliation against their opponents and the allies of the Indian state was no less brutal (Puri *et al.* 1999, Pritam Singh 2001). The entire effort of the administration during the governor's rule was directed towards defeating the Sikh insurgency.[51] The development of the industrial and service sector suffered a setback and the ruralization of the Punjab economy was further strengthened (Kumar 1991). The Government of India eventually succeeded in crushing the Sikh militancy, but at a very heavy human cost. The majority of the Punjabi Sikhs who died in the battle between the Indian security forces and the Sikh guerrilla organizations were young men in the prime of their productive life span.

Post-1991 developments

An election to the Punjab state assembly was held in February 1992 despite a boycott call by all militant and almost all the moderate Akali Sikh groups. The boycott benefited the Congress party as it had expected and wished for (Chaudhry 1994: 402). The Congress candidates got elected, in some places without any contest, in large numbers. However, the poor voter turnout of merely 20 per cent of the total electorate deprived the new Congress party government of the legitimacy it needed to restore civilian administration (Verma 1994). The new government's claims of having restored peace in Punjab were partially justified because of the drastic decline in militancy-related violent incidents after 1993. The militants, however, struck back in 1995. They assassinated Punjab's Congress chief minister Beant Singh on 31 August 1995 by using a suicide bomber. This raised the spectre of the revival of militant activity in Punjab. But Punjab largely remained free of any serious militancy-related violence in the late 1990s. In 1997, the moderate Akali Dal led by Parkash Singh Badal came back into power with a massive victory.

The new Badal government succeeded in persuading the central government to write off the huge debt Punjab owed to the centre due to the expenditure incurred on deployment of central security forces in Punjab during the 1980s and 1990s. The government also did some serious rural development work such as the construction of road networks in the rural areas. It also provided some economic relief to the farming Sikh community by providing free water and electricity for agriculture. It failed, however, to initiate any serious measures towards industrial and tertiary-sector development of Punjab. The general perception that the Badal government was pro-rural sector turned urban Hindu voters against it in the February 2002 elections. It lost marginal support even among the rural Sikh voters because of the widely shared perception that many ministers and the officials of the government were indulging in corruption (Kumar and Kumar 2002). It lost the election, though narrowly, to the Congress party led by Amarinder Singh, who was respected among Sikh voters because he had resigned in 1984 as a member of India's parliament and from the Congress party in protest against Operation Blue Star. Later on, he had joined the Akali Dal and had became the agricultural minister in the Barnala government, from which he resigned in protest against Barnala's decision to send the police into the Golden Temple complex in April 1986. He eventually left Akali Dal and rejoined the Congress after the Akali Dal president Badal denied him the ticket to contest the Punjab assembly elections in 1997 as an Akali candidate.[52] Amarinder Singh as the chief minister of Punjab (2002–2007) was involved in a legal and political battle with the central government over the question of digging the SYL Canal through Punjab to divert Punjab's river waters to Haryana (Sharma 2004). The new Akali-led coalition government that came into power in 2007, with Badal as the chief minister, has vowed to continue the fight for Punjab's river water resources (Pritam Singh 2007b: 55, 2007c: 37–39). The river water dispute strengthened the forces of Punjabi regional nationalism in both the main political parties of Punjab (Pritam Singh 2007a). It appears that the situation regarding the centre–state conflict in Punjab has reverted back to the stage when the Akali Dal and the Communist Party of India (Marxist) had started the *nehar roko morcha* in 1981, with all the tragic developments that followed thereafter. This highlights the durability and gravity of inter-regional horizontal conflicts as well as centre–state vertical conflicts in a multi-national federal entity such as India.

Summary and conclusions

The present Punjab in India was constituted as a geographical entity in 1966 as a result of reorganization of Punjab as a Punjabi-speaking state. The Sikhs, who are only 2 per cent of India's population, constitute about 60 per cent of the population of Punjab. The evolution of the Sikh community has had a crucial impact on Punjab's relations with the Delhi-based central rule in India. The religion of the Sikhs was founded by Guru Nanak (1469–1539), who was born in a village of West Punjab, now a part of Pakistan. His teachings in the Punjabi language advocated gender and caste equality. With its egalitarian features and roots in the language and culture of Punjab, the Sikh faith soon acquired a distinct identity from the two competing religions of India, Hinduism and Islam. By the time of the fifth guru, Sikhism had acquired its own holy book and its own holy centre, the Golden Temple in Amritsar. The gurus also popularized the Gurmukhi script for writing the Punjabi language. The increasing influence of Sikhism attracted the attention of the Mughal administration.

The death of the fifth guru, through brutal torture ordered by the Mughal emperor Jehangir, turned the Sikh community from a religious and social reformist movement into a political community engaged in an armed conflict with the Mughal empire. The tenth guru, Gobind Singh, gave the final shape to this transformation when he created the Khalsa in 1699. The Khalsa was an egalitarian community of 'saint-soldiers'. Before his death in 1708, Guru Gobind Singh announced that, after his death, the tradition of living guruship would come to an end and he announced the conferment of the status of guru on the Sikhs' holy book, Guru Granth Sahib, which contained the teachings of the gurus up to the ninth guru and also those of some Muslim Sufi saints and Hindu *bhaktas*.

The eighteenth century was a period of struggle for survival and aspirations for political power by the Sikh community and by 1799 the Sikhs had succeeded in capturing political power in Punjab. Punjab existed as a sovereign state for fifty years from 1799 until it was annexed in 1849 by the expanding British empire in India. Punjab was one of the last provinces in India to become a part of the British empire in India and, therefore, remained under British rule for a shorter time than most other regions in India.[53] Far-reaching and rapid economic, political, social and cultural changes took place in Punjab during British rule. A large number of Sikhs and Muslims from the peasant communities became soldiers in the British army; canal irrigation networks were developed in some regions of Punjab; the landed elites of all the three main religious communities co-operated with each other in seeking mutually beneficial arrangements by collaborating with the British authorities; sections of the Sikh and Muslim peasantry resorted to economic and political radicalism; all the three communities – Sikh, Hindu and Muslim – went through very powerful religious reform movements as a reaction against Christian missionaries and these reform movements sharpened their distinctive religious identities. The Sikhs won a successful non-violent battle for the community's democratic control over its gurdwaras against the pro-British priests who had controlled them for decades. The struggle for India's independence witnessed competing and conflicting interests in Punjab. The landed elites of the three communities, with their loyal collaboration with the British rule, were hostile to the Congress party-led independence movement. These elites were also opposed to the religious/communal partition of India and even toyed with the idea of an independent country of Punjab. The urban Hindu middle class was the most active supporter of the Congress party. The Sikh peasantry and urban middle class participated vigorously in the independence movement but mostly under the umbrella of the Sikh Akali Party. The Muslim peasantry and urban middle class eventually became supporters of the pro-Pakistan Muslim League. A section of the intelligentsia from all three communities moved to secular Marxist radicalism and provided leadership to student and peasant activism. At the end of British rule, Punjab was partitioned into two parts with East Punjab going to India and the West Punjab to Pakistan.

The partition of India resulted in the creation of a number of Sikh majority districts in East Punjab. It was eventually with the creation of a Punjabi-speaking state in 1966 that the Sikhs, for the first time in their history, became the majority community in the new Punjab. Though a Sikh maharaja had ruled over Punjab for almost fifty years in the nineteenth century, the Sikhs were a minority in a Sikh-ruled state. The 1966 Punjab looked as close as it could possibly be to the Sikh aspiration of self-rule. After the first election to the state assembly in the post-1966 Punjab, the emergence of the Sikh Akali Party as the dominant component of the alliance that came to power reinforced the perception of the close proximity to Sikh self rule. This perception was, however, soon shattered by the realization of the constitutional arrangement of centre–state relations in India and those of the party political arrangements in this federalist structure. The Akali Dal soon realized that political control of a state government did not give the government much room for economic and political decision-making due to the limited economic and political autonomy of the states in India's constitutional and political arrangement. Policies nationally determined by the central Government of India and its planning commission on the priorities of industrial and agricultural development could only be tinkered with by a state government. Regarding the budgetary decisions of revenue and expenditure, a state government was critically dependent on the centre's budgetary decisions. The Akalis found that there was not much they could do regarding the central government's priority of focusing on agriculture in Punjab to increase food output in order to meet the national politico-economic goal of self-sufficiency in food availability. If the centre had chosen to prioritize agriculture in a state, the state government there could do very little to shift the priority to industry.

The overthrow of a succession of Akali-led ministries through political manoeuvring encouraged by the central political leadership of the Congress party made the Akalis reflect more seriously about the limits of the achievement they had made in getting a Punjabi-speaking state created and winning an electoral victory in that state. This led them to the conclusions which are articulated in the Anandpur Sahib Resolution they adopted in 1972–73. This resolution called for drastic devolution of powers to the states.

The Anandpur Sahib Resolution and the unfinished business around the time of creating the Punjabi-speaking state regarding the limbo status of the capital city of Chandigarh and disputes regarding water and territory became the background for Akali–Congress and Punjab–centre confrontation that started in the early 1980s. The Indian army's Operation Blue Star action at the Golden Temple and the assassination of Mrs Gandhi by her Sikh bodyguards were the tragic culmination of that confrontation rooted in the political economy of federal arrangements in India. The decade of the Indian state's battle to suppress Sikh militancy following the 1984 confrontation pushed the Indian federal arrangements in Punjab to the limit. At many times during this period, the possibility that the Indian military might be used for a large-scale genocidal massacre of Sikh youth terrified many Sikhs and non-Sikhs in India. Peace has apparently returned to Punjab since the mid-1990s but at a terrible human cost, lost economic opportunities and the ethical degradation of the political process. The re-emergence of the river water dispute since 2004 is a reminder that the federal conflicts over resources that contributed to the manifold unrest in Punjab in the 1980s are still to be resolved.

In the next chapter, we shall look more closely at the structure and evolution of centre–state relations in India and their implications for the development path that India followed until 1991.

3

FEDERALISM, NATIONALISM AND INDIA'S DEVELOPMENT STRATEGY

An historical overview and analytical framework

Introduction

In the last chapter, I provided an account of the evolution of Punjab's Sikh community. I highlighted that in the post-1947 period, there have been varying degrees of tension in the relationship between the Punjab-based Sikh–Punjabi nationalism and the Delhi-based centre as the architect of Indian nationalism. In order to locate this Punjab–centre relationship in the context of the over-all framework of centre–state relations in India, in this chapter I aim to provide an historical overview of the evolution of centre–state relations in India. I will relate the evolution of centre–state relations in India to the evolution of Indian nationalism and India's development strategy, and emphasise that in post-colonial independent India the centre's strategic interventions in the Indian political economy have been oriented towards the goal of constructing India as one unified nation. In particular, I highlight the fact that the economic role of the centre in India's development strategy has been integral to the political objective of building a unified Indian nationhood. In the narrative provided below of the evolution of centre–state relations in India, my focus will be on the post-colonial independent India. However, I will also discuss the colonial period, and briefly mention the pre-colonial period as well, in order to provide an historical background to the evolution of centre–state relations in post-colonial India.

Before India gained its independence in 1947, the British ruled over India from the mid-1700s for about two centuries, and the Mughals had ruled from the mid-1400s until then. The Mughal rule and the British rule have both had an impact on the shaping of contemporary patterns of centre–state relations in India.

Centre–province relations in ancient and medieval India

In the ancient period before Mughal rule, there seemed to exist a fairly high degree of decentralization. In those ancient empires 'each province led its own life, continued its old familiar system of government (though under the agents of the central power) and used its own language'.[1] Another historical account of the ancient period states that 'the conquered states generally continued to retain their identity, and were ready to emerge into independence at a suitable opportunity' (Sastri 1987: 116).

During the Mughal rule, the states continued to enjoy regional autonomy, except in the reign of the last Mughal ruler, who 'made a strong bid for complete centralisation and abolition of traditional diversities and autonomy of the regions' (Govt of India 1988: 5). Soon after his death, the regional forces re-asserted their independence.

Centre–province relations during the British rule

The British colonization of India was completed by 1858. A few remaining sovereign states were annexed one by one by the expanding British empire. Punjab was annexed in 1849, Jhansi, Nagpur and Hyderabad in 1853, Awadh in 1856, and the 'Sepoy Mutiny' was defeated in 1857.[2] During the 1857 conflict, the British discovered that 500-odd princely states in India could be allies of the British rule in India. As a result, the earlier British colonial policy of expansion through 'direct rule' in the sub-continent was substituted partially by one of 'indirect rule' for these princely states. There came to exist, a dual system of direct rule in British Indian provinces and indirect rule in the princely states. The remote and inaccessible areas with strong local tribal customs and beliefs, and a long history of isolation, retained varying degrees of autonomy (Govt of India 1988: 6). The British rulers also discovered that an overly centralized administration was incompatible with the size and diversity of the country, and that it resulted in administrative inefficiency and local discontent. Some degree of decentralization, therefore, became inevitable. The first small but significant step in this direction was taken by the Indian Councils Act 1861. It reversed the centralizing trend that had been set by the Charter Act of 1833.[3] It provided for participation by non-officials in the Legislative Council of the Governor-General. Similar provisions were made for the Legislative Councils of the provinces. The principle of indirect election to these Legislative Councils was established in 1892, and the functions of these councils were enlarged to include the right of discussion of the budget and intervention in matters of public interest.

The process of decentralization of finances, starting with the Mayo Scheme in 1871, was continued until it was formalized by the Government of India Act 1919, which contributed further to the evolution of a 'dispersed' political system in India. The association of Indians with local self-government through elected municipalities and district boards was initiated in 1882 by Lord Rippon. The authority conceded to these institutions was, however, very limited.

The emergence of the Indian National Congress in 1885 and the consequent growth of Indian nationalism forced the British rulers to respond by devolving more powers to the states with the purpose of giving the Indian people some feeling of participation in power. It is useful to note here that the rising Indian nationalism in its early phase demanded decentralization of power, in order to weaken the political power of the colonial rulers. However, as I will show later, a strong pro-centralization tendency emerged in the Indian nationalist movement in its later phase, when it became clear that the movement would be victorious and that India would become an independent nation state. The Indian National Congress, the main Indian nationalist party, became a strong votary of centralization after India emerged as an independent state (Santhanam 1960: chapter V).

To continue with this account of the evolution of centre–state relations, it is important to mention here the passing of the Indian Council Act 1909, popularly known as the Morley Minto Reforms. This Act further extended the association of the Indians with state power, though with separate electorates, narrow franchise and indirect election. This increased association of the Indians with state power can be interpreted in two ways. One interpretation of this could be that it was a continuation of the British policy of co-opting some Indians into state power in order to take the steam out of the nationalist aspiration for self-rule. Another interpretation could be that it reflected the growing bargaining power of Indian nationalism in extracting some concessions from the British rulers for the participation of Indians in state power.

The next most significant step taken by the British, to introduce the devolution of power to the states, was the Government of India Act 1919.[4] By the Devolution Rules framed under the Act, the 'dyarchical' system of centre and provinces was proposed, which provided for delegation of powers to the provinces not only in the administrative but also in the legislative and financial spheres. For this purpose, separate Central and Provincial Lists of subjects were drawn up. The subjects in the Provincial List were further subdivided into 'reserved' and 'transferred' subjects. The departments dealing with the 'transferred' subjects were placed in the charge of elected ministers responsible to the provincial legislature, while the departments in respect of 'reserved' subjects were administered by the governor with the assistance of an executive council nominated by him. Although with respect to 'transferred' subjects, the provinces derived substantial authority by devolution from the central government, yet the governor-general in council remained in control at the apex of this centralized system ultimately responsible to the secretary of state for India in the UK. Finance was a 'reserved subject' in the charge of a member of the nominated executive council. The main instruments of administration, namely the Indian civil service and the Indian police, were under the control of the secretary of state and were responsible to him and not to the minister. The governor had the discretionary power of not acting on the advice of the ministers. No bill could be moved in the provincial legislature without the permission of the governor-general. No bill could become law without his assent. Though the 1919 Act formally devolved some powers to the provinces, in reality the structure of centre–province relations remained unitary with the governor-general in council effectively in ultimate control.

The failure of the extremely limited devolution set in motion by the 1919 Act to meet Indian nationalist demands for power-sharing forced the British government to appoint a Statutory Commission under Sir John Simon in November 1927 in order to consider the extension of some more power to the Indians. But the composition of the Commission – all the seven members were British – provoked a boycott of the Commission by almost all Indian political tendencies. The Indian National Congress pressed the British government to accede to the national demand for the convening of a Round Table Conference or Constituent Assembly that would determine the future constitution of India.

The British government published a White Paper in 1933, embodying the principles of constitutional reforms in India. This eventually led to the 1935 Government of India Act, which provided a new framework for centre–state relations by dividing the governmental subjects into three lists: Federal, Provincial and Concurrent. As a follow-up of this act, elected governments (responsible to legislature) assumed offices in 1937. However, as a protest against the centre's continuous intrusion into provincial autonomy, the Congress Party-led governments in the provinces resigned in 1939.

In March 1942, Sir Stafford Cripps brought with him British government proposals for a constituent assembly, elected through proportional representation by provincial legislatures that would frame a new constitution of India after the end of the Second World War. It was also suggested that the British government would accept the new constitution, *inter alia*, on the condition that any province could opt out of it and retain its constitutional position as in the 1935 Act. This strong pro-decentralization proposal was rejected by the Congress Party and the other Indian nationalist political currents. Indian nationalism was now turning away from its earlier pro-decentralization stance towards a pro-centralization perspective as the prospects for the emergence of an independent Indian nationalist state were growing. The rejection of the Cripps proposals by the dominant tendencies in the Indian nationalist movement led to a new initiative by the British government, namely the announcement of the British Cabinet Mission Plan by Clement Atlee, the British prime minister, on 16 May 1946. It envisaged a central government with very limited powers, and relatively strong provinces having a considerable degree of autonomy with all the residuary powers. Given the tilt in favour of centralization in the political vision of the Indian nationalist leadership, this plan was not liked by the leadership, in particular the dominant Nehruvian tendency. However, the Indian National Congress hesitatingly accepted the Cabinet Mission Plan, mainly in the hope that this would lead the Muslim League to abandon its demand for a separate Muslim-majority Pakistan. The Objective Resolution moved by Jawaharlal Nehru on 13 December 1949 in the Constituent Assembly expressed the hesitant support for this Plan. After the failure of all negotiations on the question of the Muslim League's demand for Pakistan, the British government announced its decision on 3 June 1947 to partition the country. Jalal (1985) has argued that the main reason behind the partition of the country, leading to the creation of Pakistan, was the resistance of the

Indian nationalist leadership to the central idea of the Cabinet Mission Plan regarding the creation of a federation with a weak centre. The partition of the country led to a marked reversal in the approach of the Constituent Assembly regarding centre–state relations. It abandoned its earlier hesitant approach in favour of greater provincial autonomy to one which was in favour of a strong centre. This change is expressed in the Second Report of the Union Powers Committee, dated 5 July 1947:

> Now that the partition is a settled fact, we are unanimously of the view that it would be injurious to the interests of the country to provide for a weak Central authority which will be incapable of ensuring peace, of co-ordinating vital matters of common concern ... and that the soundest framework of our Constitution is a federation with a 'strong centre'.
>
> (Cited in Govt of India 1988: 7)

Once the partition plan of India was accepted, some of the leading figures in the Indian nationalist movement looked on it as an opportunity to push forward their vision of creating a centralized political framework for India. Let me quote K. M. Panikkar, one of the leading figures in the Constituent Assembly. He wrote in May 1947:

> Federation with limited powers for the centre, was an unavoidable evil in India, so long as the Muslim majority provinces had to be provided for in an all-India centre.... It is no longer necessary to provide for the very large measure of power for the units, which a full union with the Muslim majority provinces would have rendered unavoidable
>
> (Quoted by Bhattacharya 1992: 99)

This seemed to reflect a sense of relief that the Muslim bargaining power had vanished and that the centralizing agenda could now be implemented without any resistance. Nehru expressed similar views:

> The severe limitations on the scope of central authority in the Cabinet Mission's plan was a compromise accepted by the Assembly much, we think against its judgment of the administrative needs of the country in order to accommodate the Muslim League. Now that partition is a settled fact we are unanimously of the view that it would be injurious to the interests of the country to provide for a weak central authority...
>
> (Quoted by Bhattacharya 1992: 96)

Many Hindu nationalists also argued for strong centralization with the objective of creating a strong nation state. There were many voices of protest in the Constituent Assembly debates against the pro-centralization proposals for the Indian constitution. These voices articulated the interests of the states and the minorities, and the views of those who thought that the pro-centralization features of the proposed constitution could pose a threat to democratic institutions and practices (Pritam Singh 2005). Regarding the opposition of the Sikhs of Punjab to the centralization proposals, Justice Ajit Singh Bains, a retired judge of the Punjab and Haryana High Court, has highlighted the well-known historical fact that '[t]he Sikh representative in the Constituent Assembly did not sign the Constitution of India as it had not given any autonomy to the states' (Bains 1996: 179). Hukam Singh, a Sikh representative, had stated at the time:

> the Sikhs feel utterly disappointed and frustrated. They feel that they have been discriminated against. Let it not be misunderstood that the Sikh community has agreed to this Constitution. I wish to record an emphatic protest here. My community can not subscribe its assent to this historic document.... In our Constitution, each article tends to sap the local autonomy and make the provinces irresponsible.... The minorities and particularly the Sikhs have been ignored and completely neglected. The Provincial units have been reduced to Municipal Boards ... there is enough provision in our Constitution ... to facilitate the development of administration into a fascist state.
>
> (Constituent Assembly Debates 1949: 753)

Another Sikh representative Bhupinder Singh Mann (spelt wrongly in the *Constituent Assembly Debates: Official Report* as Man) said:

> I will be failing in my duty if I do not give the reactions of my own community, the Sikhs of East Punjab, so far as this Constitution goes. Their feeling is that they can not give unstinted support or full approval to this Constitution.
>
> (Constituent Assembly Debates 1949: 722)

Bains has argued that the Sikh unrest in Punjab since 1947 and especially in the 1980s and the 1990s can be attributed to this unitarist constitution which empowers the centre vis-à-vis the states (Bains 1996).

India was partitioned on 15 August 1947 into two separate countries: the Muslim-majority Pakistan and the Hindu-majority 'Bharat' (the name given to India in its constitution). However, the leaders of the new countries both proclaimed to follow secularism in the policies of their new states.[5] India became a new republic on 26 January 1950 after adopting a new constitution. During the transition period of 15 August 1946 to 26 January 1950, two sets of considerations can be identified as having influenced the framers of the new constitution in their opting for a 'strong-centre'-oriented constitutional framework: the need to deal with immediate problems and, more importantly, the need to realize some long-term political objectives. The immediate problems were: the large-scale sectarian violence against Muslims in India and against Hindus and Sikhs in Pakistan, the rehabilitation of these mainly forced refugees, armed intervention in Kashmir to secure its accession for India, the use of military and diplomatic means to secure the accession of some of the princely states aspiring to set up their own sovereign states, and the military suppression of the armed Communist uprising in Telengana in the south of India. The immediate and short-term contingent developments contributed to the strengthening of pro-centre institutional structures, such as the military and the centralized bureaucracy, and also generated a general political climate in the country (and a general opinion among the constitutional framers) that was strongly inclined towards introducing a pro-centre bias in the constitutional framework.

The long-term politico-economic vision of the dominant and majority group among the members of the Constituent Assembly could be ascribed the following constituent views: (a) a strong centre is necessary to build one unified Indian national identity out of the multiple national and ethnic identities in India;[6] (b) a strong centre is more effective than the provincial governments in shaping a state capitalist path of development;[7] (c) a strong centre is necessary to reduce regional inequalities and thus foster a spirit of balanced national development;[8] and (d) a strong centre is more likely than the provincial governments to be able to reduce class inequalities and thus make the socio-economic system stable and enduring.[9]

The long-term politico-economic vision shared by the majority among the constitution makers reinforced the tendency towards centralization set in motion by the need for strong central intervention to deal with immediate contingent problems.

Centre–state relations since 1950

The constitution of India, adopted on 26 November 1949 by the Constituent Assembly and brought into operation from 26 January 1950 onwards, describes 'India, that is Bharat' as a 'Union of States'.[10] These states are specified in the First Schedule to the constitution.[11] Articles 2, 3 and 4 enable the central parliament by law to admit a new state, obliterate the identity of an existing state, and alter the boundaries, area or name of any state. 'A special aspect of the Indian Union is that the Union is indestructible but not so the States' (Govt of India 1988: 8) and 'this is a departure from a federal feature which obtains in a classical federation like the U.S.A.' (Govt of India 1988: 9). The inherent centralist bias in the Indian constitution was also reflected in a deliberated decision on the question of the designation of India. A motion in the Constituent Assembly to designate India as a 'Federation of States' was rejected in favour of India as a 'Union of States' (Govt of India 1988: 9, Rath 1984: 35). Dr B. R. Ambedkar, Chairman of the Drafting Committee, while introducing the Draft Constitution, explained the significance of this decision as follows:

> [...] though India was to be a federation, the federation was not the result of an agreement by the States to join in a federation, and that the federation not being the result of an agreement, no State has the right to

> secede from it. The federation is a Union because it is indestructible. Though the country and the people may be divided into different States for convenience of administration, the country is one integral whole, its people a single people living under a single *imperium* derived from a single source. The Americans had to wage a Civil War to establish that the States have no right of secession and that their federation was indestructible. The Drafting Committee thought that it was better to make it clear at the outset rather than to leave it to speculation or to disputes.
>
> (Constituent Assembly Debates 1949: 43)[12]

The contestation over the use of the word 'Federation' or 'Union' in the Indian constitution to characterise the Indian republic was not a mere semantic quibble, it signified a sharp ideological conflict between the centralist tendencies and the decentralist, federalist tendencies in Indian politics. According to a leading constitutional scholar, 'The choice of "Union of States" and not "Federation of States", as Article I of the Constitution was deliberately made to emphasise the centralized bias of an "Indestructible Union"' (Ray 1966: 18). The political tendency that envisaged India as one unified nation argued for 'Union of States', while the political tendencies that argued for regional nationalisms, with a vision of India as a multi-national entity, argued for 'Federation of States'. The words 'Union' and 'Federation' are signifiers of competing politico-economic tendencies. The conflict over the use of these words has continued in independent India. For example, in a Memorandum on centre–State Relations issued in 1977, the Left Front-led Government of West Bengal vehemently opposed the term 'Union of States', and proposed that the preamble to the constitution should be amended to include the word 'Federal' in the description of the republic of India (Rath 1984: 35).

The centralist bias that designated India a union was one that was consistently adhered to in the process of defining citizenship in India. The constitution provides for a single citizenship for the whole territory of India. In some other federations, for example the American federation, there is one citizenship for the country as a whole, and in addition to that, a diversity of citizenship rights across the different states (Govt of India 1988: 9).[13] In contrast with that, the Indian constitution does not provide for different citizenship rights in the various states of India. Dr B. R. Ambedkar had highlighted these differences between the American and the Indian constitutions and had argued for a single citizenship for India.[14] An explanation and justification of these two different systems of citizenships, in the contexts of their different historical backgrounds, has been attempted by the Sarkaria Commission. According to the Commission, the American federation was the result of an agreement between the pre-existing independent states whereas, before 'the formation of the Indian Union, its units did not have the status of sovereign independent States' (Govt of India 1988: 9). This explanation is only partially valid as far as India is concerned. It is true that at the time of Indian independence in 1947, there were no sovereign independent states. However, before the British colonization of India, there existed several sovereign independent states; one of the last sovereign states to be annexed by the British was Punjab in 1849. Since colonization led to the loss of the sovereignty of many states, the anti-colonial nationalist movement (after its successful conclusion) could have been expected to restore the sovereignty of those states. That would have been the logical culmination of the process of decolonization in India. On the contrary, centralist tendencies – as exemplified in the decision on citizenship – gained strength in the nationalist movement, especially in the post-partition phase. This was due to the politico-economic developments specific to those conjunctures and not the result of the alleged non-existence of sovereign states 'before the formation of the Indian Union'.

The institutional foundations for the centralist-bias in centre–state relations in independent India were firmly laid when the constitutional framers provided for such a structure of distribution of powers between the centre and the states that 'gave weightage to the Union, allocating to it dominant and relatively larger powers' (Govt of India 1988: 9). In the following sections this distribution of powers will be briefly described, with specific regard to the legislative, administrative and judicial spheres. The next chapter will deal with the distribution of financial powers.

Legislative powers

The Union Legislature or Parliament has two Houses, the Council of States (Rajya Sabha) and the House of the People (Lok Sabha). Unlike in most federations where the states have equal or near equal representation in the Council of States, in India representation in both Houses is on the basis of population, through indirect election to the Rajya Sabha and direct election to the Lok Sabha. This population-based system of representation reinforces the centralist-bias in the structure of legislative power – discussed below – because the most populous states in India are in the Hindi heartland of the country,[15] and these states, due to their dominant position in the structure of power derived from this population-based system of representation,[16] are strong supporters of the centralization of power.

In the Seventh Schedule of the Indian constitution, the subjects of legislative power have been classified into three lists: the Union List (List I), the State List (List II) and the Concurrent List (List III). Parliament has the exclusive power to legislate on matters in the Union List. The state legislatures, however, do not have the exclusive power to legislate in respect of matters in the State List, since the parliament can legislate, under certain conditions, even for matters in the State List if it decides that to do so is in 'the national interest'.[17] Both parliament and the state legislatures have the power to make laws on any matter in the Concurrent List, but the constitution provides for overriding powers to the parliament in a situation of inconsistency between the laws made by the parliament and the laws made by the legislatures of the states (whether in the State List or Concurrent List).[18] The power of a state legislature in legislating for a matter in the State List is further limited by the constitutional provision that confers overriding power to the Parliament 'to make any law for the whole or *any part of the territory of India*' in order to give effect to international agreements.[19]

Articles 256 and 257 make it obligatory for the states to comply with Union laws and, under Article 365, if a state is perceived to be not complying with the directions given by the centre, the president of India is entitled to hold that a situation had arisen in which the government of the state could not be carried on in accordance with the provisions of the constitution, therefore warranting action under Article 356, which stipulates that the president 'may by proclamation assume to himself all or any of the functions of the Government of the State'.

The constitution further provides for exclusive power to the parliament, referred to as the residuary power of legislation, to make laws and impose taxation regarding any matter not enumerated in the State List or the Concurrent List.[20]

Administrative powers

Article 258(1) enables the president to entrust a government of a state, with the consent of that government, functions in relation to any matter to which the executive power of the centre extends. Similarly, Article 258A enables the governor of a state to entrust to the centre, with the latter's consent, functions regarding a matter to which the executive power of the state government extends. To this extent, there is symmetry in the power relations between the centre and the states. However, the actual asymmetry and inequality in centre–state relations gets reflected in the way the powers of parliament vis-à-vis those of the state legislature are stipulated in Clause (2) of Article 258. Under Clause (2) of Article 258, parliament may by law impose duties on a state government even if it concerns a matter with respect to which the state legislature has no responsibility. Under this clause, the consent of the state government is not considered as a necessary pre-condition, for the imposing of such duties on a state government (Govt of India 1988: 10).

The constitution does not, however, confer any powers on the state legislature to legislate for the entrusting of any functions, duties or responsibility to the centre. This asymmetry and inequality in the power relations between the centre and the states is a result of the concentration of administrative power in the hands of the centre, as that has been structurally built into the constitution.

Subordination of the state legislation to the executive power of the centre

The constitutional provision for the necessity of seeking the assent of the president of India, under certain circumstances, for legislation by the legislature of a state even on a matter under the jurisdiction of the state legislature, further erodes the limited autonomy of the state legislature and subordinates the latter to the executive power of the central government.[21] There are a number of special provisions, many of which have been inserted by the subsequent constitutional amendments, which require that certain types of state bills dealing with some matters be reserved for the consideration of the president (which, in effect, means for the consideration of the Central Cabinet).[22]

Another unique centralist feature of the constitution is that it enables the central parliament to legislate with respect to a matter in the State List if the Council of States (the Rajya Sabha) declares by a two-third majority of the members present and voting, that 'it is necessary or expedient in [the] national interest' to do so.[23] Such a resolution remains in force initially for a period up to one year and can be extended for another one year.

Another feature of the constitution that opens the avenue for central government to assume extra powers is the provision that requires only two states to pass a resolution through their legislatures in order for parliament to legislate on a matter in the State List. Any act so passed by the parliament may also be adopted by the legislature of the other states.[24] Although such a resolution is not binding on the other states its passing acts as a pressure on them to fall in line.

Emergency provisions empowering the centre vis-à-vis the states

The constitution confers special emergency powers on the president, which in effect means to the council of ministers at the centre, since the president is bound by the constitution to 'act in accordance with such advice' as 'tendered' by the council of ministers headed by the prime minister.[25] Articles 352, 353, 354, 358 and 359 specify such powers when 'a grave emergency exists whereby the security of India or of any part of the territory thereof is threatened, whether by wars or external aggression or armed rebellion'.[26] During the 'grave emergency' period, the centre can take over all the executive and legislative powers of the states.[27] The consent of the state government is not needed for the centre to assume executive and legislative powers (Govt of India 1988: 11).[28] Even under non-emergency situations, Articles 355 and 356 empower the centre to take over the administration of a state if the governor of a state sends a report to the centre that 'a situation has arisen in which the government of the state cannot be carried on in accordance with the provisions of this Constitution'.[29] Article 360 provides for special financial powers to the centre during a period of 'financial emergency' when 'a situation has arisen whereby the financial stability or credit of India or of any part of the territory thereof is threatened'. Article 354 also provides for special financial powers to the centre during a period of 'grave emergency' as defined above.

The judiciary's role in strengthening centre vis-à-vis the states

Article 131 provides for the jurisdiction of the Supreme Court, the highest judicial court in India, in any dispute 'between the Government of India and one or more states'. However, the central parliament has enormous powers to amend the constitution if or when such an amendment is needed by the centre in a situation of centre–state conflict and, due to 'the comparative ease with which the Constitution can be amended' (Govt of India 1988: 12), the scope for judicial intervention by the Supreme Court is severely curtailed. Meghnad Desai has also highlighted the ease of the constitution amendment process: 'The Constitution is ... very easy to amend, unilaterally by the Union legislature. This weapon of easy amendment has been used frequently by elected governments either to cancel a judicial decision which it did not like or to abridge some right which came in its way' (Desai 2005: 66). Because of the ease with which the constitution can be amended, and has been amended, there are only a few judgments of the Supreme Court dealing with centre–state disputes. 'A review of these judgements would show that most of them have, in effect, upheld the primacy of the Union vis-à-vis the States' (Govt of India 1988: 12). This strongly pro-centralist role of the Supreme Court can be attributed to two main factors: the procedure for appointing the Chief Justice and judges of the Supreme Court is such that the Central Cabinet exercises a decisive role in these appointments;[30] and the acceptance by the Supreme Court of the overarching ideology of the Indian state: that in building one unified Indian nationalism out of diverse and multiple nationalisms in India a strong centre is necessary.[31]

Centralization, Indian nationalism and the planned development strategy

The centralist structure of the Indian constitution, the growing trend towards centralization, the political project of nation building, and the strategy of planned development followed by the Indian state until 1991, are all linked with each other in a mutually reinforcing relationship. My discussion above has shown that in the process of constitution-making, the deliberate choice regarding the characterization of the Indian republic as a 'Union' (and the rejection of the alternative characterization of the republic as a 'Federation') was guided by the political project of building one unified Indian nationalism as opposed to the alternative perspective of building India as a geographical space of co-existing multiple nationalisms. I have also shown that the creation of Pakistan is also linked with the Indian nationalist leadership's unwillingness to accept a vision of a multinational India. The creation of Pakistan gave a further boost to the political perspective of centralization and unified nation building. The framing of a constitution with a strong centralist bias was a logical outcome of this perspective of unified nation building.

The strategy of economic development followed by the Indian central state, which has been characterized as a state capitalist path of development by some scholars (Bettelheim 1968, Chattopadhyay 1970, 1992, M. Desai 1975, A. R. Desai 1984), accorded a strategic role to central planning. The importance accorded to central planning in this state capitalist path of development gave enormous economic and political power to the centre vis-à-vis the states. The centre had the legal and constitutional mandate of the centrally biased Indian constitution to assume the powers that it assumed in the pursuit of this state capitalist path of development. It is not surprising therefore that, although the setting up of the central Planning Commission did not have the formal sanction of the Indian constitution, its setting up was never judicially questioned. The Planning Commission was not merely an economic instrument to shape the development priorities in the country it was also a political instrument of nation building (Santhanam 1960, Paranjape 1964). In giving key importance to the objective of reducing inter-state inequalities in economic development, the Planning Commission was performing a strategic political role in the project of nation building.

In analysing the implications of centre–state relations for Punjab's development pattern in the chapters that follow, the mutually reinforcing relationship between the centralist-bias in the Indian constitution, the political project of Indian nationalism and the planned strategy of development forms an overarching framework. I have not only used this framework to inform my discussion on Punjab's development pattern, but also elaborated further the different components of this framework in the course of studying the development pattern in Punjab.

Conclusions

The British rule in India gave a big fillip to the creation of a centralized administrative structure for political and economic governance in India. The centralized structure of colonial administration suited the strategic military, economic and political objectives of the British rule in India. The colonial rulers did demonstrate some strategic flexibility in dealing with the complex diversities that characterized the political landscape of India. The creation of a different sort of politico-administrative arrangement with the several pre-existing princely states was evidence of this strategic flexibility within the overall centralized administration. As the nationalist movement for India's independence grew, the British rulers initiated gradual reforms in the centralized administration to accommodate nationalist aspirations. The Indian National Congress, the main party of Indian nationalism, was a strong votary of decentralization during its conflict with the centralized colonial administration. However, the nationalist perspective of the Congress Party turned it increasingly towards supporting a centralist perspective for India, once the prospects for India's independence grew. It is this pro-centralist perspective of the Congress Party which eventually resulted in the creation of the Muslim-majority Pakistan. The 1947 partition, in turn, strengthened the pro-centralist tendencies in Indian politics. The framing of the Indian constitution with a strong central bias was the result of the increased political weight of the pro-centralist tendencies in Indian politics. Centralization was seen by both the secular and the Hindu variants of Indian nationalism as necessary for forging one unified Indian national identity. The importance given to central planning, in the Indian central state's strategy of economic development, further increased the political and economic power of the centre. The interlocking and mutually reinforcing relationship between centralization, Indian nationalism and planned development strategy became the chief driving force of Indian political economy until 1991. The relationship between the centre and the states worked itself through this drive towards centralization, which was guided by the project of building a unified Indian nationalism and influenced by the strategy of planned development.

My next chapter takes up the implications of the workings of centre–state relations in India for Punjab's state finances.

4

FEDERAL FINANCIAL RELATIONS IN INDIA AND THEIR IMPLICATIONS FOR CENTRE–PUNJAB FINANCIAL RELATIONS

Introduction

Financial relations between the centre and Punjab are crucially shaped by the Indian constitutional provisions regarding centre–state financial relations and by the pattern of these latter relations since Indian national independence. This chapter, therefore, is divided into three parts dealing with the three issues examined here: the Indian constitutional provisions regarding centre–state financial relations, the pattern of evolution of these relations and the implications of these relations for Punjab. In examining all the three issues, especially the implications for Punjab's state finances, the focus is on the period 1966–1991.

The first section of this chapter highlights the most significant Indian constitutional provisions regarding the division of financial powers and responsibilities between the centre and the states. The main point that emerges from my discussion here is that the structure of the constitution is heavily biased in favour of financial powers for the centre. In the second section of this chapter, I discuss the pattern of evolution of centre–state financial relations since the adoption of the Indian constitution in 1950. This section constitutes the bulk of the material covered in this chapter, since the implications for Punjab follow from the general pattern of the evolution of centre–state financial relations. My analysis demonstrates that the bias in favour of the centre has been further reinforced and intensified. The power acquired by the Planning Commission in India's development strategy has significantly contributed to the strengthening of the trend towards centralization of financial powers.

Finally, I attempt to draw out the implications of these analyses for centre–Punjab financial relations. The implications of centre–state financial relations for Punjab's state finances cannot be completely separated from the implications of centre–state economic relations for Punjab's agriculture and industry. There is an interconnection between Punjab's state finances, agriculture and industry but, for analytical purposes, each aspect has been covered within a separate chapter. My discussion on Punjab's state finances in this chapter shows that due to agricultural prosperity achieved by Punjab, the transfer of financial resources from the centre to Punjab was low in proportion to Punjab's share in India's population. I have argued that this disproportionally low share of financial resources devolved to Punjab was the necessary outcome of the political economy of Indian nationalism. The project of building a unified Indian nationhood demanded that the states with relatively low per capita income deserved a higher share from the central resources.

The centrist bias of the Indian constitution in the distribution of powers between the centre and the states

The present politico-geographical identity of the Indian national state is the result of a long historical process of its boundaries being drawn and redrawn as a consequence of the emergence of a number of independent nation-states (Burma, Sri Lanka, Pakistan and Bangladesh) out of the larger geographical identity that may be called old historical India. The states and provinces as geographical–political–cultural identities in post-colonial India have been emerging at an uneven pace as the homelands of various nations and potential nations.

Not only India as a whole but even some of the regional national identities experienced divisions and sub-divisions. The two most well-known cases are of Punjab and Bengal. India's partition in 1947 was basically a partition of Punjab and Bengal (Spate 1947). Punjab was partitioned into Indian Punjab and Pakistani Punjab, and Bengal was partitioned into Indian Bengal (called West Bengal) and Pakistani Bengal (now the sovereign nation-state of Bangladesh, since 1971). Because nationalism has played a key role in the emergence of sovereign states in South Asia and in the emergence of states and provinces in India, centre–state relations in post-1947 India have been crucially shaped by the centre's strategic objective of building India as a unified nation. This strategic objective of the centre played a key role in the making of the Indian constitution and the stipulation of the powers between the centre and the states in the constitution.[1]

The constitution of India that came into force in 1950 has defined India and its states as follows:

1 India, that is Bharat, shall be a Union of States.
2 The States and the territories thereof shall be as specified in the First Schedule.
3 The territory of India shall comprise:
   a the territories of the States;
   b the Union territories specified in the First Schedule; and
   c such other territories as may be acquired.

The First Schedule lists 25 states and seven Union territories.[2]

Regarding the distribution of the powers between the centre and the states, the constitution mentions 97 entries in List I (the Union List, under the jurisdiction of the centre), 66 entries in List II (the State List) and 47 entries in List III (the Concurrent List, under the joint jurisdiction of the centre and the states). The items in the Union List include defence, atomic energy, foreign affairs, railways, national highways, shipping, airways, post and telegraph, telephone, wireless, broadcasting, currencies, public debt of the Union, Reserve Bank of India (RBI), lotteries, foreign trade, inter-state trade within India, banking, insurance and financial corporations (except co-operative societies), stock exchanges and futures markets, patents, quality control, industries (declared by parliament to be in the national interest), oil, petroleum, mineral resources, inter-state rivers (declared by parliament to be in the national interest), fishing and fisheries beyond territorial waters, salt, audit of accounts of the Union and of the states, income tax (except on agricultural income), corporation tax, custom duty, export duty, excise duty on tobacco and other goods (except alcoholic liquors, opium, Indian hemp and other narcotics), taxes on capital value of assets (except on agricultural land), estate duty on property (except agricultural land), taxes on sale and purchase of newspapers and advertisements published therein.

The items in the State List include public order (but not the use of the military), police, prisons, local government, public health, alcoholic liquors, road and water transport (except those parts that are under the centre's jurisdiction), agriculture (including income tax, estate and succession duty), irrigation, water management (except inter-state rivers), industries and mines (except those of national interest), gas and gas works, trade within the state, co-operative societies, rural debt, public debt of the state, land revenue, tax on sale and consumption of electricity, tax on advertisements (except those in newspapers and radio or TV), tax on road transport and inland waterways, and entertainment tax.

The items in the Concurrent List include criminal law (except regarding use of armed forces), preventive [*sic!*] detention, personal law, property transfer (except agricultural land), forests, economic and social planning, population control and family planning, commercial and industrial monopolies, trade unions, social security, education, professions, charities, ports (except of national importance), trade in food stuffs, cattle fodder, cotton, raw jute and the products of any industry (except those of national interest), price control, factories, boilers, electricity, newspapers, books and printing presses.

The constitution also provides for exclusive powers to the parliament, called the residuary powers of legislation, to make laws and impose taxation with respect to any matter not enumerated in the State List or the Concurrent List.[3] The constitution further provides for a legislation by the parliament even for matters in the State List if the 'national interest' so demands[4] and for over-riding powers to the national parliament in a situation of inconsistency between laws made by parliament and the laws made by the legislature of the states[5] and for giving effect to international agreements.[6]

From the items mentioned in the three lists above and from the constitutional provisions which mandate that the centre's control can be extended to even those items which are not in the Central List if this control is deemed to be necessary in the 'national' interest, it is very clear that the constitution enables the centre to exercise control over the most significant spheres of the economy. The control over some spheres like defence and foreign trade rightfully belongs to the centre as it would in any federal arrangement. However, it is the control of some other spheres such as agriculture and industry which are formally listed as subjects in the state sphere but have come increasingly under central control due to the invoking of the provision of 'national' interest that has strengthened the centralist bias of the Indian federal arrangements. I will discuss agriculture and industry in the next two chapters. In the next section of this chapter, I shall examine the ways in which the centralist bias inherent in the constitution has manifested itself in the actual operation of centre–state financial relations. Finally, the implications for Punjab's state finances will be examined.

The trend towards centralization in the evolution of centre–state financial relations in post-independence India

The constitutionally defined financial powers and responsibilities have played a major role in the concentration of financial resources in the hands of the centre (see Mitra 1983, 1987, S. Ali 1989). Right from the beginning of Indian national independence, it was clear that the constitution had so defined the functional responsibilities of the states that due to their inadequate financial powers, the states would have to depend on transfer of funds from the centre to discharge those responsibilities (Gulati 1987: 2). Furthermore, it was stipulated in the constitution that a Finance Commission, to be appointed by the president of India every five years or earlier, would make recommendations for intra-federal transfer of budgetary funds.[7] These recommendations, once accepted by the parliament, were to have a statutory sanction.[8] Transfers affected in this way are called *statutory transfers*.

There are two other kinds of transfers, which are called *non-statutory transfers* because they are made outside the framework of the Finance Commission. These are:

a Plan transfers – transfers in the form of Plan assistance by the centre to the states affected through the Planning Commission to help the states to finance their state plans;[9]
b discretionary transfers – transfers effected through the ministries and departments of the central government.

Transfers are called 'discretionary' by various scholars using two different lines of reasoning. According to one set of scholars these transfers are 'discretionary' because there are no known criteria for affecting these transfers. 'Discretionary' in this set of views implies arbitrariness.[10] This set of views considers that the statutory transfers affected through the Finance Commission (FC) are based on a criterion, but leaves Plan transfers in an ambiguous category without either calling them discretionary or based on a criterion.[11] The second set of views calls these transfers 'discretionary' because according to this view, there is no constitutional provision for making these transfers regularly.[12] This latter view therefore considers both Plan and discretionary transfers, as defined in point ii above, as 'discretionary transfers' (Qureshi 1989: 50). A clearer definition of a discretionary transfer, in our view, is a transfer which the centre can refuse to a state and the concerned state cannot take any recourse to constitutional provisions to force the centre to effect that transfer. By this definition, only the transfers made by the Financial Commission are non-discretionary (statutory) and the transfers made through the Planning Commission or the central ministries are discretionary.

The actual pattern of financial relations between the centre and the states that has evolved since national independence reveals that the statutory transfers have constituted between 31 per cent and 43 per cent of the total transfers from the centre to the states for different Plan periods during 1951–84. Taken as a whole, for the period 1951–84, more than 60 per cent of the transfers are non-statutory or discretionary (see Table 4.1).[13] The implications of the relative weighting of the three types of transfers in the total transfers to the states from the viewpoint of centre–state financial relations are very significant. The discretionary transfers by their very nature put the states in a far more vulnerable position vis-à-vis the centre than the statutory transfers. The legitimacy of 'discretionary transfers' remains a much contested field.[14]

Table 4.1 Percentage share of statutory, plan and discretionary transfers in total transfers from centre to states, 1951–84

Plan period	*Statutory transfers %*	*Plan transfers %*	*Discretionary transfers %*	*Total Rs. crores*
First Plan (1951–56)	31.2	24.5	44.3	1,431
Second Plan (1956–61)	32.0	36.9	31.1	2,868
Third Plan (1961–66)	28.4	44.9	26.7	5,600
Three Annual Plans (1966–69)	33.3	33.1	33.6	5,347
Fourth Plan (1969–74)	35.9	23.4	40.7	15,101
Fifth Plan (1974–79)	43.0	30.5	26.4	25,278
Sixth Plan (1979–84)	41.0	29.3	29.7	54,818
Total (1951–84)	39.4	29.9	30.7	110,443

Source: Adapted from George (1987: 248).

Note
The column showing discretionary transfers refers to the transfers made through the central ministries and departments.

The Plan transfers are supposed to be based on criteria but these criteria are never made public (Lakdawala 1989: 191–194) and, consequently, the Plan transfers are also used by the centre to enforce the dependence of the states on central resources and planning priorities.[15] The officials of the state government feel so overwhelmed by the authority and power wielded at the centre that they try to please the central authorities and consequently do not put forward their case powerfully if the central authorities are seen to be unsympathetic to the state's demands.[16] The top administrative layer of the bureaucracy at the state level comes from two cadres: one recruited through the centrally controlled recruitment process called the Indian Administrative Service (IAS) and the other recruited though the state recruitment process called the Provincial Civil Service (PCS). The IAS is a nationalist adaptation of the elite civil service cadre recruited during the British colonial rule that was called the Indian Civil Service (ICS). PCS officers are lower in the administrative hierarchy than the IAS officers. The commonly accepted view among IAS officers is that the best connected among them get posted to the centre.[17] A critical factor in procuring a central posting is that the aspiring officer does not have a provincial outlook and is therefore considered to have a nationalist (read centralist) orientation. The Government of West Bengal has complained that 'the fact that officers belonging to the All-India Services generally tend to think of themselves as being under the discipline of the Union Government had led to complications' (Govt of West Bengal 1987: 602). Discontentment with IAS officers, seen as agents of the centre, has also been expressed by Tamil Nadu (Govt of Tamil Nadu 1987: 495), Punjab (Govt of Punjab 1987: 898–909), Tripura (Govt of Tripura 1987: 562) and Meghalaya (Govt of Meghalaya 1987: 382).

Finally, even the Finance Commission has been suspected of being biased in favour of the centre. The most significant indictment of the way Finance Commissions have functioned comes from within the Finance Commission itself. Justice A. S. Qureshi, a member of the 9th Finance Commission, wrote in his note of dissent to the final report of the Commission: 'it is a pity that such an important institution (Finance Commission) is devalued, downgraded and rendered ineffective due to centre's growing hunger for amassing more and more power and authority in its own hands' (Qureshi 1989: 47). He writes further:

> [The] Finance Commission has been treated as an adjunct of the Finance Ministry and subservient to it. The Finance Commission has no independence in the matter of even the appointments of its staff or managing its own finances. The Finance Commission has to go to the Finance Ministry for every trivial thing.
>
> (Qureshi 1989: 48)

He states that: 'Even the functions already assigned under the Constitution were gradually taken out and exercised by the centre in clear violation of the Constitutional provisions' (Qureshi 1989: 47). There are several others who have a

Table 4.2 Grants from the centre to the states (Rs. crore)

Period	*Total grants*	*Grants under Article 275(1) i.e. statutory transfers (%)*	*Other grants (%)*
1 First Plan (1951–56)	190	12.6	87.4
2 Second Plan (1956–61)	711	21.5	78.5
3 Third Plan (1962–66)	1,315	22.2	77.8
4 Three annual plans (1966–69)	1,522	27.7	72.3
5 Fourth Plan (1969–74)	3,903	18.9	81.1
6 Fifth Plan (1974–78)	5,771	35.8	64.2
7 Two annual plans (1978–80)	4,735	19.6	80.4
8 Sixth Plan (1980–85)	18,428	11.0	89.0
9 Seventh Plan (1985–90)	43,747	14.1	85.9
(1985–86)	6,609	14.8	85.2
(1986–87)	7,258	12.0	88.0
(1987–88)	9,041	13.2	86.8
(1988–89) RE	9,939	12.7	87.3
(1989–90) BE	10,900	17.2	82.8
Total (1951–90)	80,322	16.0	84.0

Source: Adapted from Justice Qureshi's Note of Dissent to *Second Report of the Ninth Finance Commission* (for 1990–95) (Govt of India 1989: 50).

Note
Compensatory grants in lieu of the repealed tax on railway passenger fares are not included.

somewhat similar assessment of the Finance Commission (see Gulati 1987a: 63–85).[18] Justice Qureshi's view that the Finance Commission is being marginalized is validated by the evidence adduced by him in support of his view (see Table 4.2). By employing the strict constitutional criteria of considering only those grants that are made under Article 275 as statutory and all other grants as discretionary grants, Justice Qureshi shows that the discretionary grants work out to be as high as 84 per cent of total grants for the period 1951–1990.

Two points need emphasizing: first, the very high component of discretionary transfers in the total transfers from the centre to the states forces the latter into a position of weakness and dependence on the former. Second, the erosion in the independence of the Finance Commission robs even the statutory transfers of the importance they otherwise would have had. As a result, the institutional arrangement of transfers from the centre to the states by increasing the financial dependence of the states on the centre provides a perpetual source of conflict between the aspirations of the states for more autonomy and the ongoing tendency towards centralized control representing the interests of unified and integrated Indian nationalism.

Table 4.3 Total resource transfers from the centre to the states as percentages of the Union's aggregate resources

Period	*Aggregate amount raised by the centre (Rs. crores)*	*Aggregate transfers from the centre to the state (Rs. crores)*	*Amount transferred as percentage of the resources raised at the centre*
1	*2*	*3*	*4*
1951–56	3,412	1,431	42
1956–61	8,080	2,868	36
1961–66	17,654	5,600	32
1966–69	16,714	5,347	32
1969–74	41,380	15,101	36
1974–79	82,422	25,278	31
1979–84	n.a	n.a	33

Source: Adapted from Gulati (1987: 18).

It is significant to note that not only does the centre (through its control over the institutions of resource transfer) exercise a relationship of dominance over the states, but it also increases its own relative financial power by cornering the major share of the resources raised by it. The states' share in the resources raised by the centre witnesses a declining trend from 42 per cent to 33 per cent during 1951–84 (see Table 4.3).

The amount transferred from the centre to the states for 1974–79 was mentioned by Gulati as Rs.25,578 crores. I have corrected the figure to Rs.25,278 crores in the table above after cross-checking it with George 1987 (see Table 4.1) and West Bengal government memorandum data (in Govt of India 1987: 603). West Bengal estimates for the percentage transferred (compare figures in column 4 in Table 4.3) are: 1951–56: 36.4, 1956–61: 32.3, 1961–66: 31.3, 1966–69: 31.4, 1969–74: 36.4, 1974–79: 30.7, 1979–84: 32.6 (Govt of West Bengal, 1987: 604).

West Bengal data do not give the absolute figures for the aggregate sources raised by the centre but the percentage transferred to the states is based on including deficit financing in the centre's aggregate resources. Gulati's data for centre's aggregate resources (Table 4.3) do not mention whether it is inclusive of deficit financing or not. Both, however, show a declining trend in the amount transferred as percentage of the resources raised at the centre.

The states' dependence on the centre is highlighted by the fact that though the centre transfers up to as low as 31 per cent of its aggregate resources to the states (1974–79), these resources constitute a significant part of the state's total expenditure. The aggregate financial resources transferred from the centre as a percentage of the total expenditure by the states rose from 38 in 1951–56 to 46 in 1985–86 (Govt of West Bengal 1987: 603, Govt of Punjab 1987: 907).

A closer look at the sources of revenue and expenditure by the states for a few years in the mid-1980s for which I have more detailed data from the Punjab government memorandum to the Sarkaria Commission further confirms my observation about the financial dependence of the states on the centre. For 1985–86, the resource transfers from the centre, including both devolution (statutory) and discretionary transfers, financed nearly 46 per cent of the states' overall expenditure. The states' own receipts finance nearly 52 per cent of the total expenditure. The balance of expenditure (1.87 per cent in 1983–84, 5.3 per cent in 1984–85 and 2.4 per cent in 1985–86) is deficit financed. In the past even the accumulated deficit had to be financed to a large extent initially by the centre by periodically granting medium-term loans to the states to clear their unauthorized overdrafts from the Reserve Bank of India (RBI). The centre extended such loans in 1972–73 (Rs.421 crores), 1978–79 (Rs.555 crores), 1982–83 (Rs.1,743 crores), 1983–84 (Rs.400 crores) and 1985–86 (Rs.1,628 crores).[19] If the centre were to adhere strictly to its scheme for the elimination of states' unauthorized overdrafts introduced in 1985–86, there would be no more central loans to the states to enable them to clear the overdrafts from the RBI.[20] This would effectively choke off the main source of funds for financing the states' overall deficit. Since the states are unlikely to be able to make up for this by augmenting their own receipts due to the existing structures of financial relations between the centre and the states, they will have to either restrain their own expenditure further or depend even more heavily on resource transfers from the centre.

The states' dependence on the centre for financing their revenue expenditure

For financing their revenue expenditure, the dependence of the states on resource transfer from the centre is close to 40 per cent. The Punjab government memorandum to the Sarkaria Commission on Centre–State Relations looked more closely at the data in the central government budget papers to work out the proportion of devolutionary transfers and discretionary transfers in the 40 per cent contribution of the central transfers to the financing of states' revenue expenditure. The Punjab government estimate showed that about 24 per cent of these central transfers were through devolutionary (statutory) transfers and about 16 per cent were discretionary (Plan and non-Plan) transfers.[21] This means that even to finance ongoing current (revenue) expenditure, the states are dependent on about 16 per cent of that expenditure from the discretionary transfers from the centre. I will now look at the financing of states' capital expenditure.

The states' dependence on the centre for financing their capital expenditure

The states' dependence on the centre for financing their capital expenditure is much greater than for financing revenue expenditure. The states' own net capital receipts, after meeting repayment obligations on past loans from the centre, could finance no more than a very small proportion of their capital expenditure. The percentage of their capital expenditure financed by the states was 28.7 in 1983–84, 18.6 in 1984–85 and 21.5 in 1985–86.[22]

A very high and rising proportion of the total capital expenditure had to be financed by new loans from the centre. According to one estimate, nearly 70 per cent of the total capital expenditure of the states in 1983–84, 1984–85 and 1985–86 was financed by loans from the centre.[23]

All loans and advances from the centre to the states are discretionary: if the centre stops altogether or decreases the volume of loans, the states cannot take any recourse to constitutional provisions to force the centre to advance loans. The dependence of the states on the centre for financing their capital expenditure is highlighted by the fact that a substantial proportion of the states' capital receipts classified as the states' own receipts is, in fact, subject to the consent of the Government of India in accordance with Article 293 of the constitution (Govt of India 1987: 278). Under Clause 3 of the Article 293, a state may not without the consent of the Government of India raise any loan if any previous loan to it granted or guaranteed by the central government was still outstanding. The original purpose of this constitutional clause might have been to enforce fiscal discipline on the states. If the centre too had followed the practice of fiscal discipline, this clause could have been interpreted as a useful device to bring about fiscal discipline both at the centre and the states. However, since the centre has borrowed liberally within the country as well as abroad without any constitutional restrictions, the enforcement of this clause has led to unequal power relations between the centre and the states. Since all the states are heavily indebted to the centre, the approval of the central government is necessary for all borrowing by the state governments.[24]

Factors accounting for financial dependence of the states

The states' heavy financial dependence on the centre has been the result of factors that have since Indian national independence either required the states to incur expanded revenue and capital expenditure, or have prevented them from increasing their own revenue and capital receipts in accordance with the increase in their expenditure. A discussion of such factors follows below.

Factors accounting for growth of states' expenditure

Constitutional responsibilities entrusted to the states as mentioned in the entries in List II above, have meant that states have had to discharge responsibilities which have entailed rapid growth of revenue and capital expenditure. A contributory factor for this trend has been the generally low efficiency of public expenditure in the states on development projects like irrigation, road transport, housing and urban development and public health to name a few.[25] This has necessitated a more than reasonable outlay to obtain the desired physical results.

Two views have been generally put forward to explain this enormous increase in the states' development expenditure. According to one, the provisions of the constitution relating to state finances strongly suggest that the constitution makers severely underestimated the public expenditure requirements implied in the development responsibilities entrusted to the states (Govt of Punjab 1987: 910). In particular, this view holds that the constitution makers seemed to have had little perception of the large quantity of the capital outlays required of the states. It looks as if the large majority of the members of the Constituent Assembly either did not seriously believe in planned development or had little awareness of its implications in the Indian context, with regard to the growth of public expenditure. The evidence is consistent with a failure to foresee that the states would need to undertake and assist investment in a big way along with incurring growing maintenance and development expenditure on revenue account on state and state-aided services. Rapid growth of states' revenue and capital expenditure is considered a direct consequence of this state-interventionist path of development which was not fully anticipated by the constitution makers.[26]

The second view (Gulati 1987) is that, given the fact that Nehru and several others who actively participated in the constitution-making exercise were ardent advocates of economic planning, it is unlikely that they did not envisage the active role of the central state in the development process. This view holds that Nehru and others must have thought that the constitution was flexible enough to accommodate planning and that centre–state financial relations could be re-adjusted to ensure adequate resources at the disposal of the states to enable them to participate adequately in the process of planned economic development. According to this view, this expected re-adjustment has not taken place due to subsequent developments in the Indian political economy, resulting in a huge gap between states' high development expenditure and insufficient resources (Gulati 1987: 3).

The implication of both the explanations which needs to be emphasized here is that the Indian nationalist strategy of a state capitalist path of development has necessitated a massive increase in states' revenue expenditure.

Factors accounting for growth of states' non-development expenditure

There has also been a rapid growth of states' non-development expenditure. Interest payments, police, collection of taxes and duties, pensions and other retirement benefits, secretariat general services, and district administration, compensation and assignment to local bodies and Panchayati Raj institutions (rural local government) and maintenance of government buildings (public works) are the principal items that have shown a high rate of growth of non-development revenue expenditure and now account for the bulk of this expenditure. On capital account, the principal items of non-development expenditure are repayment of debt (mainly of loans from the centre) and loan advances to government servants. These details are as given in Table 4.4.

Interest payments and debt repayments are now by far the largest items of states' non-development expenditure. These accounted for 41.1 per cent, 45.6 per cent and 43.3 percent of such expenditure during 1983–84, 1984–85 (RE) and 1985–86 (BE), respectively. This item reflects the states' growing indebtedness particularly to the centre – a point which I have already referred to earlier. A major factor for rapid growth of states' indebtedness has been that as much as 70 per cent of the central assistance to the states is being given as loans.[27] Since a large proportion of these loans has been invested in social and economic infrastructural facilities – schools, hospitals, roads, social housing, government

Table 4.4 Non-development expenditure (percentage distribution) of states

		1983–84 (Accts)	*1984–85 (RE)*	*1985–86 (BE)*
A	**On Revenue Account**	**77.3**	**75.0**	**78.1**
1	Interest payments	22.1	23.6	24.7
	a on loans from the centre	13.5	14.1	15.0
	b on other debts	8.6	9.5	9.7
2	Police	15.7	13.8	13.0
3	Pensions and retirement benefits	7.1	6.8	7.3
4	Collection of taxes and duties	7.3	6.6	6.3
5	Secretariat general services and district administration	4.3	3.7	4.7
6	Compensation and assignments to local bodies and Panchayat Raj institutions	3.4	2.7	2.7
7	Public works[1]	2.4	2.2	2.3
8	All other items	15.0	15.6	17.4
B	**On Capital Account (gross of debt repayments)**	**22.7**	**25.0**	**21.6**
1	Repayment of debts[2]	19.0	22.0	18.6
	a Loans from the Centre[2]	16.2	16.6	14.4
	b Market loans	2.0	4.6	3.5
	c Other debts	0.8	0.8	0.7
2	Loans and advances to state governments	2.1	1.8	1.6
	a To government servants	1.8	1.5	1.4
	b To others	0.3	0.3	0.2
3	Non-development capital outlay	1.6	1.2	1.4
C	**Total non-development expenditure (A + B)**	**100.0**	**100.0**	**100.0**

Source: Adapted from RBI Bulletin cited in Punjab government memorandum (Govt of India 1987: 911–912).

Notes
1 Mainly maintenance of government buildings.
2 Excluding repayment of ways and means advances from the centre.

administrative and residential buildings, irrigation, soil conservation, area development, multi-purpose river projects and so on – these investments never directly yield the surplus needed to meet the repayment obligations on these loans and the structure of taxation available to the states does not compensate the states for the experienced resource gap.[28] Consequently, the states' indebtedness to the centre increases.

The states' interest liabilities have increased even faster than the growth in their indebtedness due to the high interest rate policy used by the centre to control inflation. The centre has used its control over monetary institutions to persist with this monetary policy and high interest rates have been maintained even when in the international capital market the interest rates have been relatively lower (see Table 4.5). It may be seen that the rate of interest intended for loans taken from various external sources varied from 0.5 per cent to 14 per cent. The average rate of interest which the central government was paying to the external creditors worked out to only 2.4 per cent. The central government has been passing on this credit to the state governments as part of central assistance to the state plans at 7 per cent rate of interest.[29] For a Training and Visit Scheme which was assisted by the World Bank for improving agricultural production, the Indian government had obtained a loan at the rate of 0.75 per cent but it was passed on to the Tamil Nadu state government at the rate of 5.5 per

Table 4.5 Interest rates paid by the Government of India in the international capital market

Lending countries/institutions	*Average rate of interest (%)*
France	4.8
West Germany	1.7
Japan	4.2
Holland	1.9
Britain	0.6
America	2.2
International Development Association	1.0
World Bank (IBRD)	14.0
Kuwait	6.0
Saudi Arabia	0.8
United Arab	–
Russia[1]	3.3
IMF Trust Fund	0.5
Others	–
All countries/institutions	2.4

Source: Adapted from Table A in the Tamil Nadu Government Memorandum to the Commission for Centre–State Relations (Government of India 1987: 516).[2]

Notes

1 It actually meant USSR.

2 Though the Tamil Nadu Memorandum did not specify the relevant year for this data, the discussion in the text suggested that it was 1984–85.

cent. Similarly, on the commercial side, for a state public sector enterprise, Tamil Nadu Newsprint Papers Ltd, the Indian government obtained a loan from World Bank at the rate of 10.08 per cent on an average but passed it on to the Tamil Nadu government at 14 per cent rate of interest. A more glaring case of manipulation of central government control over foreign aid and grants is the case of a full grant by the Swedish International Agency to the Indian government for implementing a Social Forestry Scheme. The Indian government converted this grant into 70 per cent loan and 30 per cent grant to the Tamil Nadu state government and charged 7 per cent rate of interest on the loan.[30]

Apart from interest payments, the other major source of non-development expenditure of the states is on police (see Table 4.4), which has grown in those states where the militant opposition movements articulating the nationalist interests/aspirations of the nations based in those states – for example Punjab, Kashmir, Assam, Nagaland and Mizoram have challenged the authority of the centralist Indian State.[31] From Table 4.6, we can see that in terms of the number of policemen per 10,000 of population, Nagaland (Rank #1), Manipur (#2), Mizoram (#3), Sikkim (#4), Arunachal Pradesh (#5), Meghalaya (#6), Jammu & Kashmir (#7), Tripura (#8), Punjab (#9) and Himachal Pradesh (#10) are the top ten states. Except Himachal Pradesh, all the remaining states are the sites of conflict between state-based nationalism and the centralist Indian nationalism.

In terms of the number of policemen per 100 square kilometres in area, Punjab (Rank #1), Nagaland (#2), Kerala (#3), West Bengal (#4), Tripura (#5), Goa (#6), Haryana (#7), Uttar Pradesh (#8), Assam (#9) and Manipur (#10) are the top ten states. In this grouping, with the exception of Goa, Haryana and Uttar Pradesh, all the states are either those states which have witnessed anti-centre nationalist movements (Punjab, Nagaland, Tripura, Assam and Manipur) or those that have long-established Left movements (Kerala, West Bengal and Tripura), which have often come in conflict with the centre. Tripura has witnessed both state-based nationalist as well as Left movements that have often come in conflict with the centre. The relatively higher concentration of police deployment in the states that have nationalist conflicts with the centre is also mirrored in greater human rights violations in such states.[32]

Factors accounting for states' inadequate budgetary receipts

States' growing expenditure on revenue and capital account has not been matched by a commensurate expansion of the budgetary receipts thus forcing them to depend increasingly on the centre for financial support. The states' inadequate budgetary receipts may be attributed to: a narrow tax base; constraints on additional taxation; low returns on investment and enterprise; and the central government's relentless drive for large capital receipts.[33]

Table 4.6 The policing of the states in India, 1990

States	*Number of policemen per 100 square kilometres in area*	*Rank*	*Number of policemen per 10,000 of population*	*Rank*
1 Andhra Pradesh	22.1	18	1.0	17
2 Arunachal Pradesh	4.6	25	4.7	5
3 Assam	52.7	9	1.7	13
4 Bihar	43.3	12	0.9	18
5 Goa	70.2	6	2.1	11
6 Gujarat	28.6	16	1.4	14
7 Haryana	65.7	7	1.8	12
8 Himachal Pradesh	20.6	20	2.3	10
9 Jammu and Kashmir	12.9	24	3.9	7
10 Karnataka	24.1	17	1.0	17
11 Kerala	87.7	3	1.1	16
12 Madhya Pradesh	19.5	22	1.4	14
13 Maharashtra	40.6	13	1.7	13
14 Manipur	50.4	10	6.3	2
15 Meghalaya	32.6	14	4.3	6
16 Mizoram	19.8	21	6.0	3
17 Nagaland	96.6	2	14.4	1
18 Orissa	21.0	19	1.1	16
19 Punjab	98.7	1	2.5	9
20 Rajasthan	14.7	23	1.1	16
21 Sikkim	31.5	15	5.1	4
22 Tamil Nadu	45.0	11	1.0	17
23 Tripura	79.4	5	3.4	8
24 Uttar Pradesh	54.4	8	1.2	15
25 West Bengal	81.3	4	1.1	16

Source: Compiled from the data collected by National Crime Records Bureau, Ministry of Home Affairs, Government of India, and presented in Table 211 of the *Statistical Abstract India, 1992* (Govt of India 1994: 485).

Note
Ranking of the states has been done by author.

Narrow tax base for the states

The states have not lagged behind the centre in their efforts for additional tax mobilization. This is evident from Table 4.7, which shows that the states have kept up their share of tax mobilization since Indian national independence except for a blip during 1961–73. The crucial factor for states' financial dependence on the centre is, therefore, their *very narrow tax base* in relation to their revenue expenditure as well as the centre's tax base. This is shown in Table 4.8. Row 2 in Table 4.8 shows that the revenue expenditure of the states, including the Union territories (UTs), has been considerably higher than the centre's revenue expenditure (excluding grants to the states and UTs for development and non-developmental purposes). On the other hand, the revenue receipts of the states (see row 1) excluding the states' share in central taxes were generally no more than one-half of the centre's tax revenue. Clearly in spite of having to finance considerably large revenue expenditure, the states have a much narrower tax base. The result has been that, as shown in row 4 (Table 4.8), the centre's tax revenue has invariably exceeded its own revenue expenditure (excluding grants to the states and UTs). The excess has been 36.8 per cent in 1975–76, 26 per cent in 1980–81, 17 per cent in 1983–84, 7.3 per cent in 1984–85 (RE) and 4.5 per cent in 1985–86 (BE). The excess shows a declining trend as the centre's gross tax revenue has been growing more slowly than its revenue expenditure. The declining trend could be partly the result of regressive taxation policy followed by the centralist Indian state. This is indicated by the data shown in Table 4.9, which show that there have been mounting income-tax arrears, which the centralist Indian state has not tried to recover. This reluctance to recover such huge tax arrears could be attributed mainly to the regressive anti-redistributive tax policies of the centralist state and to a lesser extent to the fact that the centre does not have much incentive to recover these arrears because it has to transfer 85 per cent of the collected income tax to the states as per the recommendations of the Finance Commission. The centralist state's anti-redistributive bias can be seen 'from a number of tax deductions it has allowed in respect of the individual income tax and the frequent exemptions granted'.[34] In contrast with the centre's excess of tax revenue over its revenue expenditure, the revenue from the state taxes has been generally less than one-half of their revenue expenditure (see Table 4.8, row 3). Moreover this proportion has shown a declining trend.

Table 4.7 Tax revenue of the centre, states and Union territories (%)

Period (fiscal years)	*Centre*	*States and Union territories*	*Total*
1950	64.6	35.4	100.0
First Five-Year Plan (1951–55)	64.8	35.2	100.0
Second Five-Year Plan (1956–60)	65.3	34.7	100.0
Third Five-Year Plan (1961–65)	69.8	30.2	100.0
Annual plans (1966–68)	68.4	31.6	100.0
Fourth Five-Year Plan (1969–73)	68.7	31.3	100.0
Fifth Five-Year Plan (1980–84)	65.7	34.3	100.0
1986 (BE)	64.6	35.4	100.0

Source: Adapted from the Ministry of Finance data cited in Govt of India (1987: 914).

Note
Since the data for the states and the Union territories were not available separately, the combined data have been used. This, however, does not significantly alter the picture as the Union territories with legislature account for only a tiny fraction of the total tax revenue.

Table 4.8 Relative tax base of the states and the centre

Ratios (percentage)	*1975–76*	*1980–81*	*1983–84*	*1984–85 RE*	*1985–86 BE*
1 States' taxes revenue / Central Tax Revenue	47.0	50.6	52.1	51.9	54.8
2 States' expenditure on revenue account / Central expenditure on revenue account	114.2	132.6	126.1	120.5	120.0
3 States' tax revenue / States expenditure on revenue account	56.2	48.1	48.4	46.2	47.7
4 Central Tax Revenue / Central expenditure on revenue account	136.8	126.0	117.0	107.3	104.5

Source: Compiled from the data provided in the *Report of the Commission on Centre–State Relations* (Govt of India, 1987: 918).

Table 4.9 Income tax arrears

Year	*(Rs. crore)*
1984–85	1,168.40
1985–86	1,215.83
1986–87	1,439.20
1987–88	1,631.68

Source: Adapted from Note of Dissent by Justice AS. Qureshi, *Second Report of the Ninth Finance Commission* (Qureshi 1989: 53).

The main conclusions that emerge from the discussion above are the following:[35]

1 The centre's gross tax base is more than commensurate with its revenue expenditure (excluding grants to the states and UTs). If the centre did not have to share some of its taxes with the states or to provide grant assistance to the states and the UTs with legislature, the centre's tax revenue alone would yield it a tax surplus, and its non-tax revenue would further add to that surplus.
2 The centre has been following a regressive taxation policy and is not taking steps to ensure that its gross tax revenue grows at least at the same rate along with its revenue expenditure. The excess of the former over the latter is, therefore, getting progressively eroded.
3 The states have too narrow a tax base for meeting their revenue expenditure needs. The states' dependence on the centre for additional resources by way

of share of taxes and grants is thus structurally inherent in the existing provisions with regard to centre–state financial relations.

Main reasons for states' narrow tax base

Indian constitutional divisions of financial powers and responsibilities between the centre and the states are primarily responsible for the narrow tax base of the states. This becomes clear if we look at the distribution of the tax revenues between the centre and the states (see Table 4.7), which has had only minor changes since the constitution came into force in the fiscal year 1950–51. However, in order to discharge their responsibilities, the states have had to step up their revenue expenditure to the level where it exceeds the centre's revenue expenditure (exclusive of grants to the states and UTs) by a considerable margin (see Table 4.8, row 2). The financial dependence of the states on the centre for transfers from the centre to the states is, therefore, rooted in the disproportionalities between the revenues and expenditures of the centre and the states, which follow from the constitution itself.

Low returns on investment and enterprise in the states

An estimate of the states' non-tax revenue as a percentage of the states' revenue expenditure worked out to be 17.5 in 1983–84, 16.5 in 1984–85 and 16.1 in 1985–86. The ratio of the states' non-tax revenue to the states' revenue expenditure shows a slightly decreasing trend. The major sources of non-tax revenue of the states are interest receipts and dividends, receipts from forests, mines and minerals and irrigation works and receipts from departmentally run commercial schemes like water-supply schemes, milk schemes and industrial schemes. Though interest receipts have been positive, dividends from equity investments have been very low, the receipts from forests are likely to decline because of the restrictions contained in the Forest (Conservation) Act 1980, and the receipts from the mines and the minerals have been fairly low. The worst performance has been from the states' departmental commercial undertakings (e.g. irrigation projects, multi-purpose projects, road and water transport services, dairy development, industry) and non-departmental undertakings (state electricity boards, road transport corporations).[36] This is one area which seems to be entirely the states' responsibility. If states' non-tax revenues have to be raised, and states' financial dependence on the centre has to be decreased, states' departmental commercial and non-departmental undertakings must be run efficiently enough to generate increased returns.

The economic instruments used by the centre to raise capital receipts and their implications for the states

The states' disadvantage relative to the centre is much more serious with regard to capital receipts than it is with regard to revenue receipts. The centre had always had the major share in the public sector capital receipts. The principal instruments employed by the centre to secure for itself the bulk of the public sector's capital receipts are:

a external assistance;
b special credits from abroad;
c commercial borrowings from abroad by central government;
d deficit financing (through the RBI);
e market borrowings;
f bond issues by central undertakings;
g special deposit schemes;
h the Public Provident Fund;
i the National Deposit Scheme;
j deposits of the surplus funds of the oil and other public sector undertakings;
k small savings.

Space limitations prevent me from going into the full details of each of these instruments. However, I have highlighted the most significant aspects below.[37]

External assistance

The centre is the sole recipient of external assistance to the public sector.[38] During the 35-year period (1951–1985), the centre had received a total of Rs.27,257 crores (at current prices) as budgetary receipts corresponding to external assistance. This amount is equivalent to two-thirds of the centre's total net lending (lending less repayments) to the states during this period.[39]

Special credits from abroad

These credits are in the nature of commercial borrowings from abroad by the central government. The data on annual receipts of special credit are not available but the size of annual repayments (e.g. Rs.90.88 crores in the 1986–87 budget estimate) suggests that the former is possibly a substantial amount.

Commercial borrowings from abroad by central government

Another source of substantial addition to central government funding is commercial borrowing and equity participation from abroad, mainly the former, secured by central autonomous undertakings. Private sector companies have also been availing of external commercial loans to finance the foreign exchange cost of specific projects. Starting initially with the conventional syndicated loans, managed by American, European and Japanese banks, India started raising funds in the 1980s in the international bond market. Financial institutions and public sector undertakings have been the main participants in the bond market. Japan

Table 4.10 Approvals of external commercial borrowings

Year	*Central public sector undertakings (Rs. crores)*	*Total (Rs. crores)*	*Share of public sector (%)*
1980–81	810	1,038	78
1981–82	391	1,204	32
1982–83	1,544	2,026	76
1983–84	459	1,086	42
1984–85	1,086	1,906	57
1985–86	951	1,700	56
1986–87	784	1,396	56
1987–88	1,598	2,654	60
1988–89	2,413	4,314	56
1989–90	2,189	3,317	66

Source: Adapted from *Economic Survey 1989–90*, Ministry of Finance (Govt of India 1990: 128).

has emerged as an important creditor to India with the latter actively participating in the Japanese bond market by subscribing to public 'Samurai' bonds and private 'Shibosai' bonds (Govt of India 1990: 128). Since all proposals for commercial borrowing abroad, including those from public sector undertakings, require approval by the Indian central government, the approvals may be taken as a broad, even if not a precise, indicator of the commercial borrowings. See Table 4.10 for the details of these approvals. It is clear that a major part of the commercial borrowing has been raised by central public sector undertakings. The available evidence suggests that the central government has not used this source of funding to support the public sector undertakings of the state governments.[40] If the central government further liberalizes its policy towards commercial borrowings, the latter may become an important source of funds for the central undertakings. This is an example, par excellence, of the role of international capital in the development of state capitalism in India and, through that, in strengthening the power of the centralist state against the states.

Deficit financing

Deficit financing, or net borrowing from the RBI, has been another source of funds for the central government. There is no constitutional limit on the centre with respect to the amount of deficit finance that it might undertake. Any limit on it has to be only self-imposed namely, that imposed by parliament by law under Article 292. The parliament is fully competent to raise or to abolish altogether any such limit by law. No such limit is operative at present. The central government is constrained only by the economic limit of keeping deficit financing at a level that does not trigger off spiralling inflation. Because of the flexibility of this limit, the RBI has 'indeed been a bountiful milch cow for the Central Govt.'.[41] From Rs.3,569 crores in 1970–71 as central government's net borrowing from the RBI, the figure had gone up to Rs.38,920 crores in March

1986. In other words, over a period of 15 years, the central government had used the RBI to raise a sum of Rs.35,351 crores to add to the central government finances. This amount exceeds by Rs.3,728 crores the total amount of net lending (Rs.31,623 crores) to the states undertaken by the centre during this period.

The states have no similar opportunity for augmenting their financial resources. The states can borrow from the RBI only in two ways: by means of loans and advances, and by drawing down their cash balance with the RBI. The states have been given authorized limits on ways and means of advances from the RBI. In the past, when the states' pressing need for cash could not be contained within the authorized limits, they continued to draw on the RBI even beyond these limits.

Towards putting an end to this practice, the central government introduced the Overdraft Regulation Scheme in 1972–73. It was modified in 1978. Nevertheless, this practice continued and was adopted by more states. On several occasions (1972–73, 1978–79, 1982–83 and 1983–84), the central government provided ad hoc loan assistance to state governments to clear their overdrafts with the RBI. But every time, almost immediately afterwards, the problem again surfaced. The government doubled the authorized limits in 1982 but the practice of unauthorized overdrafts continued.

The central government finally overcame the problem in 1985–86. The centre granted medium-term loans to the states to an aggregate amount of Rs.1,628 crores (equivalent to 90 per cent) of the overdraft level of Rs.1,809 crores reached on 28 January 1985 to clear their overdrafts with the RBI. They were required to clear the balance 10 per cent themselves. The centre had also stipulated that with effect from 1 October 1985, the states shall not run overdrafts with RBI for more than seven continuous working days. This was strictly enforced. No overdraft was outstanding against any state in March 1986.

The RBI's former responsibility to grant loans to state governments to enable them to participate in the share capital of co-operative credit societies has passed on to the National Bank for Agriculture and Rural Development (NABARD) after the new bank started functioning in July 1982.

As a result of the developments discussed above, at the end of March 1986, the state governments' net borrowing from the RBI stood at Rs. (–19) crores as against Rs.237 crores at the end of 1970–71. Over the 15-year period 1971–86, the addition to state governments' net borrowing, their deficit financing, has been a negative amount to the extent of Rs.256 (–19 + –237) crores. The Reserve Bank of India has increasingly become a source of liberal funding for the central government and a strict disciplinarian institution for the states.

Market borrowings

Market borrowing, or borrowing by the central and state governments and their enterprises and local bodies (excluding financial institutions) from the capital market against negotiable dated securities, is an important source of funds for financing the central and state plans. Over the successive Plan periods, this source of the Plan finance has tended to gain in relative importance as shown in Table 4.11. As for the states, their share in the total market borrowing has been drastically reduced as shown in Table 4.12.

Two factors have made it possible for the centre to raise its share in the total market borrowing to over three-quarters. First, Article 293 (3) of the constitution

Table 4.11 Ratio of market borrowings to public sector plan outlay in different plan periods

Plan period	*Public sector outlay (Rs. crore)*	*Market borrowings (Rs. crore)*	*Column 2 as % of column 1*
0	*1*	*2*	*3*
First Five-Year Plan	1,960	204	10.4
Second Five-Year Plan	4,672	772[1]	16.5
Third Five-Year Plan	85,777	823	10.9
Fourth Five-Year Plan	15,779	2,135	13.5
Fifth Five-Year Plan[1]	40,712	6,388	15.7
Sixth Five-Year Plan[2]	110,821	22,120	20.0
Seventh Five-Year Plan (original)	180,000	30,562	17.0
Annual Plan 1985–86 (estimates)	32,239	6,700	20.8

Source: Adapted from Govt of India 1987: 923.

Notes

1 Includes investment by the State Bank of India out of Public Law 480 funds.

2 Actual for 1980–81 to 1983–84 and budget estimates for 1984–85.

Table 4.12 States' share in total market borrowing (actual)

Plan period	*Total market borrowing in Rs. crores*	*States' share in market borrowing in Rs. crores*	*Column 2 as % of column 1*
0	*1*	*2*	*3*
First Five-Year Plan	204	155	76.0
Second Five-Year Plan	772	356	46.1
Third Five-Year Plan	823	516	62.7
Fourth Five-Year Plan	2,135	568	26.6
Fifth Five-Year Plan	6,388	2,529	39.6
Sixth Five-Year Plan	22,120	4,719	21.3
Seventh Five-Year Plan (original)	30,562	9,942	32.5
Annual Plan 1985–86 (BE)	6,700	1,600	23.9

Source: Adapted from Govt of India 1987: 924.

has made it obligatory for a state which has an outstanding loan or a part of a loan granted or guaranteed by the Government of India to secure the latter's consent to any borrowing within the territory of India on the security of the Consolidated Fund of the State. Since, as I have already mentioned earlier, all the states have outstanding loans granted to them by the centre, Article 293 (3) effectively bars independent access to capital markets to all of them. They can borrow on the capital market only to the extent agreed to by the centre. Market borrowing has ceased to be an independent source of finance for the state plans. The centre has used the opportunity thus provided to allocate the lion's share of market borrowing to itself. Over the 35-year period 1951–1985, the centre has raised a net amount (measured by the total market loans raised less the market loans repaid) of Rs.34,050 crores as market loans. In contrast, the state governments have raised no more than around Rs.5,800 crores. This financial imbalance on this account is the logical extension and another clear manifestation of the centralist bias inherent in the Indian constitution.

Second, over the years, the centre has extended its ownership or control over all the financial institutions that subscribe to all but a fraction of the total market borrowing by the centre and states. In the case of borrowing by the states, these institutions are the commercial and co-operative banks, the Life Insurance Corporation (LIC), the general insurance companies and the non-government provident funds. The state governments have at best some influence over the state co-operative banks and the provident funds of exempted establishments. Even in these cases, the central government (through RBI) wields considerable control and influence. All other financial institutions are fully under the control of the central government. In the event, even if under the constitution no sanction of the central government were required for states' market borrowing, it is doubtful if any states could have raised adequate amounts this way without the approval and support of the central government and RBI.

Finally, the centre not only appropriates for its own use the bulk of market borrowing, it also determines, through the Planning Commission in a completely arbitrary manner, the amount of market borrowing each state is allowed to undertake.[42]

Bond issues by central undertakings

In the mid-1980s, some central undertakings started resorting to a new method of resource mobilization by going to the capital market with their bonds, which were secured against their fixed assets and carried market rates of interest and the usual tax incentive but were not guaranteed by the central government. For instance, in 1985–86, the Indian Telephone Industries issued bonds for Rs.100 crores. The success of this issue encouraged the central government to set higher targets amounting to a total of Rs.1,130 crores for such bond issues in 1986–87 (Govt of India 1987: 925).

The states' undertakings have not yet ventured into this source of funds. Even if they do, first, they will require the clearance of the central government's Controller of Capital Issues as in the case of debenture issues by private companies; second, they will face an unequal competition with vastly powerful central undertakings and are, therefore, unlikely to register any significant success.

Special deposit schemes

This scheme of special deposits with the central government, started in July 1975 (and another one in 1980), is a mechanism by the central government to divert funds of financial institutions such as the non-government Provident Fund, the Life Insurance Corporation, the General Insurance Corporation and its subsidiaries, Unit Trust of India, Employees Provident Fund, superannuation and gratuity funds from investment into centre–states' shareable schemes like market borrowings and the Small Savings Scheme to exclusive central government control. The one started in 1975 has led to net accretion of special deposits of the amount of Rs.5,600 crores by 1984–85; the first estimates for the year 1986–87 were Rs.1,500 crores but it is likely to be higher because the rate of interest was raised from 10 per cent in 1975 (and 11 per cent in 1983) to 12 per cent in 1986–87. The second scheme started in 1980, had led to net accretion of deposits of Rs.320 crores in the year 1985–86 and was expected to net the same amount in 1986–87. By adding to the centre's resources and depleting states' resources, this scheme further reinforces states' dependence on the centre.

Public provident fund

This fund under central government control started in 1968 is meant especially to tap the savings of self-employed persons all over the country who are not covered by any other Provident Fund scheme and thus further extends centre's financial jurisdiction into states' territories. Net accretion to the Fund in 1985–86 (RE) and in 1986–87 (BE) has been estimated at Rs.105 crores. In order to further augment its resources, the central government increased the rate of interest – a monetary mechanism exclusively under central control – on this Fund from 10 per cent to 12 per cent in 1986–87.

National deposit scheme

The centre instituted the National Deposit Scheme in July 1984. The deposits were for a period of four years and carried a 10.5 per cent rate of interest. The major feature of these deposits was the exclusive income and wealth tax benefits over and above those available on other approved savings. The annual net receipts in 1985–86 (RE) and 1986–87 (BE) were estimated to be Rs.200 crores.

Deposits of the surplus funds of the oil and other public sector undertakings

The central government has been resorting to increase in the prices of oil and oil products to generate extra surplus from oil undertakings. This extra surplus is then wholly appropriated by the central government. The purpose of generating extra surplus can also be achieved by raising the excise duty – the revenue from which is shareable with the states in accordance with the recommendations of the Finance Commission. This practice of raising the administered prices rather than raising the excise duty even when the oil prices in the world market had shown a declining trend is a mechanism used by the centre to deny the states their due share of the Union excise duties while, at the same time, prop up its own surplus funds. This arbitrary increase in oil prices reduces the earnings of electricity boards and transport corporations in the states and thus puts further strain on the resources of the states.[43]

Small savings

The net collections from small savings are entirely a capital receipt of the centre. Two-thirds of the net collections in a state are given by the centre to that state as long-term loans not under any constitutional obligation but as a discretionary resource transfer to the states. The vigorous effort by each state to increase the small savings collections (70 per cent of which are from the households) will therefore, only ensure more indebtedness of that state to the centre. The present position means no more than that a proportion of the central loans to the states is linked to their small savings collection just as another proportion of these is linked to the central assistance for state Plans. The entire amount of net collections of small savings is, therefore, very much the centre's net capital receipt and the states can merely be borrowers on this source.

The inadequacy of the states' capital receipts and their consequences

It follows from the above discussion that the states' capital receipts are meagre in relation to their very large and growing requirement of capital funds to finance investment in areas of development that are, under the constitution, within their jurisdiction. This makes them depend heavily on loans from the centre. Indeed, the states' dependence on the centre for capital funds is much more severe than for revenue transfers. While the constitution has provided for devolution of revenues from the centre to the states on the basis of the recommendations of the Finance Commission to be appointed every five years or earlier, it has made no provision for comparable institutional arrangements to examine and finance their requirements of capital funds. The financing of the states' resource gap in relation to their Plan expenditure on capital account still remains very much a matter for the centre's discretion. The states' dependence on the centre – which has been growing – follows, therefore, from the structure of the Indian state as shaped by the Indian constitution after Indian national independence.

Consequences for centre–Punjab financial relations

The overall picture of the dependence of the states on the centre that we have drawn above is applicable to Punjab also. In addition to the general structure of centre–state financial relations in India, two developments specific to Punjab that have cast a long shadow on centre–Punjab financial relations are the vicissitudes in the destiny of Punjabi nationalism, and the specific form of incorporation of Punjab into a centrally selected development strategy. I have discussed the trajectory of Punjabi Sikh nationalism and its relationship with the centre in the previous chapter. In the following two chapters, I will be discussing the incorporation of Punjab's agriculture and industry into the Indian national development strategy shaped by the centre. But a few brief comments are worth making here about the significance of the two above-mentioned developments for Punjab–centre financial relations.

The victory of Indian nationalism and Pakistani nationalism in creating two independent nation-states in 1947 meant a vertical split in Punjabi nationalism (and also Bengali nationalism) (Spate 1947). One part of Punjab which was tagged on to the Indian state, the part which further went through another internal partition in 1966 to emerge as the present Indian Punjab, had to be given a special consideration during the tenure of the First Finance Commission to cope with the massive problems of two-way migration of population, refugee rehabilitation and administrative readjustment. Beginning with the mid-1960s, the incorporation of Punjab into the central government's strategy of increased food production also necessitated a special consideration of Punjab. The violent conflict between Punjabi Sikh nationalism and the centre which started in 1978 and intensified from 1984 onwards also put Punjab into another special situation. Punjab was under direct central rule from October 1983 to February 1992 except for a brief interregnum from August 1985 to May 1987. The centre ruled over Punjab indirectly through a weak though democratically elected Chief Minister (Barnala) during this brief interregnum (the details of this have been discussed in the previous chapter).

One difficulty in analysing centre–Punjab financial relations is the almost complete absence of any scholarly studies on the subject.[44] This absence of scholarly investigation is in sharp contrast with widespread though conflicting views about the centre–Punjab relations. One view shared by a large number of Punjabi and Sikh nationalists is that Punjab and the Sikhs are 'discriminated' against by the centre.[45] The opposing view, widespread among Indian and Hindu nationalists, is that Punjab and the Sikhs have been excessively pampered by the centre.[46]

It will, perhaps, stretch the scope of my work beyond the present concern to examine the reasons for the gap between the weakness of scholarly work and the strength of beliefs about centre–Punjab relations. The conflicting opinions, however, reflect the fragmented and selective reading of the complexity of centre–Punjab financial relations. I have attempted below to construct an integrated picture of these relations to overcome as far as possible the fragmentariness of the views offered so far.

Interpreting the significance of the relatively high per capita income status of Punjab

The first important point worth observing is that since Indian national independence Punjab has been among the top three states in terms of per capita income status.[47] This fact could be interpreted to argue that since Punjab has improved its relative position in the post-1947 period, the centre's contribution, if any, must be a positive and favourable one to Punjab's economic development. Such an interpretation, however, would suffer from two weaknesses. First, a relatively high per capita income status of a region does not by itself tell us anything about the structure and pattern of development of a region. There might be serious flaws in the structure and pattern of development of a region showing a relatively high per capita income. The example of Nigeria is well known. Its per capita income shot up during the oil price boom in the 1970s but as a result of the lack of diversification in the economy, the fall in oil prices later on pushed Nigeria into a serious economic crisis (Todaro and Smith 2003: 72–73). Todaro and Smith have argued that the high oil price boom was itself responsible for the neglect of other sectors of Nigerian economy (especially its agriculture) and the development of an economic crisis later on. Second, a relatively higher level of per capita income of Punjab does not necessarily imply that it has been favourably treated by the centre. My discussion in the next chapter shows that the investment made in Punjab agriculture, especially in its irrigation network, by the British colonial authorities had played a key role in raising the rural income levels in Punjab. The historical legacy of agricultural development during the colonial period had played a critical role in raising Punjab to the level of development it had reached by the time of India's independence in 1947. The colonial mode of development in Punjab raised its per capita income levels but embedded an agrarian-oriented development pattern in Punjab that became a hindrance to its industrialization (I. Ali 1989, Islam 1994, Pritam Singh 1994).

The Indian central state has carried on with this agrarian development model in Punjab even though the objectives of the Indian central state in pursuing this model of development were different from those of the colonial state. The colonial state's main objective was revenue maximization (I. Ali 1989) while the Indian state's main objective was raising food output to achieve the national goal of food self-sufficiency (see the next chapter for details of this argument). Though Punjab achieved a relatively high per capita income status, both during the colonial and the post-colonial periods, this status obscured the structural flaw in Punjab's development pattern, namely, a lack of diversification of the economy. I have explored this argument further in the next two chapters.

I now return to the implication of Punjab's high per capita income status for the pattern of the centre's financial transfers to Punjab.

Inter-state comparison of centre's transfers

In the earlier part of this chapter, our focus was on highlighting the vertical financial relations between the centre on the one hand and all the states on the other. In order to examine centre–Punjab financial relations, we will now examine the pattern of horizontal transfers: the pattern of distribution of the total states' share between the different states. In order to contextualize the pattern of transfers to the states, it is important to emphasize that the centre as the architect of Indian nationalisms has a political project in determining the pattern of these transfers. The centre looks on these financial transfers as a politico-economic tool to reduce inter-state inequalities with the purpose of welding all states into a unified Indian nationhood. Nanjundappa and Rao have summarized the equalizing objective of these transfers in the following apolitical and economistic way:

> The fundamental objective of the resource transfer from the centre to the States, as recommended either by the Finance Commissions or by the Planning Commissions from time to time, is to equalize and promote levels of infrastructural development and services in the different States.
>
> (Nanjundappa and Rao 1987: 236)

Within this broader politico-economic context, the character of centre–Punjab financial relations becomes clearer when a comparison of centre's transfers to different states is made (see Table 4.13).

Transfers (through Finance Commission) mentioned in column 3 are statutory transfers and the other transfers are discretionary transfers. Looking at column 3, it is clear that Punjab had the lowest percentage (1.68) of devolution by Finance Commissions to a state's state domestic product (SDP). The figure for central plan assistance (column 4) shows Punjab's percentage to be the next to the lowest (the lowest was for Maharashtra, another high income state). Column 6 shows that the percentage of expenditure on centrally sponsored projects to SDP for Punjab is one of the three lowest figures (Punjab 0.99 per cent, Maharashtra 0.88 per cent and W. Bengal 0.86 per cent). Similarly column 7 shows that the percentage of investment in central government non-departmental undertakings to SDP is the lowest for Punjab. The picture is slightly different for percentage of plan outlays to SDP (column 5). However, plan outlay is not a transfer from the centre. It is the sum of a state's own plan resources and

Table 4.13 Transfer of resources from centre to states, 1969–70 to 1984–85

States	*Per capita net state domestic product (SDP) at current prices (Rs)*	*% of devolution by Finance Commission to SDP at current prices*	*% of central plan assistance to SDP at current prices*	*% of plan outlay to SDP at current prices*	*% of expenditure on central and centrally-sponsored projects to SDP at current prices*	*% of investment (1970–71 to 1983–84) in central government non-departmental undertakings to SDP at current prices*
(1)	*(2)*	*(3)*	*(4)*	*(5)*	*(6)*	*(7)*
Andhra Pradesh	17,976	3.97	1.93	5.72	1.56	3.38
Assam	16,024	5.55	4.64	6.05	1.49	6.58
Bihar	12,454	5.87	2.80	6.01	1.62	5.48
Gujarat	25,125	2.72	1.34	7.20	1.18	1.82
Haryana	28,984	2.03	1.33	8.30	1.22	1.05
Karnataka	18,988	3.41	1.64	5.86	1.17	2.98
Kerala	17,939	4.44	2.17	6.18	1.05	1.41
Madhya Pradesh	15,198	4.58	2.38	7.94	1.82	5.45
Maharashtra	27,542	2.44	1.00	5.91	0.88	3.66
Orissa	14,333	6.75	3.34	6.93	2.49	4.88
Punjab	35,542	1.68	1.04	6.21	0.99	0.92
Rajasthan	17,567	4.38	2.30	5.94	1.85	1.13
Tamil Nadu	17,793	3.81	1.56	6.15	1.23	2.25
Uttar Pradesh	14,536	4.87	2.43	6.92	1.51	1.32
West Bengal	22,004	3.39	1.16	4.62	0.86	2.22

Source: Adapted from Prasad 1989: 111.

centre's assistance. But even here, Punjab's percentage is bettered by Gujarat, Haryana, Madhya Pradesh, Orissa and Uttar Pradesh.

A composite picture that emerges is that Punjab is lowest on the scale. A juxtaposition of Punjab's highest per capita income with the lowest resource transfer from the centre may appear to be contradictory. But if the interventionist role of the Indian centralist state as the articulator and builder of Indian nationalism is kept in mind, this apparently contradictory position becomes very logical in character.

The Indian centralist state in order to foster Indian nationalism and to strengthen and legitimize its role as central to building Indian nationalism has to follow a policy of reducing regional inequalities. A study aimed at examining the impact of central budgetary transfers on inter-state inequalities, emphasizes:

> Thus, if a generalization is to be attempted, while the relative position of low income States can be said to have shown a tendency to improve somewhat with the passage of time, and the position of high income States has suffered a slight setback ... with regards to statutory transfer receipts from the centre.
>
> (Gulati 1987: 277)

Another study based on assessing the role of all central transfers to the states in reducing regional inequality concludes even more emphatically that 'the share of the poor States in such transfers has been, on the whole, higher than that of the rich States' (Prasad 1989: 108).

A confidential document produced by the Punjab government to which I was allowed access, highlighted another aspect of the low share of Punjab in a revenue generating source over which the central government exercises distributive control. This source was market borrowings. Market borrowings refer to borrowings raised by the central and state governments from the capital market against negotiable dated securities. I have already showed in Table 4.11 that market borrowings have increased in importance over time as a source of revenue generation, and that the central share from market borrowings has also increased (Table 4.12). Out of the total share of all the states, the central government allocates the share of each state. The confidential papers of the Punjab government highlighted the decreasing share allocated to Punjab as shown in Table 4.14.

The confidential papers estimated Punjab's share in India's population as 2.47 per cent.[48] Punjab government data show that the 2.03 per cent share of Punjab in market borrowings between 1979–80 and 1987–88 was less than Punjab's share in India's population and that in the last three years (1985–86 to 1987–88); this share had been reduced to even less than 2 per cent. Taking an overall view, the Punjab government document argued that more weighting had been given to 'redistributive criteria' than 'compensatory criteria' in transferring central resources to the states. By 'redistributive criteria' it meant criteria that

Table 4.14 Punjab's share in market borrowings, 1979–80 to 1987–88

Year	*Market borrowings (in crores of rupees)*		*Share of Punjab as percentage to total of all states*
	All states	*Punjab*	
1979–80	296.60	8.63	2.91
1980–81	327.65	8.60	2.62
1981–82	495.99	13.34	2.69
1982–83	553.60	13.21	2.39
1983–84	766.77	16.70	2.18
1984–85	1,240.62	26.06	2.10
1985–86	1,428.31	28.33	1.98
1986–87 (RE)	1,442.00	22.00	1.53
1987–88 (BE)	1,624.65	29.21	1.80
Total	8,176.19	166.08	2.03

Sources: Confidential.

recommend allocation of greater share of central resources to the poorer states and by 'compensatory criteria' it meant criteria that recommend giving back resources to the states according to their contribution to the central pool. A greater weighting of the 'redistributive criteria', the document argued, amounts to penalizing 'disciplined' states like Punjab.[49]

Another pressing factor from the viewpoint of political geography of the Indian centralist state is that the poorest states – the states with the lowest per capita SDP like Bihar, Uttar Pradesh, Rajasthan and Madhya Pradesh – constitute the Hindi-speaking central heartland of India (see Table 4.15).[50] These states, the most populous states in India (see Table 4.16), are also in the forefront of defending Indian and Hindu–Hindi nationalism.

It is a political necessity of the Indian state and its ideology – Indian nationalism – to pursue policies that reduce the economic backwardness of these states. These states continue to be backward and had the centre not intervened through its policies to reduce regional inequalities, these states would have remained even more backward. In the absence of institutions such as the Finance Commission and Planning Commission, the logic of free market economy would have prevailed without any control and regulation. The poorer states would have been in a far worse competitive situation in a free market economy system. The accentuation of regional inequalities would have been a threat to the centre's political project of building a unified Indian nationalism. The opposite side of the centre's endeavour to help the poor states is that it leads to central policies which act against the interests of high income states. The Indian centralist state is thus forced to pursue policies which become an institutional constraint on the further development of relatively well-off states. It is, therefore, a logical extension of the political economy of the centralist state in India that while on an average (the national average), the centre finances 40 per cent of the revenue

Table 4.15 Population in India by languages, 1971[1]

Language	*Population in lakhs*[2]	*Percentage to total population*
Hindi	2,642	39.9
Bengali	542	8.2
Telgu	515	7.8
Marathi	496	7.5
Tamil	447	6.8
Urdu	353	5.3
Gujarati	332	5.0
Malayalam	269	4.1
Kannada	259	3.9
Oriya	229	3.5
Punjabi	186	2.8
Assamese	32	0.5
Kashmiri	19	0.3
Sindhi	1	N
Others	292	4.4
All languages	6,615	100.0

Sources: Adapted from data provided by Registrar-General and Census Commissioner, Census of India, 1971, and cited in *Statistical Abstract of Punjab* 1988 (Govt of Punjab 1989: 76).

Notes

1 Figures for Sikkim not included. The percentage of the Hindi speaking population had further increased to 41.7 in the 1991 Census (Govt of Punjab 2005: 106).

2 Lakh = 100,000.

expenditure of the states, in Punjab it only finances 23 per cent of Punjab's revenue expenditure (data for 1984–85, 1985–86, 1986–87).[51] The conflict between Punjabi nationalism and Indian nationalism is, therefore, rooted in the ideology and the political economy of the role of the Indian centralist state in building Indian nationalism.

We have discussed in the previous chapter the complex set of economic, political, social and cultural factors that contributed to the violent conflict between Punjabi Sikh nationalism and Indian nationalism between 1978 and the mid-1990s. The enormous costs of the security operations against the Punjabi Sikh nationalists put further financial burden on the state administration in Punjab. Another confidential document prepared by the Punjab government to which I was given access estimates that the costs of local police operations in Punjab between 1989 and 1995 would be Rs.6,208.56 crores. The Ninth Finance Commission (for 1990–95) observed that 'special loans to the tune of Rs.2,300 crores were given to Punjab during 1984–89' and one of the reasons for this loan was 'the high costs of combating terrorism' (Govt of India 1989: 39). This loan increased the debt burden on Punjab. This further increased tensions between Punjab and the centre. Punjab–centre relations seemed to be caught in a vicious circle. The logic of Indian nationalism required 'discrimination' against Punjab. This 'discrimination'

Table 4.16 Population in India, 1971 and 1981 (in lakhs)

	States	*1971 census*	*1981 census*
1	Andhra Pradesh	435.03	535.50
2	Arunachal Pradesh	4.68	6.32
3	Assam	146.25	–
4	Bihar	563.53	699.15
5	Goa	7.95	10.07
6	Gujarat	266.97	340.86
7	Haryana	100.37	129.23
8	Himachal Pradesh	34.60	42.81
9	Jammu and Kashmir	46.17	59.87
10	Karnataka	292.99	371.36
11	Kerala	213.47	254.54
12	Madhya Pradesh	416.54	521.79
13	Maharashtra	504.12	627.84
14	Manipur	10.73	14.21
15	Meghalaya	10.12	13.36
16	Mizoram	3.32	4.94
17	Nagaland	5.16	7.75
18	Orissa	219.45	263.70
19	Punjab	135.51	167.89
20	Rajasthan	257.66	342.62
21	Sikkim	2.10	3.16
22	Tamil Nadu	411.99	484.08
23	Tripura	15.56	20.53
24	Uttar Pradesh	883.41	1,108.62
25	West Bengal	443.12	545.81
	All states	5,430.80	6,774.98
	Union Territories	50.80	76.87
	All India	5,481.60	6,851.85

Source: Adapted from the data of the Census of India 1971 and 1981 cited in *Second Report of the Ninth Finance Commission* (Govt of India 1989: 80–81).

Note
The 1991 and 2001 census data shows that the Hindi-belt states continued their status of dominance in population size (see Appendix).

contributed to violent opposition to the centre. In order to suppress the violence, the centre had to give special loans to Punjab. These loans accentuated the debt burden on Punjab. The increased debt burden, in turn, led to more resentment and the vicious circle went on. Despite change of several governments at the centre and in Punjab in the last 15 years, the issue of resolving this debt burden is still mired in controversy.

Conclusions

The shaping of centre–state financial relations in India is closely linked with the politico-economic logic of building India as a unified nation. The constitutional provisions regarding the greater powers of the centre in financial dealings with the states are the result of a political perspective that saw the centre's increased power as necessary to enable the centre to play the role of a nation-builder. The introduction of centralized planning in the Indian strategy of development and nation-building further reinforced the power of the centre. The centre pursued policies to reduce the economic disadvantages of poorer states so as to generate and strengthen feelings of association of these states with the Indian nationhood. The central policies favouring the poorer states bred resentment among the richer states such as Punjab. This resentment eventually fed into the violent conflict between Punjabi Sikh nationalism and Indian nationalism in the 1980s. That violent conflict necessitated an increased expenditure on security operations in Punjab. The central loans to Punjab to meet this increased expenditure further exacerbated the debt burden on Punjab.

In the next chapter, I shall explore the implications of centre–state relations in agriculture for the pattern of agricultural development in Punjab.

5

CENTRE–STATE RELATIONS IN AGRICULTURE AND THEIR IMPLICATIONS FOR PUNJAB AGRICULTURE

Introduction

The structure of centre–state relations in India, with regard to agriculture, has crucially shaped the pattern of agricultural development in Punjab. My analysis shows that the centre has had overwhelming powers in deciding the agricultural policies that a state government pursues. This power to shape the pattern of agricultural development in the states goes beyond even the constitutional powers granted to the centre for intervening in the agriculture sector. The political discourse of 'national interest' is commonly used to expand the power of the centre vis-à-vis the states. In this chapter, I first examine the constitutional provisions regarding centre–state relations in agriculture, in order to provide the overall legal and political framework for the respective roles and powers of the centre and the states in agriculture. I then discuss the implications of the centrally directed policies for Punjab agriculture. This discussion highlights the role of the centre in reinforcing an agrarian oriented development pattern in Punjab. In particular, I examine the impact of the centre's politico-economic decision of achieving 'national' self-sufficiency in food availability, on Punjab agriculture. I have highlighted the two-crop (wheat and rice) dependent nature of Punjab agriculture, which emerged as a result of centre's introduction of the Green Revolution strategy in Punjab, the aim of which was to make India self-reliant in meeting the food needs of its population.

Constitutional provisions regarding centre–state relations in agriculture

The Seventh Schedule of the Indian constitution has three lists. List I refers to the departments, activities and subjects under the centre or Union; List II refers to the State List; and List III refers to the Concurrent List, where the states and the centre are co-sharers of power and responsibility. Entry 14 of the State List mentions the item relating to agriculture: 'Agriculture, including agricultural education and research, protection against pests and prevention of plant disease'. If we were to deduce from this that agriculture is a state subject under the constitution, that would be formally correct. However, some other provisions of the constitution in the Union List and in the Concurrent List have provided legal justifications for central interventions in the sphere of agriculture. In general, national goals and imperatives were invoked in order to use these Union and Concurrent List provisions. In some cases, the central intrusions into agriculture were made even without any constitutional sanction. S. P. Singh (1973: 37) has rightly remarked that, 'stating merely that "agriculture is a state subject", as provided under Entry 14 of the State list would be an over-simplification'. The states can be constitutionally deprived of all powers, including in the sphere of agriculture, under some provisions mentioned in Part XI of the constitution, dealing with 'Relations between the Union and the States'.

Under Article 248 in Part XI, the centre has the residuary powers of legislation relating to any item which is not mentioned in any of the three lists. Under Article 249, the central parliament has the power of legislation regarding any subject, even in the State List, if the centre considers this to be necessary 'in the national interest'. According to S. P. Singh (1973: 37), '[t]here is no similar provision in any federal constitution' elsewhere, and even the 1935 Act during the British rule in India did not have a similar clause. Article 250 further reinforces this power in a situation of national emergency by stipulating that the central parliament has the power to legislate, 'with respect to any matter in the State list if a Proclamation of Emergency is in operation'. Articles 251 and 254 assert the superiority of the central parliament over the state legislature in a situation of conflict or perceived inconsistency between the acts passed by the centre and the states. In a Supreme Court decision in 1962 in a case involving the 'State of West Bengal Versus Union of India', the superiority of the centre was conceded even with regard to items in the Concurrent List (S. P. Singh 1973: 38). Article 258A provides for 'power' to the states to entrust functions to the centre in matters which are under the jurisdiction of the states. Though technically, this provision is categorized as 'power' of the states, in its implications, it amounts to surrendering a sphere of activity in state's jurisdiction to the centre. The provisions of Articles 256 and 257 require the compliance of the executive power of every state with that of the Union. This compliance requirement undermines very fundamentally the power of the state governments and, coupled with the pro-centre decision by the Supreme Court in 1962 (referred to above) in a situation of conflict between the centre and the states, it makes it unmistakably clear that the centre has overwhelming powers. I will discuss below some other provisions of the constitution which further demonstrate this overwhelming power of the centre vis-à-vis the states more specifically in the sphere of agriculture, despite the fact that formally speaking agriculture is a state subject.

Part XIII of the Constitution (Articles 301 to 307) deals with 'Trade, Commerce and Intercourse Within the Territory of India'. This also applies to the exchange and movement of agricultural goods within the states. Under Article

302, the centre can, through the Parliament, impose restrictions on the movement of agricultural goods in the national or 'public interest' and can thus encroach on a state's sphere of operation in the agricultural sector (S. P. Singh 1973: 38). Article 303 (2) empowers the Parliament to use 'any discrimination' if it is in national interest. P. M. Bakshi, in an interpretation of Article 304, cites a court ruling stating that any discrimination in the national interest should not be even considered discriminatory: 'An action which furthers the economic development of the whole of India and its unity by removing economic barriers cannot be said to be discriminatory' (2002: 248). It is a recurrent phenomenon in the provisions of the constitution that 'national interest' and 'public interest' are used interchangeably, with both then being equated with the role of the centre. This use of language reflects the mind-set of a dominant centralist tendency among the constitution makers who looked down on the states with suspicion. They viewed any devolution of power to the states as potentially divisive and agreed to the devolutionary clauses as a painful concession to the minority decentralist tendency, necessary for the purposes of carrying the latter along with them (Bhattacharya 1992, Pritam Singh 2005).

Entry 52 in the Union List relating to control of industries in the public interest authorizes the centre to control the production of certain agricultural commodities in the public interest. On the basis of this, Parliament could, for example, pass enactments controlling the dairy industry, if it were to decide that the control of milk marketing is in the public interest (Hannah 1957, cited by S. P. Singh 1973: 54). The Tea Act of 1953 and the Coir Industry Act 1953 contained a declaration that it was expedient in the public interest that the Union should take under its control these 'industries' through statutory boards. Coffee, rubber, tea and cardamom boards fall in this category. There is nothing to prevent the Union government from adopting the same argument and procedure in the case of certain other crops, such as cashew and pepper – both of these being regarded as 'industry' (S. P. Singh 1973: 54). The Sarkaria Commission has pointed out that the Industries (Development and Regulation) Act 1951 has been enacted under Entry 52 of the Central List, and that this Act covers agro-industries, for example those concerning manufacture of sugar, fertilizers, insecticides, fungicides, vegetable oils, agricultural machinery and implements, tractors or processed foods (Govt of India 1988: 440–441). This opens a very wide field of agricultural activities that are thus characterized as agro-industries to be brought under central control.

Entry 51 in the Union List empowers the centre to establish 'standards of quality for goods to be exported out of India or transported from one State to another' and this can be easily used to extend the centre's role in the agricultural sector of a state that produces agricultural commodities to be exported to other states or countries. It can be argued that the provisions of Entry 51 can be invoked to legitimize the centre's interference in the state sphere of agriculture even if only a part of the total output of an agricultural commodity is exported.

Entry 33 in the Concurrent List, as amended by the Third Amendment Act of the Constitution in 1954, empowers both the state and the Union government to legislate regarding 'trade and commerce in, and the production, supply and distribution of': foodstuffs, including edible oilseeds and oils; cattle fodder, including oilcakes and other concentrates; raw cotton, whether ginned or not ginned, and cotton seed; and raw jute. This, in accordance with the Supreme Court decision of 1962 cited above, would give the centre an overruling position despite entries 26 and 27 of the State List covering these subjects (S. P. Singh 1973: 38). Entry 26 in the State List stipulates: 'Trade and commerce within the State subject to the provisions of entry 33 of List III'; and Entry 27 states: 'Production, supply and distribution of goods subject to the provisions of entry 33 of List III'. Thus the state powers in these spheres are undermined by the provisions of Entry 33. For example, under the provisions of Entry 33, the centre can take over food production and distribution (normally under state control) if the national interest is interpreted to demand central control. This virtually amounts to moving agriculture from the State List to the Concurrent List. It will be pertinent to refer to the observations made on this subject by the study team of the Administrative Reforms Commission in 1967:

> By a constitutional amendment (Entry 33 in List III) the production, among other activities, of foodstuffs (including edible oilseeds and oils), cattle fodder, raw cotton and raw jute has become a concurrent subject. These items together form much of the largest part of agriculture produce. If the word 'production' occurring in this entry has to be given a wide import, *agriculture for the most part must be deemed to have become a concurrent subject.* In that case the amendment of this entry has introduced an element of confusion in that Entry 14 in List II reading 'Agriculture, including agricultural education and research, protection against pests and prevention of plant disease' has not been amended. If the term 'production' is to carry a limited import, it is not clear at all what the limitation is. The confusion needs to be resolved through a parliamentary review so that responsibility is clearly defined. *It appears to us that agriculture should administratively be treated as a State subject and that central encroachment in the sphere of the assumption of responsibility for substantive activity should not be permissible. However, considering the importance of agriculture to the national economy, the centre should have the right to lay down overall policies and, if necessary, legislate for them.*
>
> (Govt of India 1967: 164, italics added)

Though the study team's observations reinforce the point I made above, that Entry 33 in List III amounts to moving agriculture from the State List to Concurrent List, these observations also reveal an internal contradiction. On one hand, the study team rightly criticizes central encroachments into the state sphere of agriculture, but, on the other, it gives carte blanche to the centre for the same encroachments in the name of 'national interest'. The invoking of 'national interest', for the purposes of legitimizing central encroachments into the state sphere, is the most commonly resorted method adopted by those who favour greater central role in agriculture; and the study team also resorts to this method. S. S. Puri uses this internal flaw in the study team's observations to argue for an even stronger role for the centre in the sphere of agriculture, which he describes as 'a tied sector' (1970: 359). This description of agriculture as 'a tied sector' reflects both the pro-centre stance of Puri, a Planning Commission official, as well as his attempt to capture the pro-centre bias of many provisions of the Constitution regarding agriculture.

The Sarkaria Commission on Centre–State Relations has pointed out that the Parliament had enacted the Essential Commodities Act 1955 by using the provisions of Entry 33. This Act gives power to the central government to control production, supply, distribution, trade and commerce in essential commodities. 'This definition "essential commodity" in Section 2 of the Act includes, inter alia, Sugarcane, Foodstuffs, Edible oilseeds and oil, Raw Cotton and Raw Jute' (Govt of India 1988: 441). This observation by the Sarkaria Commission highlights that the implications of Entry 33 have a wider reach in agriculture than that which could be imagined from a literal reading of this Entry. The Sarkaria Commission has further explicated the wider implications of Entry 33, as follows:

> The Union Government has an important role to play in securing not only increased production of the items covered by Entry 33 but also in ensuring a purposive distribution and supply of the same. It is well known that some parts of the country are surplus in foodstuffs and many others are deficient. Similar is the case with oilseeds and cattle fodder. Raw cotton and raw jute, also covered by this Entry, are basic raw materials for industry and are grown in large areas of some States. They involve reconciling the interests of farmers, industry and trade through price-support, ensuring smooth supply across the States and maintaining their demand. Obviously, such matters provide scope both for action by the Union and the States, and *primacy to that of the formar* [sic] *wherever national and inter-state interests are involved.*
>
> (Govt of India 1988: 441, italics added)

It is clear that the Sarkaria Commission also justified the 'primacy' of the centre under this provision in the name of 'national interest'.

Entry 34 in the Concurrent List mentions 'Price Control'. D. D. Basu (1965), an expert on the Constitution, has interpreted this to mean an authorization for the government to fix maximum and minimum prices (cited by S. P. Singh 1973: 55). The most important use made of this power by the central government has been to fix minimum support prices for key food commodities like wheat and paddy, and to set up centrally controlled public procurement organizations, such as the Food Corporation of India (FCI). Minimum support prices and the FCI have been crucial instruments in the hands of the central government, used to bring about changes in the cropping pattern of a state like Punjab in order to fulfil the centrally decided objective of national food self-sufficiency.

The Sarkaria Commission considered Entry 34 in the Concurrent List to be functionally related to Entry 33 of this List, and suggested that it had a much wider coverage. According to the Commission, price control was a basic issue in the national economic policy, one that had special relevance in the context of India's planned development and mixed economy. In this arrangement, according to the Commission, the centre 'has to evolve policy parameters and co-ordinate the overall aspects impinging on prices' while the states have to attend to 'the details of implementation' (Govt of India 1988: 441). This interpretation of the provisions of Entry 34 again demonstrates the strategic primacy accorded to the centre in the constitutional arrangement, while the states are seen merely as implementers.

The wide ranging implications of Entry 33 and Entry 34 in the Concurrent List, in terms of central intrusions into the state's sphere of agriculture, led the state government of Tamil Nadu to demand that these entries should be transferred from the Concurrent List to the State List (Govt of Tamil Nadu 1987: 524). West Bengal's Leftist government went even further, arguing that not only the existing entries in the Concurrent List but also those in the Union List that constrict the states' jurisdiction in agriculture should be deleted, and that 'Agriculture, including animal husbandry, forestry and fisheries, should be exclusively a States subject.... The recent trend, with the centre progressively encroaching in the sphere of agriculture, must be reversed' (Govt of West Bengal 1987: 614).

Entries 42, 43 and 44 in the Union List relate to inter-state trade, and the formation of trading and financial corporations, but not to co-operatives or inter-state corporations (excluding universities). These also empower the centre to initiate and control activities that have implications for the agricultural sector.

Entries 64 and 65 in the Union List deal with scientific education and research, while Entry 66 deals with the co-ordination and determination of standards within the concerned institutions. These provisions empower the centre to set the agenda even for agricultural research and education. In 1976, during the period of Emergency imposed by Mrs Indira Gandhi, 'education' (which was an item number 11 in the State List) was taken out of the State List and included in item 25 of the Concurrent List via an amendment of the constitution (the Forty-second Amendment). This further empowered central control over education and research, with implications even for agricultural education and research, even though item 14 in the State List (on agriculture education and research) and item 15 (on animal husbandry) are technically in the states' jurisdiction.

The centre can liberally interpret the powers given to it in the constitution, in order to increase its outreach in areas which might not obviously be seen to be in its jurisdiction on a first reading of the distribution of powers between the centre and the states. One such case which can be cited is item 47 in the Union List. It mentions only one word: 'Insurance'. S. P. Singh (1973: 39) notes that a national legislation on crop insurance had been suggested under this item. Legislation on crop insurance under item 47 will have obvious implications for further encroachments of the centre into the state subject of agriculture through the possible development of a centrally controlled crop insurance scheme.

Entry 20 in the Concurrent List mentions 'Economic and social planning'. Another addition to this entry was made during the Emergency (1975–1977) by inserting entry 20A as 'Population control and family planning'. Entry 20 has provided the centre with semi-legitimacy for the creation of the Planning Commission. One commentator on the constitution characterized the wording in this entry as 'the vaguest phrase' in the distribution of centre–state powers (Jennings 1953: 62). However, it is important to note that the centre has used this vagueness to its own advantage vis-à-vis the states. Although, the creation of the Planning Commission does not have the legal sanction of a parliamentary decision, this entry can be adduced to be a semi-legal justification for its creation. The central government has used the institution of the Planning Commission 'to introduce a national bias in State policies' (Khatkhate and Bhatt 1987: 48). During the Constituent Assembly debates, a lone dissenting voice (that is, against putting this entry in the Concurrent List) was that of K. Santhanam, one of the most powerful advocates of decentralization. He had feared that the centre could use the power of planning provided by this entry to intrude even into the state subject of agriculture (S. P. Singh 1973: 55).

Article 282 makes provisions for discretionary grants from the centre. During the framing of the constitution, this Article was conceived as a 'residuary or reserve Article to enable the Union to deal with unforeseen contingencies' (Santhanam 1960: 40). However, over the years, the power conferred on the centre by this Article has been used by the centre in the central planning mechanism to go much beyond the original purpose (Santhanam 1960: 40–41). Central discretionary grants have become an increasingly important source of the revenue of the states even in normal times. Through these discretionary grants, the centre has been able to steer the agricultural policies of the states in the direction desired by the centre (S. P. Singh 1973: 39).

Entry 56 in the Union or Central List refers to: 'Regulation and development of inter-State rivers and river valleys to the extent to which such regulation and development under the control of the Union is declared by Parliament by law to be expedient in the public interest'. This gives an enormous amount of power to the centre for the control of river water resources.[1] This central power is further enhanced by the provisions of Article 262 of the constitution. This article provides the central government not only the power to adjudicate in a case of inter-state dispute over the use of inter-state river waters, but it even allows for the central government to deprive (through parliament legislation) 'the Supreme Court or any other court' from exercising 'jurisdiction in respect of any such dispute or complaint' in the adjudication mechanism set up by the centre. The Punjab Termination of Agreements Bill 2004, passed by the Punjab State Assembly in July 2004 to terminate all previous inter-state river-water sharing agreements concerning Punjab, has put the constitutional situation regarding the use of inter-state river water resources into serious dispute (S. Sharma 2004). The central government has been forced to seek Supreme Court intervention in order to resolve this constitutional dilemma. The case is pending before the Supreme Court and its resolution will have far reaching implications in defining centre–state relations on the use of inter-state river water – a critical input for agricultural production.

Entry 29 in the Concurrent List, covering the prevention of plant and animal diseases extending from one state to another, opens the possibility of central intervention in this aspect of the agricultural economy of a state. The power of intervention by the centre in this aspect of agriculture is further enhanced by entry 81 in the Central List, giving the centre the sole power of dealing with 'inter-State quarantine'.

Although entry 30 in the State List, dealing with 'money-lending and money-lenders; relief of agricultural indebtedness', gives the states the power to deal with the subject of credit in agriculture, this power gets limited with the provision of entry 9 in the Concurrent List (dealing with 'bankruptcy and insolvency'). Entry 9 opens the path for central intervention in this field. This constitutional provision has allowed the centre to shape the agricultural credit policies of the states, by providing large-scale credit facilities from central institutions to state level agencies (Hannah, cited by S. P. Singh 1973: 55).

Entry 17 'Prevention of cruelty to animals', entry 17A 'Forests' (introduced during the Emergency, 1975–1977), entry 17B 'Protection of wild animals and birds', and entry 18 'Adulteration of foodstuffs and other goods' are all in the Concurrent List and open avenues for central intervention into agriculture in all the activities covered by these entries.

A brief discussion of Article 48 of the constitution would be useful in order to demonstrate how centralization creeps in through unsuspecting doors. This article is perhaps the most opaque article in the constitution from the angle of centre–state relations. It is worded:

> **Organisation of agriculture and animal husbandry**. – The State shall endeavour to organise agriculture and animal husbandry on modern and scientific lines and shall, in particular, take steps for preserving and improving the breeds, and prohibiting the slaughter of cows and calves and other milch and draught cattle.
>
> (Article 48, bold in the original)

This article, a part of the constitution dealing with directive principles of state policy, seems on first reading to be an innocuous statement of state intention towards good scientific management of animal stock. However, if one unravels the historical context of the wording of the constitution, one begins to understand the sub-text hidden beneath the text of this article. The specific insertion of 'prohibiting the slaughter of cows and calves' in the wording of the article, was/is a reflection of the religious preferences and powers of the dominant upper caste Hindus among the constitution makers, for whom the cow was/is a sacred animal. These Hindu groups were also the strongest votaries of centralization during the process of constitution making.[2] This Article empowers the centre not only to prevent cow slaughter but also to intervene into the wider dimensions of animal management – an important area of agriculture.

The discussion above demonstrates that, though in a formal division of powers between the centre and the states, agriculture falls under the purview of the states, there are enough other provisions in the Central and Concurrent lists of the Indian constitution to open avenues for central intervention that would shape the pattern of agricultural development in any state in the Indian Union. Most of these provisions are invoked in the name of 'national interest' or 'public interest'.

In following section, I will analyse how, with the constitutional provisions legitimizing the role of the centre, the central government has pursued certain national development policies that have shaped the pattern of agricultural development in Punjab.

The centre and Punjab agriculture

I will argue in this section that the national developmental priorities and strategies set by the central government in India have crucially shaped the pattern of development in Punjab agriculture. I will first discuss the key components of the central government initiatives and policies that have had implications for Punjab agriculture, and then elaborate on the developments in Punjab agriculture that have resulted as a consequence of these central government initiatives and policies.

National development strategies and Punjab agriculture

The overwhelming feature of Punjab's development is its strong reliance on the agricultural sector. Two events of historical significance, which have shaped the direction of Punjab's economic development towards an agriculturally oriented pattern of development in the last 150 years, are the dissolution of the sovereign Punjabi state in 1840s and the incorporation of Punjab into Britain's colonial empire in India; and the emergence of an independent Indian nation state in 1947 with the key role assigned to the centre in shaping the economic policy of the new nation state.[3] Both the British colonial state and the Indian national state followed (though for different reasons as discussed below) economic policies in Punjab that contributed to the development of the agricultural sector, and to the relative neglect of the non-agricultural sectors. The development of canal colonies during the British colonial rule and the introduction of the Green Revolution strategy by the independent Indian state are the two high watermarks of the respective economic policies followed in Punjab.

I have very briefly discussed below the role of the colonial state in contributing to the agrarian-oriented development pattern. This discussion has been kept deliberately brief since the focus of my argument is on the role played by the post-colonial Indian state, particularly post-1966. The purpose of this brief discussion is twofold: to provide a historical background to the role of the Indian nationalist state in Punjab's economic development; and to point out the continuity in the agriculturally oriented economic policy of two different regime types in Punjab.

The colonial period and the historical roots of the agrarian-oriented development pattern in Punjab

Punjab was incorporated into the British Empire in 1849. Within a few decades of the consolidation of the British rule in Punjab, the colonial administration initiated an ambitious programme of canal irrigation networks in Punjab. This came to be popularly known as the canal colonies programme, because it involved the settlement of the Punjabi peasants from the East Punjab (which after the 1947 partition became Indian Punjab) into the areas of West Punjab (which eventually became Pakistan Punjab) where the canal networks had been developed (I. Ali 1999). Soldiers retiring from the army were also given land grants in these colonies. These soldiers came predominantly from a peasant social background, and these land grants were seen both by the peasants and the colonial administration as the best economic award for military service to the Empire. The development of these irrigation networks and canal colonies was one of the most impressive developmental projects that the British Empire had undertaken in India. The colonial administration had three interlocking aims behind this massive project: to increase the agricultural output, for the maximization of land revenue returns; to facilitate military recruitment from the peasantry by making military service an economically attractive route to land acquirement; and to create a loyal political base in the countryside for the British rule (Bal 1986, I. Ali 1989, Mazumdar 2003). This politico-economic development strategy generated long-term favourable conditions for an agriculturally oriented pattern of development in Punjab (Pritam Singh 1994). The implications of this British strategy for Punjab's agriculturally oriented pattern of development become clearer if we compare this strategy with that adopted in some of the coastal provinces, such as the Bombay Presidency (the present Maharashtra, Gujarat region), the Madras Presidency (the present Tamil Nadu region) and the Calcutta Presidency (the present Bengal region), which favoured some degree of industrialization in these regions (Bharadwaj 1982). This was also a fine example of an externally governed politico-economic strategy having a crucial impact on changing the internal development pattern of a region (I. Ali 1989,

Pritam Singh 1994). It demonstrated the power of the state in engineering a development path. This development path had contradictory features: it led to highly developed agriculture and the neglect of non-agricultural sectors.

Talbot (1988, 1991) has extensively examined the role of the colonial state in strengthening rural-oriented politico-economic structures in Punjab. Similarly, Fox, in a controversial and provocative work, argues that 'the British [...] in their model province, the Punjab [...] distorted agrarian conditions and classes in the interests of the capitalist world system and [...] foreign rule'; he calls Punjab's agriculture 'mainly a colonial manufacture' (1985: 11). In a retrospective study, I. Malik throws light on the long-term implications of the colonial state policy for inter-sectoral and intra-sectoral imbalances and distortions in the Pakistani Punjab economy. He argues that 'the canal-fed areas – even after almost a century, have remained totally different in their economy and resultant outlook from the *barani* region where people have generally opted for soldiery and similar other professions' (1995: 9) and that 'industrial and urban development has been equally confined to certain specific regions leading to a number of grievances from western and northern Punjab – retarding the urban-based mainstream political movement' (1995: 10). The contradictory nature of the development path engineered in Punjab by the colonial administration has been best demonstrated by I. Ali, when he argues that the co-existence of development and underdevelopment in Punjab was a logical culmination of the colonial policy of developing Punjab merely as an agrarian region. He gives a very succinct description of the consequences of this colonial policy: 'From 1885 on, the economy of the Punjab began to be reshaped by the unprecedented extension in agricultural production brought about by canal colonisation' (1989: 5). The focus of Ali's thesis of this development co-existing with underdevelopment perhaps emerges best when he argues that Punjab 'experienced economic growth' as a result of this colonial policy 'and yet remained backward, or even [...] acquired through the very process of growth further structural resistance to change. [...] That continued backwardness was entrenched because of, rather than in spite of, economic change' (1989: vii).

Having given some flavour of the agriculturally oriented path of development pursued in Punjab by the colonial state, I will now focus on the role of the Indian state in continuing and deepening this agrarian-oriented path of development in Punjab after 1947, and especially after 1966.

The agrarian-oriented path of development in Punjab after 1947 and the politico-economic agenda of the Indian nationalist state

The independent Indian nationalist state, which owed its birth to a largely successful anti-colonial struggle, had four main guiding principles of its economic policy: economic self-reliance, political non-alignment, balanced regional development, and the reduction of socio-economic inequalities.[4] The goals of economic self-reliance and political non-alignment reflected foreign policy concerns, and the goals of reducing regional and social inequalities reflected domestic policy objectives. These goals were not necessarily all mutually compatible, nor were they all successfully pursued. However, the common ideological thread running through these policy goals was the building of a unified Indian nationalism. A unified Indian nationhood was considered a pre-requisite to the building of a strong Indian nationalist state, and this strong Indian nationalist state was perceived as necessary to keep India united as a territorial and political entity (Pritam Singh 1999a). Economic self-reliance was aimed at providing economic muscle to the pursuit of independence in domestic and foreign policy design by the nationalist state. Political non-alignment was aimed at making the best possible use of the Cold War rivalry to pursue the goal of making the new nation state as strong as possible – economically and politically – by seeking economic co-operation and support of both the superpowers (USA and Soviet Union). The domestic goals of reducing regional and socio-economic inequalities were aimed at developing the self-identification of the economically weaker regions and social groups with Indian nationhood.

Central to the goal of achieving economic self-reliance and political self-dependence was the goal of food self-sufficiency. Every independent nation aims to be food self-dependent. Even in the 1960s, India was dependent on US food aid, provided under Public Law 480 programme of the US administration (Shenoy 1974).[5] The overriding concern of the Indian nationalist state in introducing the Green Revolution strategy in Punjab and some districts of other states was to achieve the goal of self-reliance through food self-sufficiency, and thus avoid 'the humiliation of accepting the conditions of US food aid' (Dantwala 1985: 115).[6] Public Law 480 food aid was cut off following the outbreak of the 1965 armed conflict between India and Pakistan. In the context of the Cold War at that time, the US foreign policy was pro-Pakistan as a counterweight against the pro-India policy of Soviet Union. The American state tried to use India's food dependence for political blackmail during the 1965 Indo-Pakistan conflict (Shenoy 1974). The political goal of non-alignment and national self-reliance hinged crucially on achieving self-sufficiency in food output availability (Chaudhuri 1971, Dantwala 1976, Frankel 1978, Dutt 1984, Chakravarty 1989, Dhar 1989). The vulnerability of the Indian state was further enhanced by the fear of food riots, as a result of the decline in domestic food production brought on by the 1965–67 drought (Patnaik 1975: 76–77, Sims 1988: 38, Jeffrey 1994: 79). If the domestic pressure to match food supply with rising domestic demand required *some* increase in food output, the foreign policy compulsions required not *simple* increase in food output but *substantial* increase to attain food self-sufficiency.

This necessitated a massive policy shift at the national central level. From the Second Five-Year Plan (launched in 1956) onwards, the national central policy was heavily oriented towards the industrialization of the country (Chakravarty 1989). The shift from a pro-industry policy to a pro-agriculture policy was therefore a national imperative, and was symbolized by the increased power of the then Food and Agriculture Minister C. Subramaniam in the economic policy decision-making process and by the introduction of the Green Revolution strategy in the mid-1960s.[7] Subramaniam was himself acutely aware of the historical role he was playing in pushing a policy shift (Subramaniam 1979, 1982).[8] Swaran Singh was replaced as the food and agriculture minister by C. Subramaniam in 1964 because Singh was seen as complacent in pursuing the strategy of increasing food output (S. P. Singh 1973: 113).

The Green Revolution strategy involved using high-yielding varieties of seeds on irrigated land, and the application of fertilizers, insecticides and pesticides. In using this package of irrigation, seeds and fertilizers, the strategists aimed at a quick increase in crop production (Randhawa 1974). N. Srinivasan, a Professor of Political Science at Delhi's Indian Institute of Public Administration, argued at a very high level conference in Delhi in 1970 that the survival of Indian nationhood depended on an increased agricultural output brought about by 'the application of science and technology'. He emphasized therefore that the development of agriculture and crop production must take 'the highest priority in our plans' (Srinivasan 1972: 128). Two other eminent political scientists, Iqbal Narain and P. C. Mathur, also highlighted the importance of 'intensive agricultural development' for attaining the 'national objective of securing self-sufficiency in food grains' (Narain and Mathur 1964: 122). Even the advocates of the earlier policy of emphasis on industry started seeing the national benefits of increased food output for Indian industry. The view that continuing low levels of food production would lead to high wage costs, with adverse consequences for industrial profitability, was accepted even by pro-industry policy-makers and turned them into grudging supporters of the shift towards pro-agriculture policies (Ahluwalia 1985, Chakravarty 1989, Dhar 1989, Nayar 1989).

Looking at Table 5.1, we can see that, in the allocation of the Indian state's resources to the agricultural sector, the marked priority was a quick increase in crop production. The policy shift adopted by the central policy planners 'reflected not only economic interests, but also *the interests and hopes of the political authorities in securing their power by facilitating rapid gains in food production*' (Kohli 1989: 75, italics added).[9] The specific politico-economic conditions of the time when the Green Revolution strategy was adopted 'reflected and contributed to the specific pattern of state intervention in India's deliberate development.' (Kohli 1989: 77).

In order to fulfil their nationally decided objectives, central policy planners deemed Punjab to be the most natural and suitable choice for the introduction of the Green Revolution strategy. Historically, Punjab was a relatively better irrigated state, and the forcibly migrated peasantry from the canal colonies after the 1947 partition had accumulated a rich experience of managing irrigated agriculture.[10] Kusum Nair (1961) highlights the positive contribution of these refugee peasants to agricultural development in Punjab, and Randhawa (1974) argues that the Sikh religion of the Punjab peasantry made Punjab the best choice for launching the Green Revolution in India. According to him:

Table 5.1 Share of crop production in total agricultural outlay in Third and Fourth Five-Year Plans (%)

	Third plan (1961–66)	*Draft Fourth plan (1969–74)*
Crop production	11.5	21.3
Major irrigation	37.3	28.6
Minor irrigation	15.3	15.4
Community development	16.5	7.7
Miscellaneous	19.4	27.0
Total	100.0	100.0

Source: Adapted from Kohli (1989: 74).

Note
There was a period of 'plan holiday' from 1966 to 1969 when, due to the conditions of 1965 Pakistan War, drought and food shortages, the Five-Year Planning process was abandoned and three adhoc annual plans (1966–67, 1967–68 and 1968–69) were adopted.

> There is no doubt that the Sikh farmer is the best farmer in India. Sikhism is a faith which brought about a social revolution in north India five centuries ago. [...] It liberated people from the ancient Brahmanical system which looked to the past for its Golden Age. The new faith promoted dignity of labour and exhorted its followers to earn their living by manual work. [...] Above all, it gave new dignity to agriculture which was declared as the best of professions.
>
> (Randhawa 1974: 33–34)

Malcolm Darling, an administrator during the colonial period, made a pioneering study of the Punjab peasantry in the early 1920s, in which he paid a similar kind of glowing tribute to the farming skills of the Jat Sikh peasantry (Darling 1947).

I have not come across any written evidence that suggests that Indian policy planners took into consideration the sociological and religious characteristics of the Jat Sikh peasantry in arriving at the decision to introduce the Green Revolution strategy in Punjab. There is some evidence to suggest that some of the policy planners were aware of the historical background of the Punjab peasantry, and would have viewed it as another factor in favour of introducing the Green Revolutionary strategy in Punjab, in addition to the objective material conditions prevailing in Punjab agriculture, such as irrigation sources and potentialities (Randhawa 1974).[11]

As a key component of its Green Revolution strategy, the central government played an active interventionist role in the setting up of the Punjab Agriculture University in Ludhiana, to support research into farming techniques for the purpose of raising food output in Punjab (Randhawa 1974). This centrally directed and assisted research into agronomical practices (cropping pattern, efficient doses of fertilizers, use of insecticides and pesticides, use of water, high yielding varieties of seeds) was aimed at increasing the food yield per acre, and played a key role in raising the total food output in Punjab (Chadha 1986, Sims 1988).

The increase in food output that resulted from the introduction of the Green Revolution strategy was hugely impressive and made India self-sufficient in food for the first time in its history. Lakdawala, once a deputy chairman of India's Planning Commission, recounting the importance of planning in India's development, highlighted that '[India's] foodgrains production has reached a stage where it can meet the effective demand of its teeming population … without the need to replenish them [government food stocks] through imports' (Lakdawala 1987: 3). The total foodgrain production in 1960–61 was 82 million tonnes, which increased to 108 million tons in 1970–71, 130 million tonnes in 1980–81, and 175 million tonnes in 1990–91 (Gill 1993: 1). It had more than doubled in a time span of 30 years.

The consequences of the Green Revolution strategy for Punjab's overall economic development in independent India have not proved to be very different from those of the canal colonies strategy during the British colonial rule: primarily, a structural imbalance in the economy, with a developed agrarian sector co-existing with a backward non-agrarian sector. The common point between the two very different historical situations, which deserves special consideration because it has remained almost completely unconsidered in the scholarly work on Punjab studies, is the absence of autonomy for Punjab to chart its own economic priorities and strategy of development in correspondence with its own resource endowments and its own stage of economic transition. In the first situation, the colonial rulers and the imperialist bourgeoisie initiated a strategy of development (canal colonies) in correspondence with their own global and local politico-economic and military objectives; in the second situation, the Indian nationalist political leadership which controlled power at the centre initiated a strategy of development (the Green Revolution) suited to their own historical agenda of achieving food self-sufficiency in order to deal with domestic and foreign policy exigencies. The point I am making is not that the colonial and the Indian nationalist strategies did not generate any gains for Punjab's rural economy. On the contrary, I am suggesting that Punjab's rural economy benefited significantly in terms of increase in agricultural output and incomes. Nonetheless, what I am trying to highlight is that these two strategies (canal colonies and the Green Revolution), through their over-reliance on agriculture, reinforced an agriculturally oriented pattern of development and contributed to creating structural impediments for the transition of Punjab's economy towards non-agricultural sectors.

The biggest damage to Punjab as a consequence of these agrarian models of development was (and is) the 'ruralization' of Punjab – even of its bourgeoisie. Imran Ali characterizes this class and the post-canal colony development process thus:

> Agricultural expansion tied this class more closely to the values of agrarian society, thereby weakening the impetus to diversify its economic activity. Agricultural expansion did not produce a social base conducive to rapid change, indeed, the reinforcement of the existing class structure created, through the very process of economic growth, a situation that was hostile to an economic transformation.
>
> (I. Ali 1989: 242)

His description also echoes some of the post-Green Revolution development processes in Punjab. In his well-documented study, G. K. Chadha observes that '[in] the post-Partition period, in Indian Punjab, there was a steady shift of power from the urban bourgeoisie to the rural elite … *the development of agriculture has been the first priority with each successive government in the state*' (Chadha 1986: 28, emphasis original).[12] He observes further that '[it] is perhaps ironic that the investible surpluses of rural Punjab have been used to the advantage of agriculture and allied activities only; a "modern industrial culture" has never emerged directly out of rural enterprise' (Chadha 1986: 34).[13] However, what is missing in Chadha's study is an examination of the role of the central government's strategies in shaping the choices of the state-based governments in Punjab – that is, towards agrarian-oriented policies in Punjab's economy, politics and culture.

The familiar joke that Punjab has no 'culture' but only 'agriculture' captures popular perceptions regarding the consequences of the agrarian models of development introduced in Punjab by the British colonial state and the independent Indian nationalist state.

The economic structure of Punjab and its inherent weakness

A comparison of the economic structure of Punjab, India and the advanced industrial capitalist economies until the early 1990s (as depicted in Table 5.2) shows that the Punjab economy was still locked in agrarian dependence and had not undergone the normal process of economic transition from the agrarian sector to non-agrarian sectors that the Indian economy as a whole (albeit with unevenness between states) was undergoing, and the advanced industrial economies (OECD countries) had dramatically undergone.

The ranking of the Indian states in the post-independent period in terms of per capita income is often used to project a better economic profile for Punjab. Aside from several fundamental methodological objections to this method of comparing economic performance, the alleged 'better' economic profile of Punjab in these terms hides the reality that Punjab owes this status primarily to its agrarian-oriented development path. From column 2 of Table 5.3, it can be observed that in 1949–50, West Bengal had the highest per capita income and Punjab (including Haryana) had the second highest. In 1960–61, Maharashtra

Table 5.2 Share of agricultural and non-agricultural sector in GSDP/NNP/GDP for Punjab, India and OECD countries between 1960 and 1994

Years	*Punjab (SDP)*			*India (NNP)*				*Advanced industrial economies (GDP)*	
	1970–71	*1980–81*	*1992–93*	*1961*	*1971*	*1981*	*1991–92*	*1960*	*1994*
Agricultural sector	58.37	48.20	46.92	49.34	42.76	35.52	28.4	6	2.1
Non-agriculture sector	41.63	49.80	53.08	50.66	57.24	64.48	71.6	94	97.9

Sources

1 For Punjab (1970–71) *Statistical Abstract of Punjab 1986* (Govt of Punjab 1987a); for Punjab (1980–81 and 1992–93) and India (1991–92), *Economic Survey of Punjab 1993–94* (Govt of Punjab 1993–94), Economic Adviser to Government of Punjab, Chandigarh, p. 45.

2 For India (except for 1991–92, for which see 1 above) V. K. R. V. Rao, *India's National Income, 1950–1980: An Analysis of Economic Growth and Change* (Delhi, 1982) quoted by Chakravarty 1989: 125.

3 For advanced industrial economies, OECD data cited by Griffiths and Wall 1997: 8.

had the highest, West Bengal the second highest and Punjab the third highest. Only since 1970–71, after the Green Revolution strategy had been introduced, has Punjab had the highest per capita income among the major Indian states. (Goa has had the highest per capita income, if we consider all the states, for the 1980s.)[14]

Although the Green Revolution did push up Punjab's relative per capita income status, the agrarian-oriented development path in Punjab based on it is handicapped in sustaining long-term growth. Punjab's decline in its relative position among the major Indian states is indicated by the annual average percentage growth of SDP at constant prices between 1969–70 and 1984–85 as shown in Table 5.4. Gujarat and Haryana surpassed Punjab during these 15 years and Andhra Pradesh was catching up. In the 1979–84 period, Punjab's SDP growth rate of 5.41 per cent was substantially lower than Rajasthan's 9.47 per cent and Tamil Nadu's 8.26 per cent and was only marginally higher than Karnataka's 5.33 per cent, Uttar Pradesh's 5.12 per cent and Madhya Pradesh's 5.05 per cent.[15]

Table 5.5 shows the SDP growth rates of 17 major states in India for the decade 1980–1990. It is very clear that there is a significant fall in Punjab's relative rank in SDP growth rate in the 1980s. Punjab's rank fell from #3 during the earlier period (see Table 5.4) to #11 in the 1980s. Punjab's growth rate of 5.14 per cent between 1980 and 1990 was not only lower than the all-India growth rate (5.60 per cent), it was lower than all the states except three (Andhra Pradesh

Table 5.3 Per capita income of Indian states at current prices (Rs.)

State (1)	*1949–50* (2)	*1960–61* (3)	*1970–71* (4)	*1980–81* (5)	*1984–85* (6)	*1985–86* (7)	*1986–87* (8) (Prov.)
1 Andhra Pradesh	229	275	585	1,358	2,039	2,205	2,333
2 Assam	–	–	535	1,221	2,037	2,068	2,204
3 Bihar	200	215	402	943	1,513	1,643	1,802
4 Gujarat	273[1]	362	829	1,967	2,952	2,775	3,223
5 Haryana	334[2]	327	877	2,361	3,230	3,748	3,925
6 Himachal Pradesh	–	–	651	1,530	2,216	2,636	2,908
7 Jammu and Kashmir	–	–	548	1,455	2,111	2,270	2,344
8 Karnataka	186	296	641	1,454	2,189	2,264	2,486
9 Kerala	234	259	594	1,385	2,104	2,140	2,371
10 Madhya Pradesh	255	252	484	1,181	1,699	1,960	2,020
11 Maharashtra	273[1]	409	783	2,244	3,177	3,549	3,793
12 Manipur	–	–	390	1,382	2,218	2,383	2,533
13 Orissa	188	217	478	1,173	1,671	1,954	1,997
14 Punjab	334[2]	366	1,070	2,620	4,103	4,536	4,954
15 Rajasthan	173	284	651	1,220	2,050	2,106	2,150
16 Tamil Nadu	229	334	581	1,324	2,173	2,514	2,732
18 Uttar Pradesh	262	252	486	1,272	1,284	2,003	2,146
19 West Bengal	353	390	722	1,643	2,576	2,767	2,988
All India	**246**[3]	**306**	**633**	**1,627**	**2,477**	**2,721**	**2,974**

Sources: Columns 2 and 3 Prasad 1989: 110; columns 4 to 8 *Statistical Abstract of Punjab 1988* (Govt of Punjab 1989: 106–107).

Notes
1 Gujarat and Maharashtra.
2 Haryana and Punjab (Punjab acquired its new territorial status in 1966).
3 For 1950–51.

Table 5.4 Annual average growth of SDP of the states at constant prices (%), (1969–70 to 1984–85)

	State	*Annual average growth of SDP at constant prices (1969–70 to 1984–85)*	*Rank*
1	Andhra Pradesh	4.12	4
2	Assam	3.55	11
3	Bihar	3.97	7
4	Gujarat	4.81	1
5	Haryana	4.47	2
6	Karnataka	3.85	9
7	Kerala	2.10	15
8	Madhya Pradesh	3.98	6
9	Maharashtra	4.08	5
10	Orissa	3.30	12
11	**Punjab**	**4.34**	**3**
12	Rajasthan	2.59	14
13	Tamil Nadu	3.75	10
14	Uttar Pradesh	3.94	8
15	West Bengal	2.89	13

Source: Adapted from Prasad 1989: 111.

Table 5.5 Growth rate of SDP at constant prices, 1980–90, per annum (%)

States	*1980–90*	*Rank*
Andhra Pradesh	4.82	12
Assam	3.91	14
Bihar	5.20	9
Goa	5.71	8
Gujarat	5.71	8
Haryana	6.68	2
Himachal Pradesh	6.10	4
Karnataka	6.10	4
Kerala	4.50	13
Madhya Pradesh	5.18	10
Maharashtra	5.98	5
Orissa	5.85	7
Punjab	**5.14**	**11**
Rajasthan	7.17	1
Tamil Nadu	6.35	3
Uttar Pradesh	5.88	6
West Bengal	5.20	9
All-India	5.60	

Source: Adapted from the data on growth rates; original source is the Central Statistical Organisation data revised with 1993–94 as the base year and cited by Bhattacharya and Sakthivel (2004: 1073).

Note
I have done the ranking on the basis of the data cited above.

4.81 per cent, Assam 3.91 per cent and Kerala 4.50 per cent). Even states like Bihar and Orissa, known to be poor states, had higher growth rates (5.20 per cent and 5.82 per cent, respectively) than Punjab. That these poorer states had higher growth rate than Punjab cannot be explained on the basis of their low base because even the richer states with higher base also had higher growth rate than Punjab. These relatively richer and industrially more advanced states such as Maharashtra, Gujarat, Tamil Nadu and Karnataka had growth rates close to 6 per cent or more than 6 per cent.

For a better analysis of inter-state differences in growth, it is important to analyse not only aggregate growth rates but also the growth rates of per capita SDP. Table 5.6 shows the growth of per capita SDP for 17 major states of India during the 1980s. It is very clear that Punjab's growth performance in the 1980s was poor not only in terms of aggregate growth rate but also in term of growth of per capita SDP which takes into account the population growth rates. The data in Table 5.6 show that the growth rate of per capita SDP in Punjab (3.19 per cent) was lower than all-India growth rate. Only six states (Andhra Pradesh,

Table 5.6 Growth rate of per capita SDP and population, 1980–90, per annum (%)

States	*Growth rate of per capita SDP*	*Rank*	*Population growth rates*	*Rank*
Andhra Pradesh	2.56	16	2.19	10
Assam	1.74	17	2.05	8
Bihar	2.97	13	2.14	9
Goa	4.08	5	1.57	3
Gujarat	3.62	8	1.94	7
Haryana	4.12	4	2.45	15
Himachal Pradesh	4.36	3	1.91	5
Karnataka	4.00	6	1.93	6
Kerala	3.04	12	1.35	1
Madhya Pradesh	2.74	15	2.41	14
Maharashtra	3.60	9	2.32	13
Orissa	3.96	7	1.84	4
Punjab	**3.19**	**11**	**1.91**	**5**
Rajasthan	4.41	2	2.53	16
Tamil Nadu	4.79	1	1.44	2
Uttar Pradesh	3.46	10	2.30	12
West Bengal	2.93	14	2.22	11
All-India	3.36		2.44	

Sources

1 For per capita SDP data, the source is the revised data produced by the Central Statistical Organisation, Government of India, and cited by Bhattacharya and Sakthivel (2004: 1073), who have used the revised data based on 1993–94 as the base year for computing the data even for the previous period (1980–90).

2 For the population data, the source is Census data for 1981 and 1991 and cited by Bhattacharya and Sakthivel 2004: 1074.

Assam, Bihar, Kerala, Madhya Pradesh and West Bengal) out of 17 had lower growth rates of per capita SDP than Punjab. All these six states, except Kerala, had higher population growth rates than Punjab. In other words, in spite of a relatively low population growth rate (1.91 per cent), Punjab's per capita SDP growth rate remained low because the aggregate growth rate was dismally poor.

The drastic fall in the growth performance of Punjab in the 1980s shows that the potential for sustaining growth on the basis of the agrarian model of development was getting exhausted.

The saturation crisis of Punjab agriculture

The analysis of the data on various aspects of Punjab's agriculture suggests that by 1991 the potentiality of Punjab's agriculture to sustain further development of the Punjab economy was getting increasingly limited. According to the *Economic Survey of Punjab 1990–91*, published by the economic adviser to the Government of Punjab, over 84 per cent of Punjab's geographical area was under cultivation (Govt of Punjab 1990–91: 45). The *Economic Survey of Punjab 1993–94* pointed out: 'Since 96 percent of the cultivable land was under plough during 1991–92 there is limited scope to bring more area under cultivation in future' (Govt of Punjab 1993–94: 55).[16] The fact that the forest area was only about 5.65 per cent of the total area in Punjab (in the Kapurthala district the forest area was as low as 1.04 per cent of the district's total area) further highlighted the extremely limited possibility of any further extension in the area under cultivation (Govt of Punjab 1992: 258).[17] With the figures for cropping intensity having reached as high as 175.7 per cent, the highest in the country, any further increase in the area under cultivation (even through intensive cultivation) was extremely limited (Govt of Punjab 1990–91: 45). A very high proportion of this cultivated land was irrigated. According to the estimates made by the Directorate of Land Records (Punjab), on the intensity of irrigation in Punjab, the percentage of gross irrigated area (of the total gross cropped area) had reached as high as 95 per cent, and in Kapurthala district it was 100 per cent. Except for the two semi-hilly districts of Hoshiarpur and Rupnagar, where this figure was 64.1 per cent and 65.5 per cent, respectively (thus indicating some possible scope for expansion of irrigation potentialities), in all the remaining districts this figure was above 93.3 per cent (in Ludhiana, Sangrur and Jalandhar, it was 99.8 per cent, 99.6 per cent and 99.1 per cent, respectively) (Govt of Punjab 1992: 214).

Profit margins on major Punjab crops were shrinking primarily because the institutions of central regulation over agriculture allowed the centre to exercise a decisive role in determining agriculture input and output prices.[18] A number of studies conducted in the 1970s and 1980s suggest an overall pattern, whereby a large majority of the farmers in Punjab were either running into deficit or else making only a small profit. According to a survey conducted by the Revolutionary Communist Party of India (RCPI), 'the small farmers were running annually a per capita loss of Rs.125 whereas the farmers with land between five and ten acres were producing a per capita profit of Rs.1200'.[19] According to another study on the years 1976–77 and 1977–78, the marginal and small farmers' households were annually running into an average deficit of Rs.1513.17 and Rs.1648.17, respectively (Azad 1980: 306). In 1982, it was noted that 24 per cent of the small farmers and 31 per cent of the marginal farmers in Punjab lived below the poverty line (Bhalla and Chadha 1982: 870). If we use the categorization employed by the All India Report on Agricultural Census 1981–81 (marginal farmers below one hectare; small farmers 1–2 hectares), then by 1985–86, 23.55 per cent of all operational holdings in Punjab were marginal and 19.08 per cent were small. Only about 6.75 per cent were 'large', above ten hectares in size.[20]

The economy of all these categories of farmers still depended crucially on wheat productivity and prices. The share of wheat in the area and production of cereal crops in Punjab remained, with occasional minor fluctuations, at around 60 per cent through the 1980s[21] and the developments in the international wheat economy suggested a bleak future for a predominantly wheat dependent agrarian economy such as the Punjab's.[22] Most observers of Punjab's agrarian economy agree that by the end of the 1980s it had reached a 'saturation point' (Govt of Punjab 1990–91: 39).[23]

The diversification of crops was recommended (see S. S. Johl 1986) and was widely viewed as a strategy to get Punjab agriculture out of its saturation crisis. There was certainly some merit in these recommendations, since they recognized that the food-dependent agrarian economy of Punjab had a bleak future, and that an alternative framework for the future of Punjab's economy needed to be developed. However, there was one fundamental weakness with this recommendation for the diversification of the cropping pattern in Punjab. There were very limited potentialities of changing the cropping pattern in Punjab, since the centre had overwhelming control over the pricing and marketing of agricultural products (especially food products). The centre still needed Punjab to continue producing foodcrops and contributing to the central food procurement stock. Therefore, the central government did not develop any incentive structure to encourage Punjabi farmers to move away from the wheat-rice cropping pattern in Punjab.[24]

Another serious, perhaps even more fundamental, criticism of the strategy of diversification of crops is that such a strategy reinforces the agrarian-dependent character of the Punjab economy. This raises the question of possible transition paths for the Punjab economy.

Potentialities of economic transition in Punjab

The only way that Punjab can keep up and improve its rate of economic growth is to make a transition towards a non-agrarian economic structure. Punjab can move out of its present poverty-stricken footloose small-scale industrial sector (see Pandit, 1985) to a modern developed industrial sector through massive central public sector investment in Punjab and/or a massive inflow of private capital (Indian or non-Indian). There is very little likelihood of this happening within the existing framework of centre–state relations. The transition to a non-agrarian economic structure also requires a dramatic shift in the agricultural policy followed within the state. The important components of the agriculture policy – cropping patterns, pricing of agricultural products and marketing of agricultural products – will have to be refashioned in order to articulate with the needs of industrial development in the state. However, the state government has a limited power to reshape these components of the agricultural policy within the constraints of centre–state relations in agriculture. The potentialities of economic transition taking place in Punjab looked very limited as seen until 1991. It is beyond the scope of this work to explore the possible implications of changes that have taken place since the launch of liberalization policy reforms from 1991 onwards. However, it is reasonable to suggest that no fundamental change has taken place in the dependency of Punjab agriculture on food crops.

Conclusions

Although the Indian constitution provides for agriculture to be a state subject, several other provisions in the constitution authorize central intervention in agriculture if such intervention is seen by the centre to be in the 'national' or 'public' interest. These central interventions have undermined the formal control of agriculture by the states and, as a result of this, the agricultural sector has in reality come increasingly under central control.

The strategic politico-economic goals of the British rule in Punjab led this province to be developed on an agrarian-oriented development path. Central government policies in India after independence (especially in the 1960s) reinforced this agrarian-oriented path of development in Punjab. The national goal of self-reliance in food availability played a key role in initiating the policy of Green Revolution in Punjab. The pattern of agricultural output in Punjab shifted crucially towards two food items: wheat and rice. The Punjab economy increasingly became a food-dependent agrarian economy and the process of economic transition towards non-agricultural sectors remained neglected throughout the 1980s.

In the next chapter, I look at the implications of centre–state relations for Punjab industry.

6

CENTRE–STATE RELATIONS IN INDUSTRY AND THEIR IMPLICATIONS FOR THE PATTERN OF INDUSTRIAL DEVELOPMENT IN PUNJAB

Introduction

At the time of its independence from British rule in 1947, India was an industrially backward country. The national leadership of independent India was acutely conscious of the need to overcome this industrial backwardness in as short a period of time as possible, in order to make India an economically and politically strong nation. The strategy of planned development initiated in the post-independence period – especially the launch of the Second Five-Year Plan in 1956 – was aimed at speeding up the process of industrialization in India.

Some states did better than others in this march towards industrialization. Punjab was one of the states that did not do as well as those industrially advanced states such as Maharashtra, West Bengal and Tamil Nadu. Even by the 1960s, Punjab was an industrially backward state in comparison with these states. From the late 1960s onwards, Punjab achieved impressive agriculture development as a result of the centre's introduction of the Green Revolution strategy at the state-level, with the aim of achieving the national goal of self-sufficiency in food availability. If the central policy of making India self-sufficient in food availability contributed positively to Punjab's agricultural development, its policy of reducing regional inter-state income inequalities led to the denial of crucial public sector investment in Punjab's industry, thus contributing negatively to its industrialization.

The goals of achieving national self-reliance in food availability and reducing inter-state income inequalities were both parts of a centrally determined national objective of making India a unified and strong nation. A food-dependent nation is perpetually vulnerable to political manipulations by food donor nations. The Indian nation state wanted to overcome this food and political vulnerability by making India a food self-sufficient country. Similarly the growth of regional inequalities can also weaken a nation, by leading to inter-regional tensions as well as to conflicts between the disaffected regions and the centre. These tensions and conflicts can adversely affect the process of nation-making and this danger is particularly acute in a newly independent country, such as India was in the 1950s. The experience of the 1947 partition had a decisive influence on the Indian political leadership in making it aware of the need to correct regional inequalities if India was to emerge as a strong unified nation. The fact that the states in India had linguistic and sub-national identities made the task of reducing regional inequalities all the more urgent from the perspective of Indian nationalism.

The two goals of achieving food self-sufficiency and reducing regional inequalities appeared compatible with each other at the national level with the view to making India a strong nation. However, the compatibility between these national goals was difficult to maintain in the process of their implementation at the level of individual states. Different states were at different levels of development and each state was being inserted differently into the national strategy of development. It was unavoidable therefore that the implementation of this national strategy of development with regard to the two goals of achieving food self-sufficiency and reduction of regional inequalities would produce conflicting implications for different sectors of the economy at the level of individual states. In the case of Punjab, the two national goals of achieving food self-sufficiency and reduction of regional inequalities had conflicting implications for the state's agriculture and industry. The goal of achieving food self-sufficiency led to strategies of increasing food output and benefited Punjab's total agricultural output, whereas the goal of reducing inter-state income inequalities harmed Punjab's industry. Since the introduction of the Green Revolution strategy in Punjab had led to a rise in the per capita income level in the state, it was logical from the viewpoint of the national strategy of reducing regional inequalities that industrial investment be directed towards economically backward states. Had the centre not directed this investment to the economically backward states in the way that it did, these states would have lagged even further behind higher per capita income states such as Punjab. This would have further exacerbated inter-state income inequalities. With the objective of reducing these inter-state inequalities, the centre played a key role not only in deciding in favour of substantial public sector investment in economically backward states, but also in addition directing private sector investment to these states, via the licensing mechanism. The implication for Punjab of this industrial policy by the centre was that Punjab was allocated disproportionately low levels of public and private sector investment. In the absence of this critical investment, Punjab in the 1950s and early 1960s had virtually no large-scale industrial unit to start with. The predominance of small-scale industry in Punjab's industrial sector was therefore a logical culmination of the centre's industrial policy.

In the first section below, I discuss the key aspects of centre–state relations in industry. I first discuss the constitutional provisions regarding centre–state relations in industry. I argue that the constitution empowers the centre vis-à-vis the states even more powerfully in the sphere of industry than it does in the sphere of agriculture which was discussed in the earlier chapter.

I then discuss the evolution of industrial development in Punjab. I argue that central policies have played a critical role in keeping Punjab relatively backward industrially until 1991. A detailed analysis of the post-1991 period is beyond the scope of this work but a preliminary look at some of the evidence from the post-1991 period confirms our analysis about Punjab's industrial backwardness.

The constitutional provisions regarding centre–state relations in industry

The constitutional provisions relating to the centre and the states' jurisdiction in industrial development and the subsequent legislative amendments have been shaped by the centrally directed development strategy of planned development in a mixed economy framework and that of ensuring balanced regional development to forge unified Indian nationalism (Prasad 1983, Ahluwalia 1985, Bardhan 1989, Chakravarty 1989, Prasad 1989).

As mentioned in Chapters 4 and 5, the Seventh Schedule of the Indian constitution stipulates divisions of power between the centre and the states. List I in the Schedule refers to the areas and subjects under central control, List II to those under the control of the states and List III, called the Concurrent List, refers to the areas and subjects under the joint jurisdiction of the centre and the states. The subject of industry is referred to as item 24 in the State List (List II) but the very wording of this item indicates the circumscribed power of the states in the realm of industry. The wording: 'Industries subject to the provisions of [Entries 7 and 52] of List I', clearly implies that the provisions of Entry 7 and Entry 52 in the central list (List I) limit the power of the states in the subject of industry. Entry 7 in the central list mentions: 'Industries declared by Parliament by law to be necessary for the purpose of defence or for the persecution of war', while Entry 52 states: 'Industries, the control of which by the Union is declared by Parliament by law to be expedient in the public interest'.

Looking at the wording of Entry 7 we can see that, in a federal structure, central government control of industries in the sphere of defence and the prosecution of war is justifiable because that is a realm that cannot be left to the individual states in a federation. However, it is the interpretation of what kind of industries can be included under the rubric 'for the purpose of defence or for the prosecution of war' that is debatable. A liberal interpretation of this provision can lead to an extension of central government control over many other industries that can be shown to have any link, even if a remote one, with defence or war needs. Similarly, the words 'public interest' in Entry 52 are also open to a very elastic interpretation that could justify central government control over any industry. In fact, the greater generality of the words 'public interest' in Entry 52 than that of the words 'for the purpose of defence or for the prosecution of war' in Entry 7 allow the former entry to be used even more than Entry 7 for the constitutional and legal-political justification for extending the control of the central government over many industries. Commenting on the provisions of Entry 52 in the central list, P. N. Dhar, who has worked as a leading policy planner with several governments at the centre, admits:

> It gives omnibus authority to Parliament to regulate and control industries in the national interest. And since economic and social planning is a concurrent subject, as it should be; it has resulted in some intrusion by the centre into fields otherwise earmarked for the States and has extended central control over national industrial development.
>
> (Dhar 2003: 76)

The Industrial Policy Resolution of 1948, the Industries (Development and Regulation) Act 1951 (called IDR Act 1951), the Revised Industrial Policy Resolution 1956, and the Monopolies and Restrictive Trade Practices (MRTP) Act 1969 have in combination decisively shaped the industrial superstructure of the country (Bhagwati and Desai 1972, Goyal 1979, Ahluwalia 1985, Harriss 1989).

The Industrial Policy Resolution of 1948, which is considered a 'landmark' document 'in the industrial development of the country' set the initial framework for extensive central government control over industry (Govt of India 1988: 407). One can see the logic of 'public interest' being used in this document to justify the extension of central government control over many industries. In general the document underlined the importance of 'rapid industrial development as an essential ingredient of the strategy for economic development', and specified that not only 'arms and ammunition industry' but also 'atomic energy' and 'railway transport' should be under central government control, for the purpose of rapid industrial development (ibid.: 407). This line of argument was further extended when the document proposed that in the establishment of industrial units in basic industries such as 'iron and steel, coal, shipbuilding, manufacture of telephone, telegraph and wireless apparatus' the public sector should have exclusive control (ibid.: 407). This highlighting of the importance of the public sector in India's industrial development policies amounts to a justification of the role of the centre in industrial development, since in the economic discourse on India during the planning era that lasted till 1991, 'centre' and 'public sector' came to be equated (Sen 1982, Bardhan 1989, Chakravarty 1989, Nayar 1989, Dhar 2003).

The Industrial Policy Resolution of 1948 was followed by a comprehensive act, the Industries (Development and Regulation) Act 1951. This was comprehensive in detailing the power of the centre in the sphere of industry, and was viewed by the Supreme Court of India in one of its judgments as severely limiting the power of the state legislature in this sphere (Govt of India 1988: 407–408). According to Dhar, 'the Industries Development and Regulation Act of 1951 is the basic law governing the central government's activities in the field of industrial development' (Dhar 2003: 76).[1]

This Act has been amended several times with the principal aim of further empowering the centre in the sphere of industrial development.[2] The Industries

(Development and Regulation) Act 1951 had a list of 37 items over whose production the central government had regulatory control. Through subsequent amendments made up until 1979, the list of such items had increased to 171 by the mid-1980s (Govt of India 1988: 409). The chief instrument used by the central government under this act, to increase its power in the sphere of industry, was licensing. The central government used its power of licensing to dictate the setting up of specific industries and in specific locations (Munshi 1973, Goyal 1979, Marathe 1986, Lakdawala 1987, Govt of India 1988: 408).

The Industrial Policy Resolution of 1956 adopted by the Indian Parliament was a revised version of the Industries (Development and Regulation) Act 1951 and can be considered as the chief policy document in Indian economic policy debates until 1991.[3] The 1956 Resolution laid heavy emphasis on the role of the public sector in initiating industrial development in India. It argued that all industries of basic and strategic importance, and all public utilities, should be in the public sector. Further, it argued that industries which required large-scale investment should also be in the public sector (Bettelheim 1968, Desai 1984, Chakravarty 1989, Byres 1994, Dhar 2003). It also made a classification of industries according to the degree of public sector control needed over an industry. In the first category were those industries that were to be exclusively in the public sector. These included: iron and steel, atomic energy, coal and lignite, mineral oils, air transport, railway transport, shipbuilding, and electricity generation and distribution. In the second category were those industries which could be in the private sector, in order to supplement the public sector, but should be progressively brought under public sector control. It was also stipulated that in this second category the government should take the initiative in setting up new units. These included machine tools, fertilizers, antibiotics and other essential drugs. The third category of industries included the remaining industries, which could be in the private sector but not without the permission of the government (Govt of India 1988: 407).

The 1956 Resolution further empowered the central government by emphasizing the need for central government to use the location policy for industries for the reducing of regional inequalities. This meant that economically poorer regions must receive a higher dose of public sector investment. Indira Gandhi, India's prime minister from 1966 to 1984 (except for a brief period of 1977–1979), in a 1976 interview with P. N. Dhar, a leading economic policy planner, made a lucid justification of this aspect of public sector investment. To a question posed by Dhar as to whether public sector investment should be located in a place which yields the highest efficiency and profitability, Gandhi replied:

> Sometimes expert groups take a very academic and narrow view whereas you have to take steps to develop States like Assam and Rajasthan which are very backward. Even though they may not be the best place for locating a particular industry, you have to make that

> much allowance – not from the prestige point of view of employment and development of the area. Otherwise, development (will be limited) in the more developed areas because they offer more facilities and it is a little cheaper (to start out) and so on.
>
> (Dhar 2003: 205).

Indira Gandhi's views here reflected a political vision of nation-building in a country where there were significant regional inequalities. This political vision transcended the narrow economic doctrine of efficiency as the primary criterion for industrial investment. In this politico-economic vision of nation-building, the location of public sector units by the centre had to be guided by the criterion of giving priority to reducing inter-state inequalities in the level of development. The persistence of inter-state inequalities was seen as a potential threat to national unity. It was feared that if the political and intellectual elites in the backward states perceived that their states would continue to suffer economic disadvantage by remaining a part of the Indian Union, this could lead to demands for autonomy and secession in these states. The political economy of nation building required that these states witness some positive gains from remaining within the Indian Union. The politico-economic strategy of Indian nationalism entailed that the centre be projected as the provider of that hope for economic advancement in the backward states. The key instrument of economic power in the hands of the centre, in terms of providing that economic hope to the poorer states, was public sector investment. The constitutional and industrial policy provisions enabled the centre to acquire that economic and political power, so as to locate the public sector units in those states where it was deemed necessary to serve the interests of the political strategy of Indian nationalism.

This political strategy of Indian nationalism was not without its contradictions. If it was hoped that the centre's power to locate public sector units in the economically backward states would strengthen feelings of national belongingness among these states, it was logical to expect that the same powers would generate feelings of estrangement in those economically better off states that were denied crucial public sector investment. In the following section, we discuss these differences in the views of the states regarding the power of the centre to shape industrial development in the country.

Differing views of the state governments regarding the constitutional provisions relating to centre–state relations in industry

Three state governments (Punjab, Tamil Nadu and Karnataka) have criticized the constitutional provisions of Entry 52 in List I which limit the power of state governments in the field of industry. The Government of Punjab in its memorandum to the Sarkaria Commission on Centre–State Relations argued that 'the obvious intention' behind subjecting Entry 24 relating to industry in the state list to the limitation of Entry 52 in the central list was to keep the central control over 'key, basic and defence industries which are obviously of national or strategic importance' but to leave 'all other industries ... within the purview of the States' (Govt of Punjab 1987: 872). However, the Punjab government memorandum pointed out that the provisions of the constitution have been misused by the central government to expand its purview in the sphere of industry beyond 'key, basic and defence industries' (ibid.). The Punjab government memorandum emphasized that this misuse of the constitution by the central government had been facilitated by the expression 'in public interest' in Entry 52.

By using this expression 'in public interest', the central government had brought in even 'essential consumer goods within the scope of the Industry (Development and Regulation) Act 1951 passed with reference to this [52] Entry' (ibid.: 872).

The Punjab Government Memorandum complained that 'industries [*sic*] has become unwittingly a Union subject' and proposed that Entry 52 of the Union List should be 'modified to limit Union's control to specified key, basic and strategic industries' (ibid.: 872). The Punjab government provided a list of such industries; the 16 industries proposed were: ferrous and non-ferrous metallurgy (pig iron, sponge iron, steel, aluminium, copper, zinc and lead); cement; newsprint; petroleum refining and natural gas processing; nitrogenous fertilizers; petro-chemical basic materials and intermediates; bulk drugs; steam and hydro turbines; power boilers; transformers (33 kilovolt amps and above); locomotives; railway coaches and wagons; naval ships, oil tankers, and cargo vessels above 10,000 tonnes DWT; communications equipment; defence weapons and materials; atomic energy materials and equipment (ibid.: 881).

By proposing this list of 'key, basic and strategic industries', the Government of Punjab was trying to limit the all-embracing role assumed by the centre under the constitutional pretext of industrialization 'in public interest'.

The Government of Tamil Nadu also criticized the expression 'in public interest' in Entry 52 because, it argued, that this expression 'is so wide that any and every industry can be brought within the scope of entry 52' (Govt of Tamil Nadu 1987: 479). The Tamil Nadu government further proposed a list of industries in 11 categories, which it argued should be specifically mentioned in Entry 52 so as to limit the centre's control to only those specified industries. These 11 categories were: metallurgical industries, fuels, steam generating plants, prime movers (other than electrical generators), telecommunications, transport (aircraft, ships and railways), fertilizers, chemicals (other than fertilizers), paper and pulp including paper products, sugar and defence industries. In each of these categories, specific industries were further identified. Having identified these specific industries for mention in Entry 52 of the central list (List I), the Tamil Nadu government proposed that Entry 24 of the state list (List II) should be amended to read as follows: 'industries other than industries specified in Entries 7 and 52 of List I' (Govt of Tamil Nadu 1987: 480). It is clear that, through this proposed amendment of the constitution, the Tamil Nadu government wanted to limit the centre's control over industrial development in the states.

The Government of Karnataka proposed that terms such as 'public interest' and 'national public interest' should be more clearly defined, so that the central government could not invoke these terms to justify its growing intrusion into the subject of industry. To highlight the unjustified intrusion of the centre into the sphere of industry, the Karnataka government pointed out certain household consumption goods which were under the purview of the Industries (Development and Regulation) Act 1951 passed by the central government. These household consumption goods included 'matchsticks, soaps, paints, varnishes, weighing machines, sewing machines, lanterns, furniture and cutlery' (Govt of Karnataka 1987: 240) – goods that were certainly not of any strategic importance to the industrial development of the country. The central government control over the production of these goods could be justified only by stretching the definition of 'public interest' to a meaningless point. These goods could be easily produced in the small-scale sector in any of the states without any licensing or regulation by the central government.

Some other state governments also argued for the deletion of a number of industrial items from the list of the Industries (Development and Regulation) Act 1951, though most of them did not advocate any constitutional amendments. The Government of Tripura, however, argued very strongly for constitutional changes so that central control should be limited only to 'Defence, Foreign Affairs Including Foreign Trade, Currency and Communication and Economic Coordination' and that '[t]he list in the Seventh Schedule should be reformulated so that the States may be given exclusive powers in respect of most of the industries' (Govt of Tripura 1987: 562)

The state governments that advocated the deletion of some items from the list provided in the Industries (Development and Regulation) Act 1951 to reduce central control of industries were: Gujarat (Govt of Gujarat 1987: 173), Haryana (Govt of Haryana 1987: 187), Jammu and Kashmir (Govt of Jammu and Kashmir 1987: 219), Maharashtra (Govt of Maharashtra 1987: 351–352), Sikkim (Govt of Sikkim 1987: 460) and West Bengal (Govt of West Bengal 1987: 611–612). The items that these state governments proposed for deletion from the purview of the Industries (Development and Regulation) Act 1951 were fairly similar to those in the list suggested by the governments of Punjab and Tamil Nadu.

The state governments that expressed their general unhappiness with increasing central intrusion into the area of industries but did not specifically mention any items that should be taken out of the purview of the Industries (Development and Regulation) Act 1951 were: Andhra Pradesh, which suggested that 'All industries except those connected with the Defence or National Security or war effort should be allowed to be regulated by the State governments' (Govt of Andhra Pradesh 1987: 58), Assam, which blamed excessive 'Central Regulation' for not allowing the adequate development of national resource industries in the state such as oil, gas and cement (Govt of Assam 1987: 85), Kerala (Govt of Kerala 1987: 291), Manipur (Govt of Manipur 1987: 376) and Meghalaya, which defended the licensing mechanism but argued for using it to support decentralization (Govt of Meghalaya 1987: 386). The chief minister of Meghalaya criticized the extension of central jurisdiction over industries 'under the cover of "public interest" or "national importance"' (Govt of Meghalaya 1987a: 388). The Nagaland government made a general argument in favour of a system of continuous central consultation with the states in all matters of policy including industrial policy (Govt of Nagaland 1987: 393–404).

A small number of governments, located mainly in the northern region known also as the Hindi belt of the country, supported the continuation of central control over industries. For example, the Bihar government argued that 'keeping the complexity of the country and the stage of development at which different States are, this [Central control over industries] is a healthy provision' (Govt of Bihar 1987: 147). The Himachal Pradesh government justified increasing centralized control over industries from the view point of using the licensing mechanism to shift investment to industrially backward states, such as Himachal Pradesh itself (Govt of Himachal Pradesh 1987: 199). The Madhya Pradesh government argued for a strong centre and criticized the recommendations of the Rajamannar Committee appointed by the Tamil Nadu government that had gone in favour of devolution of power to the states (Govt of Madhya Pradesh 1987: 305). The Madhya Pradesh government was in favour of keeping intact the existing constitutional arrangement of centre–state relations in the field of industry (ibid.: 321). The Orissa government did not suggest any decrease in central control over industries, except in consumer goods industries (Govt of Orissa 1987: 419–420) and endorsed those aspects of the central government's industrial policies that were aimed at the 'correction of regional imbalances through preferential development of industrially backward areas' (ibid.: 419). Similarly, the Uttar Pradesh government supported central government policies that would use public sector investment to bring about industrial dispersal and balanced regional development in the country (Govt of Uttar Pradesh 1987: 586–587). The Rajasthan government made a mild plea for keeping only 'core industries' under central control (Govt of Rajasthan 1987: 443) but argued very forcefully that the 'centre should be made stronger in the interests of national unity' (ibid.: 431).

We can see from this summary of the positions of various state governments in the country that neither pure economics nor pure politics can explain the patterns of similarities and differences in the approaches of these governments to the question of central control over economic policy in general and industrial policy in particular. The northern Hindi belt states feel a closer ideological affinity with the centre with regard to developing India as a unified single nation (Pritam Singh 1999a: 85–99). The fact that Hindi has been accorded a special privileged position in the centrally biased Indian constitution contributes significantly to these states' centralist orientation (Pritam Singh 2005). Most of these states (Bihar, Himachal Pradesh, Madhya Pradesh, Rajasthan and Uttar

Pradesh) are also industrially backward states. All these states favour a strong centre, which they believe is necessary for reducing inter-state inequalities and developing a feeling of one nationhood among the states. Their plea for a strong centre is motivated simultaneously by economic as well as political-ideological considerations. The economic consideration is that a strong centre could engineer industrial investments to locations in these states. Politically, the ideology of a single unified Indian nationalism is stronger in these states than in the non-Hindi speaking states. These states are also large and populous, with a very powerful political clout in the Indian parliament and the central political establishment. There is therefore a clear convergence of economic interest and political ideology in the case of these states' support for a strong centre. They are joined in this plea for a strong centre by Orissa, which is a non-Hindi speaking state but an industrially backward one. Though Orissa does not share the ideological enthusiasm of the Hindi speaking states for a strong centre-orientated Indian nationalism, it does share their economic interest, in terms of using the power of a strong centre to orient industrial investment to locations in its state territory.

At the other end of the spectrum, regarding the position on central control over industry, are the states of Tamil Nadu and Punjab. Both these states are at the forefront in arguing for reduced central control over industry. Tamil Nadu has a long history of industrial development, whereas Punjab has a weak industrial base built mainly around small-scale industry, as our discussion in the later part of this chapter will show. Though they differ in their levels of industrial development, both the states have very strong traditions of state-based nationalism in opposition to centrist Indian nationalism. The centre's policy aim of diverting public sector investment for economic and political reasons to industrially backward states is seen by a state like Tamil Nadu as a constraint on its ambition to further industrialize the state. The implications of a central policy of balanced inter-state development are such that public sector industrial investment is bound to be engineered away from the state. Tamil Nadu has therefore argued very strongly for greater devolution of power to the states in fashioning their own industrial development. Tamil Nadu's argument in favour of regional autonomy from the angle of its own economic interest is reinforced by a strong regional nationalist tradition that is opposed to Hindi dominated and centre-orientated Indian nationalism.

Similarly, Punjab can also see that due to its relatively higher level of per capita income status, generated by its developed agriculture, it is unlikely to get generous public sector investment in industry within this framework of central policy to reduce inter-state differences in the levels of development. Punjab's economic interest is therefore clearly manifested through its plea for reducing the centre's control over the regulation of industrial investment. This economic interest in the devolution of power over industry is reinforced by a politics of state based nationalism that has a long tradition of opposition to centre-orientated Indian nationalism. We discussed the conflict between the state-based

Punjabi Sikh nationalism and the centre-orientated Indian nationalism in Chapter 2.

On the question of central control over industry, between Tamil Nadu and Punjab at one end of the spectrum and the Hindi speaking states at the other end, lie the remaining states which have argued for devolution of powers on industrial regulations but not as strongly as Tamil Nadu and Punjab. This third category of states are broad-ranging in terms of their levels of economic development and their degrees of affinity with centre-orientated Indian nationalism. For example, a relatively less developed state like Assam would benefit industrially and economically from the centre's policy of reducing inter-state developmental inequalities. Judged purely from an angle of economic interest, Assam should support a strong pro-centre policy. However, the political tradition of Assamese nationalism is opposed to Indian nationalism, pulling the state away from such a possible pro-centre approach. In demanding the weakening of central regulation over industry, Assam's case demonstrates that the political opposition of Assamese nationalism to centre-oriented Indian nationalism has overpowered its narrow economic interest.

The case of Haryana is just the opposite of Assam. Haryana is located in the Hindi speaking heartland of India. It has no tradition of regional nationalism opposed to central-orientated Indian nationalism. Purely from a political and ideological angle, it would be logical to expect Haryana to support arrangements that favour the power of the centre. However, the economic interests of Haryana demand opposition to central control over industry. In the context of comparative levels of industrial and economic development of different states in India, Haryana is a high per capita income state and reasonably well developed industrially. Therefore, the central policy of diverting public sector industrial investments to backward states goes against Haryana's economic interest. As we mentioned above, Haryana is one of those states which have argued for weakening central control over industrial development. In Haryana's case, its economic interests have overtaken its political and ideological orientation, in demanding the restriction of central control over industry. The explanation I have offered here of Haryana's position can also be applied to industrially developed states like Maharashtra and Gujarat.

By way of conclusion on this section, we can say that it is by examining the complex interplay of economic and political forces, which sometimes overlap and sometimes conflict with each other, that we can understand the legal, political and constitutional arrangements that have empowered the centre in the sphere of industry on the one hand and have attracted support and opposition from various states in the Indian Union to this centralization on the other. In the case of Punjab, both its economic interests and its political situation impel it against a centralized control over industry.

In section below, I have discussed the evolution of the pattern of industrial development in Punjab. Our discussion will show that the backward and small-scale nature of Punjab industry is the product of the centre's politico-economic strategy of reducing inter-state income inequalities and building a unified Indian nationalism. I have discussed in the chapter on agriculture that it was the political economy of Indian nationalism that led to the central strategy of attaining food self-sufficiency in the country. I have argued that it was this strategy that led to the introduction of the Green Revolution strategy in Punjab which resulted in increasing agricultural production in Punjab. The increased agricultural output in Punjab manifested itself via the improvement of relative per capita income status of Punjab among the Indian states. My discussion below will show that it was precisely this income status of Punjab that resulted in the specific character of the centre's industrial policy towards Punjab. This industrial policy, guided by the political economy of Indian nationalism, resulted in disproportionately lower levels of central public sector investment in Punjab. This absence of substantial public sector investment contributed critically to keeping Punjab's pattern of industrial development confined to the small-scale sector.

The evolution of industrial development in Punjab

The Indian Punjab at the time of partition in 1947 was relatively speaking an industrially backward region (Khanna 1983, Ajit Singh 1983, Bhalla *et al.* 1990). As a result of the partition, the already existing industry experienced massive disruption. The *Statistical Abstract of Punjab, 1947–50* captured the disruptive impact of the partition on the industrial labour force, factories, raw materials and markets. It pointed out that 'the Muslim artisans who migrated to Pakistan contributed almost 90% of our skilled labour. Most of the factories and workshops, as well as small and cottage industries had to close down. A number of famous industrial institutes were lost to us, let alone the loss of raw materials and markets' (*Statistical Abstract of Punjab, 1947–50*, cited by Pandit 1978: 1935, and Ajit Singh 1983: 37). The dislocation of the banking facilities adversely affected the availability of finance capital for industry (Sandhu and Singh 1983: 132). This further accentuated the disruptive implications of the partition for Punjab's industry.

The sectoral distribution of the population in 1951 in Punjab and Patiala and East Punjab States Union (PEPSU; a union of Punjab's princely states, which subsequently merged with Punjab in 1956) was a clear indication of the industrial backwardness of Punjab and PEPSU (Khanna 1983: 85). Only 7 per cent of the population in Punjab and PEPSU depended on 'manufacturing, construction and maintenance of public utilities. If one were to consider manufacturing alone, the percentage would be still smaller – 6 percent.' (Khanna 1983: 85 and 125).

The extent of Punjab's industrial and urban backwardness is further highlighted if we note that a predominant proportion of its tiny industrial population (nearly 70 per cent) lived in the rural areas, where an overwhelming proportion (more than 93 per cent) worked on a cottage basis on their own account as independent workers. Even among the remaining people who lived in urban areas, nearly two-thirds were independent workmen who used no hired labour and generally very little mechanical power (Khanna 1983: 85–88). The data available from different sources on the number of factories and the number of industrial workers in Punjab shortly after the partition and independence give a different set of figures. However, these differences are not huge and can be explained as the result of the disruptive impact of the partition on the work of different data collection organizations. Despite these differences in the data, it is useful to look at some of the important studies on the subject to construct a picture of the nature of the industrial sector in Punjab in the early 1950s. On the basis of the Census of India 1951 data, two studies have reported that the Indian part of Punjab was left with only 547 registered factories employing 37,486 workers (Pandit 1978: 1935, Ajit Singh 1983: 37). My calculations from the data quoted by another study from another source show that in 1950 the total number of working factories was 811 and the number of workers employed in the factories submitting returns was 35,370.[4] The data on the size of factories (based on number of workers employed) for 1950, also provide us with very useful evidence to highlight the backward nature of the industrial structure in Punjab. There were only 14 factories employing more than 500 workers each and these factories employed only a little more than 1 per cent of the industrial labour force.

Almost half of the factories employed fewer than 20 workers and over 80 per cent of them employed fewer than 50 workers (Khanna 1983: 86) The over-all picture that emerges from this discussion is that there was overwhelming dominance of small-scale units in the industrial sector in Punjab at the dawn of India's independence.

Table 6.1 gives information about the relative weighting of different types of industries in the total number of working factories, the number of factories submitting returns and the average daily number of workers employed in the factories submitting returns.

This data show that in the structure of industrial production in Punjab around the time of independence, the industries involving relatively simple manufacturing processes were predominant.

Though the different studies reported above have given differing figures for the number of factories and workers employed, these differences are not substantial. The overall picture that emerges from these studies is that Punjab had very limited industrial development before Independence. It was a region with a very small percentage of the work force engaged in manufacturing, with the predominant form of organization being either the independent family labour based enterprise or small-scale industry, and with the structure of industrial production being dominated by industrial units employing relatively simple manufacturing processes.

Khanna (1983) attempted to draw a picture of Punjab's industrial development in comparison with the other Indian states on the basis of manufacturing data for three years (1948, 1949 and 1950). He used data on the number of factories registered, productive capital employed, persons employed, value of

Table 6.1 Total number of working factories and the average daily number of workers employed in the reporting factories submitting returns and arranged in descending order of working strength by type of industry, Punjab, 1950

Industry	*Total number of working factories*	*%*	*Number of factories submitting returns*	*%*	*Average daily number of workers employed in the factories submitting returns*	*%*
Textiles	183	22.56	171	22.80	15,843	44.79
Manufacture of machinery except electrical machinery	296	36.49	281	37.46	6,282	17.76
Processes allied to agriculture	100	12.33	91	12.13	3,709	10.48
Food except beverages	105	12.94	99	13.20	3,609	10.20
Manufacture of metal products	115	14.18	97	12.93	3334	9.42
Paper and products	1	0.12	1	0.13	1,652	4.67
Non-metallic minerals	11	1.35	10	1.33	941	2.66
Total	**811**	**100.00**	**750**	**100.00**	**35,370**	**100.00**

Sources: Govt of Punjab, *Report on the Factories Act, 1950*, quoted by Khanna (1983: 87).

Note

The calculations for the total and the percentage in each category have been done by me. The total for the percentages sometimes does not add up to 100 due to rounding errors.

Table 6.2 Number of registered factories in Punjab and other states in India 1948–1950

State	*Number of registered factories in existence*			*Factories from which returns were received number and %*					
	1948	*1949*	*1950*	*1948*		*1949*		*1950*	
				no.	*%*	*no.*	*%*	*no.*	*%*
West Bengal	1,408	1,484	1,444	1,351	96	1,407	94	1,360	94
Bombay	1,237	1,596	1,736	1,126	91	1,376	86	1,575	91
Madras	1,465	1,473	1,471	1,408	96	1,458	99	1,446	98
Uttar Pradesh	623	623	605	523	84	540	87	512	85
Bihar	393	403	383	333	85	368	91	370	97
Punjab	322	341	468	291	90	321	95	416	89
Madhya Pradesh	276	308	300	258	93	287	93	298	99
Orissa	109	126	135	106	98	124	98	129	96
Assam	75	79	86	73	97	77	97	88	99
Delhi	144	147	177	133	93	139	94	167	94
Ajmer	8	10	9	8	100	9	90	9	100
Vindhya Pradesh	6	9	10	6	100	77	78	7	70
Travancore and Cochin (Cochin only)	62	77	74	59	95	68	87	67	91
Pepsu	7	79	103	6	86	72	91	103	100
Himachal Pradesh	9	3	4	9	100	3	100	3	75
Rajasthan	–	–	88	–	–	–	–	52	59
Kutch	–	–	3	–	–	–	–	3	100
Total	**6,144**	**6,758**	**7,099**	**5,690**	**93**	**6,250**	**92**	**6,605**	**93**

Source: Adapted from Khanna (1983: 118).

products and by-products, and value added by manufacture, both gross and per capita, for the years 1948, 1949 and 1950, for the states then constituted.

In Table 6.2, I have reproduced the data solely on one aspect (the number of registered factories), to give a flavour of the comparative picture of Punjab's industrial development.

The data relate to factories employing more than 20 or more persons on any day and using power for the 29 industries covered in the data collected by the Census of Manufacturing and used by Khanna (1983). This table shows Punjab lagging far behind the more advanced industrial states like West Bengal, Bombay and Madras. Even Uttar Pradesh and Bihar were ahead of Punjab. Khanna (1983) showed that the comparative status of Punjab's industrial development vis-à-vis the other Indian states in terms of the number of industrial units, as captured in Table 6.2, was mirrored in terms of the other important variables, e.g. the level of fixed capital investment, the number of persons employed, gross factory value of output, and value added by manufacture (total and per person).

Central policies and the industrial backwardness of Punjab

The central government in India followed the strategy of planned economic development for the industrialization of India until 1991. Public sector investment by central government undertakings was the prime mover of industrialization during that phase, helping the growth of industrialization directly as well as indirectly. The direct contribution of public sector investment to industrialization was evident, with the opening of industrial plants, the production of industrial goods and the employment of an industrial labour force. The indirect contribution of public sector investment to industrialization was in the stimulus that this investment gave to private sector investment. Public sector investment provided key industrial inputs, such as power and steel, to the private sector on a subsidized rate. Public sector investment also created external economies of scale for private sector investment. The forward and backward linkages of public sector investments had multiplier effects on private sector investment and over-all industrialization.

Table 6.3 presents a set of very interesting data on the total volume of public sector investment in the different states during the 20-year period from 1963 to 1983. The data in Table 6.3 show that from 1968 (when the data for Punjab as reorganized in 1966 were separately available) to 1975, Punjab's share of total central public sector investment was abysmally low. Punjab's share during these years hovered around 1 per cent being more often below than above this figure. Punjab's share in India's population in 1991 was 2.39 per cent (Govt of India 1994: 28); this share has been more or less the same even before 1991. It is clear that Punjab's share in the total central public sector investment was less than half of Punjab's share in India's population during the years 1968–1975. Though it improved from 1976 onwards, it continued to be below Punjab's share in India's population (with the exception of 1979). In sharp contrast with Punjab are the states of Bihar and Madhya Pradesh. Bihar's share in India's population was 10.23 per cent and that of Madhya Pradesh was 7.84 per cent (Govt of India 1994: 28), but Bihar's share in the total central public sector investment varied from a low of 15.9 per cent in 1963 to a high of 27.8 per cent in 1974, while that of Madhya Pradesh similarly varied from a low of 13.4 per cent in 1975 to a high of 23.9 per cent in 1965. This disproportionately low share of Punjab and disproportionately high share of Bihar and Madhya Pradesh in central public sector investment was the result of the centre's politico-economic strategy of reducing inter-state inequalities. A report submitted to the Planning Commission on the politico-economic dimensions of inter-state inequalities concluded: 'disparities between states ... have to be brought to the minimum possible. *This is ... necessary to provide a material foundation for national integration*' (Khanna 1973: 6; italics added). Another study on the same subject highlighted the role of central planning: 'Reduction of regional inequalities was one of the aims of the economic policy regime of centralized planning that operated in India till 1991' (Bhattacharya and Sakthivel 2004: 1071). According to this study, the chief

Table 6.3 Percentage share of the states in cumulative investment (gross block) in central public undertaking, 1963 to 1983

Year	*Andhra Pradesh*	*Assam*	*Bihar*	*Gujarat*	*Haryana*	*Himachal Pradesh*	*Karnataka*	*Kerala*	*Madhya Pradesh*	*Maharashtra*	*Orissa*	*Punjab*	*Rajasthan*	*Tamil Nadu*	*Uttar Pradesh*	*West Bengal*
1963	0.8	1.5	15.9	0	–	Neg.[1]	3.6	0.2	23.7	2.0	21.4	2.8[2]	0.2	8.3	0.2	19.4
1964	1.0	1.8	16.9	0.1	–	Neg.[1]	3.5	1.5	23.8	2.6	19.2	2.6[2]	0.2	9.1	0.7	17.4
1965	1.5	2.1	17.7	0.1	–	Neg.[1]	3.0	1.8	23.9	2.7	17.4	2.4[2]	0.2	9.3	1.8	16.2
1966	2.4	1.5	17.0	1.4	–	Neg.[1]	2.9	2.0	23.3	3.1	15.2	2.0[2]	0.2	9.1	2.6	27.2
1967	3.0	1.4	17.2	1.4	–	Neg.[1]	2.9	2.2	21.8	3.2	14.3	1.8[2]	0.3	9.3	3.5	17.7
1968	2.9	2.0	17.8	2.9	0.3	Neg.[1]	2.7	2.6	19.6	3.5	14.8	1.2	0.7	8.9	4.8	15.3
1969	2.9	2.1	20.8	2.9	0.2	Neg.[1]	2.7	3.4	18.2	3.4	14.2	1.1	0.9	8.8	4.6	13.8
1970	2.9	2.2	23.0	2.9	0.2	Neg.[1]	2.7	3.4	16.5	3.6	13.4	1.0	1.0	9.2	4.6	13.5
1971	3.0	2.1	24.9	4.2	0.2	Neg.[1]	2.7	3.4	15.5	3.5	12.6	0.9	1.1	8.8	4.3	12.7
1972	3.1	3.1	25.9	4.3	0.2	Neg.[1]	2.8	3.3	14.8	3.6	11.7	0.9	1.4	8.4	4.2	12.6
1973	3.5	3.2	26.9	4.7	0.2	Neg.[1]	2.9	3.2	14.0	3.9	11.0	0.8	1.8	7.5	4.0	12.5
1974	3.8	3.0	27.8	4.7	0.2	Neg.[1]	3.0	3.3	13.8	3.9	10.1	0.8	2.2	6.9	4.1	12.3
1975	4.3	3.2	26.8	4.8	0.3	Neg.[1]	3.0	3.2	13.4	4.9	9.3	1.2	2.6	6.2	4.1	12.6
1976	4.2	3.6	25.1	5.8	0.7	0.2	2.8	3.3	18.2	5.0	8.3	2.2	2.5	6.7	4.1	7.6
1977	4.2	3.4	27.2	5.7	1.5	0.4	2.9	3.0	16.2	6.8	7.0	2.1	2.5	5.1	4.1	8.3
1978	4.4	3.3	25.2	5.6	1.3	0.7	3.7	2.9	16.1	8.1	5.9	2.0	2.5	5.1	4.4	9.5
1979	4.2	3.0	22.6	5.0	1.7	0.8	4.1	3.0	14.5	7.6	5.8	2.7	2.9	4.9	5.2	8.4
1980	5.1	3.4	20.7	5.8	1.6	0.8	4.9	2.8	14.7	8.6	6.2	2.3	2.2	5.0	5.3	10.2
1981	5.5	3.7	19.7	6.0	1.5	0.8	4.7	2.7	14.6	10.0	5.8	2.3	2.0	5.1	5.6	9.7
1982	5.4	5.7	18.0	5.0	1.3	0.7	4.3	2.4	14.2	13.3	5.7	2.0	2.1	4.8	6.0	8.8
1983	7.5	5.5	16.6	3.9	1.1	0.6	3.7	2.2	13.6	14.1	5.4	1.7	2.1	4.7	8.9	8.5

Source: The original source of data was from the Bureau of Public Enterprises Annual Reports on the Working of Industrial and Commercial Undertaking of the Central Government, Government of India, various issues. This was cited in Govt of India (1987: 445–446) and this table is an adaptation of the data presented in Govt of India (1987).

Notes

1 Neg. – negligible, not available.

2 Punjab and Haryana.

policy instrument used to reduce regional and inter-state inequalities during the economic policy regime of centralized planning was public sector investment: 'In the pre-reform era [before 1991], public investment was made mainly in backward states. Even private investment was directed towards backward regions by practices such as licensing etc.' (ibid.: 1075). Some other studies on the subject either emphasize the reduction of inter-state inequalities as the chief aim of the central public sector investment strategy (Kundu *et al.* 1986, Banerjee and Ghosh 1988, Meher 1999) or highlight the political goal of national integration as the key aim of the centre's policy of directing public and private sector investment to the backward regions (Paranjape 1964, Krishnaswamy *et al.* 1992). Despite the differences in the nuances of these studies, they have helped in highlighting the contribution of central public sector investment to the national aim of reducing inter-state inequalities for national integration.

It was this centrally directed politico-economic policy of nation-building, behind the aim of reducing regional inequalities, that was responsible for poor states like Bihar and Madhya Pradesh being allocated relatively higher levels of central public sector investment, and for a high per capita income state like Punjab getting allocated a relatively lower level of central public sector investment.

Table 6.4 gives data on central public sector investment for a 15-year period (1984–85 to 1999–2000) for India as a whole and for Punjab.

Though the focus of my study is limited to the period up until 1991, I have also presented data for the latter period, in order to demonstrate that there is a long-term trend regarding the disproportionately low public sector investment

Table 6.4 Investment of central projects in Punjab and India, 1984–85 to 1999–2000

Year (as on 31st March)	*Punjab gross block (Rs. crores)*	*All India gross block (Rs. crores)*	*Share of Punjab (%)*
1984–85	563.62	47,323.27	1.20
1985–86	602.78	56,806.42	1.00
1988–89	802.35	96,880.67	0.83
1989–90	836.51	113,430.90	0.74
1990–91	875.57	130,655.10	0.67
1991–92	941.49	153,893.02	0.62
1992–93	1,230.89	174,837.04	0.70
1993–94	1,200.56	198,912.48	0.60
1994–95	1,393.24	229,568.37	0.61
1995–96	1,723.07	267,259.64	0.64
1996–97	2,077.85	284,361.52	0.73
1997–98	2,435.05	319,829.16	0.78
1998–99	2,950.33	354,131.67	0.83
1999–2000	3,004.01	381,364.90	0.79

Source: Adapted from Maini (2004: 175), original source is *Public Enterprises Survey*, Government of India.

by the centre in Punjab. From the data in the two tables (Tables 6.3 and 6.4), one clear observation that emerges is that not only has there been a disproportionately low level of central public sector investment in Punjab, but further that the share of Punjab in the total central public sector investment shows a declining trend. In one of its Five-Year Plan (1974–79) documents, the Government of Punjab made a stark statement that highlights low central public sector investment in Punjab: 'so far ... only a single Central Project namely, Fertilizer Factory at Nangal has been located in the state' (cited by P. Singh 1997: 62).

This relatively low level of public sector investment by the centre has had obvious implications for the pace of industrialization in Punjab. In developing economies at the early stage of industrialization, public sector investment plays a key role in setting the pace of industrialization. At the early stage of industrialization, the private sector is weak. Its major weakness is that it does not have enough capital to invest. The weak private sector is crucially dependent on the public sector for creating the industrial infrastructure and external economies of scale for industrialization. In other words, it is public sector investment that induces private sector investment in a developing economy at the early stage of industrialization. Low public sector investment therefore also results in low private sector investment in such a developing economy. The impact of a relatively low level of public sector investment in Punjab has been that the secondary sector has remained a relatively less important sector of the state's economy. A study in 1983 reported that,

> Meagre Central investment in Punjab (2.2 per cent of the total investment and 0.9 per cent of the total investment in projects in hand) has deprived it of spread effects of such investment. The woefully deficient Central investment and its continuing deficiency have constrained industrial development of Punjab.
>
> (Johar *et al.* 1983: 172)

In order to get a better picture of the share of the industrial/tertiary sector in Punjab's economy, and to get a comparative view of the sectoral composition of Punjab's SDP, we need to look at the sectoral distribution of India's national domestic product (NDP) and also compare Punjab's SDP composition with the other states of India. Let us first look at the sectoral composition of India's NDP. Table 6.5 shows us the changing sectoral composition of India's NDP from 1970–71 to 1991–92.

The data presented in Table 6.5 reveal that the share of the primary sector in India's NDP declined from about 48 per cent in 1970 to about 36 per cent in 1991–92. This was an impressive structural change in the Indian economy. In a time period of about 20 years, the primary sector's share declined from slightly less than half of the NDP to nearly one-third of the NDP by 1991–92. The secondary sector's share improved in the same period from about 20 per cent to 24 per cent – a modest improvement but still reflecting the move away from the

Table 6.5 Sectoral distribution of India's net domestic product at factor cost (current prices), 1970–71 to 1991–92 (Rs. crore)

SECTOR	*1970–71*	*1975–76*	*1980–81*	*1985–86*	*1990–91*	*1991–92*
Primary	17,568 (47.75%)	28,223 (43.50%)	45,565 (41.30%)	77,111 (37.15%)	148,889 (35.38%)	171,263 (35.67%)
Secondary	7,279 (19.79%)	13,631 (21.01%)	25,381 (23.00%)	50,147 (24.16%)	105,766 (25.14%)	116,130 (24.19%)
Tertiary	11,940 (32.46%)	23,024 (35.49%)	39,394 (35.70%)	80,304 (38.69%)	166,121 (39.48%)	192,686 (40.14%)
Total	**36,787 (100%)**	**64,878 (100%)**	**110,340 (100%)**	**207,562 (100%)**	**420,776 (100%)**	**480,079 (100%)**

Sources: Calculated from the data provided in the *Statistical Abstract India 1992* (Govt of India 1994: 399).

Note
The *Statistical Abstract India 1992* provided the data for aggregate NDP and its nine industry components in absolute figures in *crores* (a *crore* is equal to ten millions). I rearranged the nine industry component data into three sectors – primary, secondary and tertiary, and also calculated the percentage figures for the three sectors.

Table 6.6 Percentage distribution of net state domestic product by sectors in Punjab (at current prices) 1960–61 to 1990–91

Sector	*1960–61*	*1965–66*	*1969–70*	*1970–71*	*1975–76*	*1980–81*	*1985–86*	*1990–91*
Primary	54.01	54.62	61.40	60.34	56.68	49.50	47.72	44.02
Secondary	15.63	14.98	15.00	13.34	16.61	18.47	20.38	23.80
Tertiary	30.36	30.40	23.60	26.32	26.71	32.03	33.90	32.18
Total	**100.00**	**100.00**	**100.00**	**100.00**	**100.00**	**100.00**	**100.00**	**100.00**

Sources:
1 For 1960–61, 1965–66, 1970–71, 1975–76, *Statistical Abstract of Punjab 1978* (Govt of Punjab 1979: 60).
2 For 1969–70, *Statistical Abstract of Punjab 1974* (Govt of Punjab 1975: 373–374) and *Statistical Abstract of Punjab 1975* (Govt of Punjab 1976: 365–366).
3 For 1980–81 and 1985–86, *Statistical Abstract of Punjab 1992* (Govt of Punjab 1993: 110–111).
4 For 1990–91, *Statistical Abstract of Punjab 1998* (Govt of Punjab 1999: 116–117).

Note
I had collected time-series data for the years 1960–61, 1965–66 and then for every year from 1969–70 to 1990–91. The yearly data from 1969–70 to 1990–91 represented the same trend as shown in the table above. There are some minor changes in the data for the sectoral distribution of net state domestic product as reported in the statistical abstracts for different years. This happens because the data for the previous years undergoes some minor revisions in the subsequent years in the process of updating. I have tried everywhere to use the latest data available.

primary sector. The improvement in the share of the tertiary sector is much more impressive – from slightly less than one-third of the NDP in 1970 to 40 per cent in 1991–92. Let us now look at the changes in the sectoral composition of Punjab's net SDP as shown in Table 6.6.

Though the change over a 30-year period (1960–61 to 1990–91) in the sectoral composition of Punjab's SDP shows a broadly similar trend as we noticed for India over a 20-year period (1970–71 to 1991–92), there are significant differences worth noting. While the share of the primary sector has declined in Punjab and India, the decline in Punjab is much less marked than in India. The share of the primary sector in India's NDP had declined to close to one-third (35 per cent) by 1991, but in Punjab the share of the primary sector in Punjab's SDP was still close to almost half (44 per cent). The share of the secondary sector had risen to about 24 per cent for India and for Punjab by 1991 though, as we will discuss below, Punjab's secondary sector was heavily dependent on the small industry sector. The rise in the share of the tertiary sector in India's NDP was impressive and had gone up to 40 per cent in 1991, but for Punjab the rise was much less impressive: it had risen to only about 32 per cent in 1991. This 32 per cent share of the tertiary sector in Punjab's SDP in 1990–91 was not much higher than the 30 per cent figure in the united Punjab in 1960–61. However, it did show some rise in comparison with the 24 per cent figure in 1969.

The most significant feature to emerge from this comparative view is that, *by 1991, while India as a whole was making a significant transition away from the dependence on agriculture, the Punjab economy still remained significantly dependent on its primary/agriculture sector.*

If we focus our attention on comparing the changes in the structure of India's NDP and those of the SDP of the major states in India, including Punjab for the decade 1980–1990 as given in Table 6.7, it provides us an even clearer picture of the industrial backwardness and continuing agricultural dependence of Punjab than the one we have presented so far.

In order to highlight the significance of the structural change during the 1980s as captured in Table 6.7, it is necessary to explain briefly the nature of the data that have been used in this table. The Central Statistical Organisation (CSO) of the Government of India has revised the gross domestic product series data for India and the state domestic product series data for the states with 1993–94 as the base year. With that base year, the data from 1980–81 to 1992–93 has also been revised. However, the revised data for the period before 1980–81 are still not available (Bhattacharya and Sakthivel 2004). The main difference between the revised data as presented in Table 6.7 from the data we have used in the previous tables from 1980–81 onwards is that the data in Table 6.7 are expressed in constant prices with 1993–94 as the base year, whereas the data in the previous tables were in current prices. The main implication of this is that the sectoral composition of India's NDP and that of the SDP of Punjab presented on the basis of revised data is slightly different from the composition of the NDP amd SDP presented in the current price series data in the earlier tables.

The revised series data present a better picture, since it is expressed in constant prices, but its disadvantage is that it presents data only from 1980–81 onwards. Since we also needed to construct a picture of the period prior to 1980–81, the data from that earlier period were absolutely indispensable even if expressed in current prices.

Let us now look more closely at Table 6.7 to see how the sectoral composition of Punjab's SDP is changing in comparison with the changes in the sectoral composition of the SDP of India's major states during the last decade of our study period i.e. from 1980–81 to 1990–91.

In 1980–81, among the 17 major states of India, Punjab had the 4th lowest place in terms of ranking based on the share of the secondary sector in a state's SDP. Punjab was ranked at the 14th place, with the share of the secondary sector in its SDP at only 18.94 per cent. Only Rajasthan (18.77 per cent), Orissa (17.18 per cent) and Haryana (11.00 per cent) were lower than Punjab in terms of this ranking.

By 1990–91, even these three states had risen above Punjab in this ranking. Therefore, by 1990–91 Punjab had the lowest share of the secondary sector in its SDP in comparison with all the remaining 16 major states of India. In other words, by 1990–91 Punjab was the least industrialized state of all the major 17 states in India.

I discuss below that the industrial backwardness of Punjab is emphasized further if we look closely at the structure of Punjab's industry. One prominent feature of Punjab's industrial structure is that it is highly dependent on the small-scale sector. The following section discusses this aspect of Punjab's industry.

Punjab's industrial structure – the dominance of the small-scale sector

In Table 6.8, we have data on the distribution of registered industrial units in terms of different size groups where the size is measured in terms of work force. The smallest size group is the one employing fewer than ten workers and the biggest size group is the one employing 5,000 or more workers. Each size group gives us information on the number of industrial units in that size group and the number of workers employed by the industrial units in that size group. Since my study focuses on the years 1966–1991, I collected the relevant information for 1966 and then for the five-year interval points 1970, 1975, 1980 and 1985, and finally for 1991 and 1992.

Looking at Table 6.8 we can observe that there was a preponderance of small-scale units in the industrial sector of Punjab. Until 1985, there was not even a single industrial unit employing more than 5,000 workers. Even in 1992, there was still only one factory employing more than 5,000 workers. Even this solitary big factory showed a declining trend in employment. The number of workers in this factory declined from 5,822 in 1985 to 5,457 in 1991 and 5,004

Table 6.7 Sectoral composition of SDP of 17 major Indian states, 1980–1, 1990–91 (%)

States	*Sectors*	*1980–81*	*Ranking based on the share of the secondary sector in SDP 1980–81*	*1990–91*	*Ranking based on the share of the secondary sector in SDP 1990–91*
Andhra Pradesh	Primary	41.21		34.20	
	Secondary	21.88	11	24.67	9
	Tertiary	36.91		41.13	
Assam	Primary	50.11		41.48	
	Secondary	20.17	12	24.49	13
	Tertiary	29.72		34.03	
Bihar	Primary	59.93		46.52	
	Secondary	21.89	10	24.66	10
	Tertiary	18.18		28.82	
Goa	Primary	18.45		14.30	
	Secondary	43.48	1	34.50	2
	Tertiary	38.10		51.19	
Gujarat	Primary	46.25		30.95	
	Secondary	29.90	4	34.38	3
	Tertiary	23.85		34.67	
Haryana	Primary	58.80		42.60	
	Secondary	11.00	17	24.60	12
	Tertiary	30.20		32.70	
Himachal Pradesh	Primary	47.55		35.67	
	Secondary	22.27	9	24.88	8
	Tertiary	30.17		39.45	
Karnataka	Primary	46.56		33.10	
	Secondary	24.54	8	27.59	6
	Tertiary	28.89		39.31	
Kerala	Primary	42.31		31.26	
	Secondary	25.38	7	21.47	16
	Tertiary	32.32		47.27	

Maharashtra	Primary	28.75		21.80	
	Secondary	35.41	2	35.26	1
	Tertiary	35.84		42.94	
MP	Primary	50.71		38.42	
	Secondary	29.60	5	28.56	5
	Tertiary	19.70		33.01	
Orissa	Primary	49.79		42.43	
	Secondary	17.18	16	22.90	15
	Tertiary	33.03		34.67	
Punjab	Primary	47.87		46.31	
	Secondary	18.94	**14**	21.12	**17**
	Tertiary	33.18		32.57	
Rajasthan	Primary	51.93		42.47	
	Secondary	18.77	15	24.65	11
	Tertiary	29.30		32.64	
Tamil Nadu	Primary	24.64		22.83	
	Secondary	34.78	3	34.03	4
	Tertiary	40.58		43.15	
UP	Primary	49.53		36.74	
	Secondary	19.54	13	24.17	14
	Tertiary	30.93		39.09	
West Bengal	Primary	33.15		31.82	
	Secondary	27.46	6	25.58	7
	Tertiary	39.39		42.60	
All-India	Primary	39.64	32.91		
	Secondary	24.36	28.03		
	Tertiary	35.99	39.06		

Source: Adapted from Bhattacharya and Sakthivel (2004: 1071).

Note
Ranking done by author.

Table 6.8 Registered working factories and workers employed there in respect of submitting return in the state of Punjab, 1966 to 1992

Factory size by no. of workers	*1966*		*1970*		*1975*		*1980*		*1985*		*1991*		*1992*	
	A	*B*	*A*	*B*	*A*	*B*	*A*	*B*	*A*	*B*	*A*	*B*	*A*	*B*
Less than 10	626	3,987	1,087	6,429	1,176	7,044	722	4,669	445	2,835	398	3,339	340	1,940
10–19	1,092	14,208	1,176	15,115	1,031	13,596	845	11,288	526	7,124	437	7,774	408	5,604
20–49	568	17,701	546	16,930	641	19,819	595	18,408	359	11,829	263	10,466	292	8,954
50–99	178	13,030	182	13,054	172	11,711	159	11,175	134	10,005	107	9,089	123	8,284
100–499	89	17,992	90	16,831	107	20,885	120	23,422	98	24,441	122	27,723	128	29,025
500–999	12	8,325	15	9,462	12	8,013	15	9,593	20	14,677	32	24,437	29	21,108
1,000–4999	7	12,700	6	11,995	9	18,084	16	31,909	13	29,668	16	27,178	18	34,850
5,000 or more	–	–	–	–	–	–	–	–	1	5,822	1	5,457	1	5,004
Total	**2,572**	**87,943**	**3,102**	**89,816**	**3,148**	**99,152**	**2,472**	**110,464**	**1,599**	**106,401**	**1,376**	**115,463**	**1,339**	**114,769**

Source: Adapted from the *Statistical Abstract of Punjab 1993*, (Govt. of Punjab 1994: 378–379).

Note
'A' denotes the total number of factories and 'B' denotes the total number of workers in each size group.

in 1992. After 1992, this factory seems to have either disintegrated or eventually gone down in status to the next lower category – employing 1,000 or more workers. The *Statistical Abstract of Punjab 1997* reported that for the years 1993, 1994, 1995 and 1996, there was no factory in Punjab in the category employing 5,000 or more workers (Govt of Punjab 1998: 390–391). Similarly the *Statistical Abstract of Punjab 1998* reported no factory in this category for the year 1997 (Govt of Punjab 1999: 392–393) and the *Statistical Abstract of Punjab 2002* reported no factory in this category for the years 1999, 2000 and 2001 (Govt of Punjab 2003: 394–395). However, the latest *Statistical Abstract of Punjab 2004* reported one factory in this category for the year 2002 (employing 6,848 workers) but again no factory in this category for the year 2003 (Govt of Punjab 2005: 398–399). It will be interesting in the coming years to observe the fate of this solitary big factory which once existed but according to the latest information available does not exist anymore.

There was a marginal and faltering increase in the number of factories employing over 1,000 or over 500 workers. There were seven factories employing 1,000 or more workers in 1966 (same as in 1950, see Khanna 1983: 86). This figure decreased to six in 1970, increased to 16 in 1980, again declined to 13 in 1985 and rose to the maximum figure of 20 in 1990 (the figure for 1990 is not shown in the Table 6.8 but I have taken it from the *Statistical Abstract of Punjab 1992*: 378–379). It declined to 16 in 1991 and increased marginally to 18 in 1992. I calculated the total figure for all the factories which employed more than 500 workers, which could be considered medium-sized factories. This figure rose from 14 in 1950 (Khanna 1983: 86) to 19 in 1966, to 52 in 1990 (the highest ever reached) and then declined to 48 in 1992.[5] In contrast with the vacillating and marginal increase in the number of these medium-sized factories, the factories employing 20 or more workers but fewer than 50, and the factories employing 50 or more workers but fewer than 100, experienced an impressive increase in their numbers. The Government of India's Ministry of Industry defines a small-scale enterprise as one employing 50 or fewer workers when using power, or 100 or fewer workers without power (Ajit Singh 1983: 45–46, Pandit 1985: 23). Since the *Statistical Abstract of Punjab* did not give information whether the factories on which the data have been shown in Table 6.8 used power or not, I am including, for the purpose of our analysis here, all factories employing fewer than 100 workers in the category of small scale. Using this definition of small scale, it is clear that in Punjab between 1966 and 1992 the most impressive increase took place in the number of small-scale units. The picture of the dominance of the small-scale sector in Punjab's industrial sector emerges much more clearly if we look at the proportions of different size groups in the total number of registered industrial units. In Table 6.9, I have computed the percentage share of each size group in the total number of factories for the years 1966 and 1992 in order to get a snap shot view of the change during our study period.

We had noted earlier, while discussing the nature of the industrial sector in Punjab shortly after India's independence, that in 1950 almost half the factories

Table 6.9 Percentage distribution of different size groups of factories (by no. of workers) in Punjab's industrial structure, 1966 and 1992

No. of workers	*1966*		*1992*	
	A	*B*	*A*	*B*
Fewer than 10	24.34	4.53	25.39	1.69
10–19	42.46	16.16	30.48	4.88
20–49	22.08	20.12	20.81	7.80
50–99	6.92	14.82	9.20	7.22
100–499	3.46	20.46	9.56	25.29
500–999	0.46	9.47	2.18	18.39
1,000–4,999	0.27	14.44	1.34	30.67
5,000 or more	–	–	0.07	4.36
Total	**99.99**	**100.00**	**99.03**	**100.00**

Source: Computed from the data provided in the *Statistical Abstract of Punjab 1993* (Govt of Punjab 1994: 378).

Note
The total does not add up to 100 due to rounding errors. The data in column A refers to the percentage share of the different size groups of factories in the total number of factories and the one in column B refers to the percentage share of different size groups in the total number of workers.

employed fewer than 20 workers and over 80 per cent employed fewer than 50. If we compare that situation with the one in 1966 or 1992, we can see interesting patterns of similarity. Looking at Table 6.9, we can see that in 1966 and 1992, the proportion of the factories that employed fewer than 20 workers had increased to 66.80 per cent and 55.87 per cent, respectively. The proportion of the factories that employed fewer than 50 workers was 88.88 per cent in 1966 and 76.68 per cent in 1992. These statistics highlight a significant aspect of Punjab's industrial sector, namely that the pattern of the preponderance of the small-scale sector in Punjab's industrial sector, in terms of the share of the small-scale units in the total number of units, had not undergone any significant change either from 1950 to 1992 or from 1966 to 1992.

Ajit Singh compares the performance of small-scale units with medium and large units in Punjab between 1973–74 and 1979–80. He took four variables into comparison: the number of units, fixed investment, production and employment. His data showed that by 1979–80, the small-scale sector dominated the industrial sector of Punjab not only in terms of the number of units but also in terms of its share in total industrial output and employment. It was only in fixed investment that the medium- and large-scale sector had an edge over the small-scale sector, and Singh attributes this better performance of the medium- and large-scale sector to the investment by the state government of Punjab in 'food processing and agro-based industries' (1983: 46). Singh's comparison of the small-scale sector with the medium- and large-scale sector was a highly valuable contribution to the understanding of the structure of Punjab industry. The data he had used for the study were not publicly available. It was made available to him by the officials of the Punjab government. In view of the special importance of these data, and the fact that they cover a part of my study period, I have used some relevant materials from Singh's study in Table 6.10. The comparative data on the small-scale sector and the medium- and large-scale sector became publicly available for the first time in 1993.[6]

Using the data made available in 1993, I was able to construct the comparative picture of the small-scale sector and the medium- and large-scale sector in Punjab industry from 1980–81 to 1990–91. These data are presented in Table 6.11.

The data presented in Table 6.11 reveal that in the 1980s the small-scale sector in Punjab's industry had expanded in terms of working units at an annual rate of growth which was almost six times higher than that of the medium- and large-scale units. In 1990–91, the total number of units in the small-scale sector was phenomenally higher (by 430 times) than that in the medium- and large-scale sector. Similarly, in terms of providing employment, not only was the rate of growth in the small-scale sector much higher than that of the medium- and large-scale sector, but also the total volume of employment in the small sector was much higher than that in the large-scale sector. It is only in fixed capital investment and total production that the small-scale sector was lagging behind the medium- and large-scale sector by 1990–91, though the rate of growth of fixed capital investment and production in the small-scale sector was higher than that in the medium- and large-scale sector in the decade 1980–81 to 1990–91. The *Economic Survey of Punjab 1993–94* concluded rightly that 'Small scale industry is the backbone of the industrial structure of the State' (Govt of Punjab 1993–94: 64). Pandit (1985) highlighted the importance of the small-scale sector in Punjab by pointing out that the average employment size of industrial units in Punjab was smaller than the all India average, whether the comparison was done specifically for the small-scale sector or for all the factories taken together. He showed that if one were to compare data for all the industrial establishments for which the data are collected by the Annual Survey of Industries, then in 1979–80 the average number of employees per factory in Punjab was 48.8 while the all India average was 80.7 (1985: 40). If the comparison is done specifically for the units in the small-scale sector, the average for India worked out to be 11.84 while the average for Punjab and Haryana taken together was 8.42 persons. Since the average size for Haryana was noted to be higher than Punjab, the average for Punjab would be even less than 8.42 (Pandit 1985: 46). Ajit Singh had observed that the small-scale sector was much more important in Punjab's manufacturing sector (in terms of its share in the total employment and total value added in the manufacturing sector) than in any other large state in India, especially highlighting this aspect by comparing Punjab with some of the more industrialized states like Maharashtra and Tamil Nadu (1983: 41). Similarly, Sandhu and Singh pointed out that in 1973–74 the share of the small-scale sector in the total industrial production in Punjab was more than 60 per cent of

Table 6.10 Number of small-scale units, production, investment and employment in Punjab, 1973–74 to 1979–80 (production and investment at 1973–74 prices)

Item	*Years*							*Average annual rate of growth (simple)*
	1973–74	*1974–75*	*1975–76*	*1976–77*	*1977–78*	*1978–79*	*1979–80*	
A. Small-scale sector								
Number of working units	30,691	32,968	34,776	36,737	38,652	42,233	47,437	9.09
Fixed investment (Rs. Crores)	–	–	–	148.28	180.47	210.83	237.26	–
Production (Rs. Crores)	408.25	393.83	439.01	453.33	573.32	584.18	653.13	9.99
Number employed	233,660	249,939	254,456	262,776	275,727	298,925	333,090	7.09
Fixed investment per unit (Rs. lakhs)	–	–	–	0.40	0.47	0.50	0.50	
Value of production per unit (lakhs)	1.33	1.19	1.26	1.23	1.33	1.38	1.38	0.63
Output per worker (Rs.)	17,472	15,757	17,253	17,252	18,617	19,543	19,608	2.04
B. Large- and medium-scale sector								
Number of units	122	132	144	160	175	188	203	11.06
Fixed investment (Rs. crores)	73.69	89.92	159.73	205.03	241.57	296.44	523.33	118.3
Production (Rs. crores)	282.83	254.54	313.70	375.63	473.49	552.76	625.24	36.9
Number employed	56,537	57,891	63,291	69,942	77,971	91,551	98,376	12.3
Production per unit (Rs. crores)	2.32	1.93	2.18	2.35	2.71	2.94	3.08	5.4
Output per worker (Rs.)	50,026	43,969	49,656	53,706	60,726	60,377	63,556	4.5

Source: Adapted from Ajit Singh (1983: 45).

Note
The definition of 'small scale' used here is: 'enterprises employing 50 or less workers when using power or 100 or less workers without power' (ibid: 46). A lakh is equal to 100,000 (0.1 million) and a crore is equal to 100 lakhs (ten million).

Table 6.11 Number of small-scale units and large- and medium-scale units in Punjab, 1980–81 to 1990–91 at current prices

Item	*Years*							*Average annual rate of growth (simple)*
	1980–81	*1985–86*	*1986–87*	*1987–88*	*1988–89*	*1989–90*	*1990–91*	
A. Small-scale sector								
Number of working units	43,338	97,517	108,913	119,888	132,962	146,443	160,368	13.98
Fixed capital (Rs. crores)	332.12	738.94	830.02	943.49	1,084.21	1,217.72	1,348.78	15.04
Number employed	264,869	464,809	503,397	545,560	594,354	633,964	668,845	9.71
Production (Rs. crores)	1,118.44	2,150.99	2,358.63	2,681.53	3,108.59	3,504.10	4,049.82	13.73
Fixed investment per unit (Rs. lakhs)	0.76	0.75	0.76	0.78	0.81	0.83	0.84	1.01
Value of production per unit (lakhs)	2.58	2.20	2.16	2.23	2.33	2.39	2.52	–0.24
Output per worker (Rs.)	42,226	46,276	46,854	49,151	52,301	55,272	60,549	3.67
B. Large- and medium-scale sector								
Number of units	228	292	306	322	335	355	373	2.48
Fixed capital (Rs. crores)	727.42	1,489.72	1,701.25	2,066.77	2,451.96	3,082.70	4,003.08	10.39
Number employed	109,767	132,174	142,381	151,199	160,609	169,801	187,311	3.55
Production (Rs. crores)	1,141.07	2,534.53	3,184.73	3,777.53	4,378.39	5,458.15	7,163.96	10.95
Fixed investment per unit (Rs. crores)	3.19	5.10	5.55	6.41	7.32	8.68	10.73	12.89
Production per unit (Rs. crores)	5.00	8.68	10.41	11.73	13.07	15.37	19.21	14.41
Output per worker (Rs.)	103,953	191,757	221,148	249,838	272,612	321,444	382,463	13.91

Source: Adapted from the data provided in the *Statistical Abstract of Punjab 1992* (Govt of Punjab 1993: 402–403).

Notes

1 The *Statistical Abstract of Punjab 1992* did not provide the definition of small-scale enterprise used here. However, *the Economic Survey of Punjab 1993–94* (Govt of Punjab 1993–94) gave a definition of a 'small scale unit' as one 'having fixed investment of not more than Rs.60 lakhs (Rs.75 lakhs in case of ancillary units) in assets, plant and machinery' (p. 125). This definition of a small-scale unit is different from the one used by Ajit Singh (1983) in Table 6.10. The information provided in this table is therefore not strictly comparable with the one provided by Singh in Table 6.10.

2 There was an error in the data presented in the *Statistical Abstract of Punjab 1992* Table 16.10 (p. 402) on production and investment in the small-scale industries. The data was given in lakhs (Rs.). It should be in crores (Rs.). The data has been correctly presented from the *Statistical Abstract of Punjab 1993* onwards.

3 The average annual rate of growth data shown in the last column was my calculation.

the total industrial production in the state while at an all-India level this figure was only 40 per cent (1983: 133–134).

I have tried to demonstrate in this section that Punjab's industrial backwardness by 1991 was reflected not only in the relatively low share of the secondary sector in Punjab's SDP but also through the structure of the industrial sector, which was heavily dependent on the small-scale sector. The relatively low volume of central public sector investment in Punjab has contributed to the negligible presence of large industrial units in Punjab. The inducement that large-scale public sector investment provides for the growth of large-scale industry, both, in the public sector and in the private sector, has been missing in Punjab. The absence of large-scale industry had other adverse consequences for the Punjab economy. One of the notable adverse consequences has been that the savings generated through the rise in incomes brought about by agricultural development in Punjab were not used within Punjab. These savings have been channelled through the banking network in the country to more industrially advanced states. Table 6.12 gives data on deposits and advances in different states and brings out the stark fact of the low advances – deposits ratio for Punjab.

Table 6.12 shows that the advances-deposits (or credit-deposit) ratio for Punjab in 1970 was 35.16 per cent, which was less than half of the all India average of 75.97 per cent. Punjab's ranking on the basis of advances–deposits ratio was 14, which meant that of the major 15 states it was above only Bihar. The states which had advances – deposits ratio higher than the all India average were: Tamil Nadu (133.05 per cent, rank # 1), Andhra Pradesh (109.09 per cent, # 2), West Bengal (93.34 per cent, # 3), Maharashtra (90.92 per cent, # 4) and Karnataka (78.40 per cent, # 5). All these states had a well-developed large-scale industrial sector, which created the major source of demand for large volumes of bank credits and advances. Punjab's advances–deposits ratio had improved in 20 years to 45 per cent in 1990 but Punjab still remained at the same ranking place of 14th, just above Bihar (the state with the lowest ranking). The low credit-deposit ratio of Punjab is an effect of its low level of industrialization. It reflects the absence of large-scale industrial units, which would have needed large bank loans. The fact that the bank deposits in Punjab are used for loans in industrially advanced states leads to a drain of resources from Punjab to these states. Just in one year (1990), it led to a drain of 4,725 crore Rupees (deposits 8,668 crore Rupees minus credit 3,943 crore Rupees) from Punjab. In the year 1990, nearly 50 per cent of the bank deposits mobilized in Punjab was invested in the other states of India. The constitutionally given power of the centre in regulating the national banking network means that no state can legally stop the flow of banking funds from one state to another.[7] This also points to the economic and constitutional power of the centre to determine one unified monetary policy that might have uneven consequences for different states. For example, a policy of low interest rates, which would be advantageous to industrially advanced states needing large bank credits, is not in the interest of a state like Punjab, which would lose on the savings on its deposits.[8]

Table 6.12 Deposits and advances of scheduled commercial banks (15 major states), December 1970 and March 1990

State	*Deposits (Rs. crores)*		*Advances (Rs. crores)*		*Advances/deposits ratio (%)*			
	1970	*1990*	*1970*	*1990*	*1970*	*Rank*	*1990*	*Rank*
Punjab	**273**	**8,668**	**96**	**3,943**	**35.16**	**14**	**45.49**	**14**
Maharashtra	1,453	32,803	1,321	26,145	90.92	4	79.70	5
West Bengal	841	16,846	785	9,245	93.34	3	54.88	12
Gujarat	510	10,182	302	6,238	59.22	9	61.26	9
Kerala	184	6,498	131	4,158	71.20	6	63.99	7
Haryana	77	3,436	47	2,103	61.04	8	61.20	10
Tamil Nadu	351	11,231	467	11,169	133.05	1	99.45	1
Karnataka	301	8,218	236	7,476	78.40	5	90.97	2
Andhra Pradesh	198	9,354	216	8,151	109.09	2	87.14	3
Uttar Pradesh	502	17,903	264	8,414	52.58	12	47.00	13
Rajasthan	110	4,604	61	2,863	55.45	10	62.20	8
Madhya Pradesh	152	6,573	95	4,509	62.50	7	68.60	6
Bihar	231	8,253	80	3,304	34.63	15	40.03	15
Assam	49	1,891	23	1,050	46.94	13	55.53	11
Orissa	46	2,350	25	1,911	54.35	11	81.12	4
All-India	6,026	172,759	4,578	113,592	75.97		65.75	

Source: Adapted from the data provided by the Centre for Monitoring Indian Economy (CMIE) (1990: Table 13.2).

Notes

1 I have provided here the data for the major States only. However, the all-India figure here includes the data for the smaller states and the Union territories also, which have not been mentioned here. The data on the absolute figures of deposits and advances has been taken from the CMIE source. I have calculated the percentages and the rank.

2 The states were not mentioned here according to the alphabetical order but according to the ranking based on per capita deposits in March 1990. I followed the procedure adopted by CMIE in presenting the data on this aspect. The data on per capita deposits is shown in greater detail in Table 6.13.

Table 6.13 Per capita deposits and advances of scheduled commercial banks in 15 major states, December 1970 and March 1990

States	*Deposits (Rs.)*		*Advances (Rs.)*	
	1970	*1990*	*1970*	*1990*
Punjab	201	4,422	70	2,012
Maharashtra	288	4,421	262	3,524
West Bengal	189	2,600	177	1,427
Gujarat	191	2,520	113	1,544
Kerala	89	2,188	61	1,400
Haryana	77	2,121	46	1,298
Tamil Nadu	85	2,016	113	2,005
Karnataka	103	1,843	80	1,676
Andhra Pradesh	45	1,480	49	1,290
Uttar Pradesh	57	1,339	30	629
Rajasthan	42	1,058	23	658
Madhya Pradesh	36	1,042	23	715
Bihar	41	974	14	390
Assam	33	772	15	429
Orissa	21	760	11	618
All-India	100	2,101	84	1,381

Source: Adapted from the CMIE source cited in Table 6.12 above.

The reverse side of the low advances-deposit ratio in Punjab was that Punjab had a high level of bank deposits. Table 6.13 shows the ranking of the states on the basis of per capita deposits in 1990.

The relatively high level of per capita bank deposits in Punjab was a reflection of the relatively high per capita income level in the state. Agricultural development, as a consequence of the introduction of the Green Revolution strategy, had contributed to this high per capita income status of the state. The fact that the bank savings generated by this growth in per capita income level could not be adequately invested in the state implied that agricultural development in Punjab was not contributing adequately to the industrialization of Punjab, but was instead providing a stimulus to the growth of industry in other industrially advanced states. The contribution of Punjab's agricultural development to Punjab's industrialization was limited to a few agro-industries, either providing inputs to agricultural production or processing some of the agricultural products (Sidhu 1996). Though it seems logical that Punjab should have agro-industrialization, the type of agro-industrialization that has taken place has failed to either mop up agrarian savings for investment into Punjab's industry or open up the process of transforming Punjabi farmers into industrial entrepreneurs (Sukhpal Singh 1999). The bulk of the consumer goods consumed in the rural and urban sector were imported from the other states or from abroad (Ajit Singh 1983, Khanna 1983, Bhalla *et al.* 1990). Similarly the capital goods used in Punjab agriculture were produced mainly in the other states of India. Johar *et al.* found that, 'An examination of inter-activity employment brings out the fact that manufacturing activity in other states is the main beneficiary of expanding rural market in Punjab' (1983: 172). Similarly Gill (1983: 292) also highlighted that the expanding rural market in Punjab was benefiting mainly the industrial sectors of states other than Punjab.

I discussed in the earlier chapter on agriculture that the central government policy approach towards agriculture development in Punjab (the Green Revolution) led to a pattern of agricultural production which was extremely narrow in product range. It was basically confined to two crops – wheat and rice. The narrowness of product range in industrial production in Punjab bears some resemblance to this narrowness of the product range in agriculture. Sandhu and Singh (1983: 135) have demonstrated that eight industries – woollen textiles and hosiery, steel re-rolling, cotton textiles including spinning, cycles and cycle parts, cotton ginning and pressing, agricultural implements and machine tools, sewing machines and parts, and sports goods – claimed a 78.12 per cent share of the total production in the small-scale sector in 1973–74, rising to 90.8 per cent by 1978–79. Some of these industries (hosiery, cycles and cycle parts, sewing machines and parts, and sports goods) were characterized as footloose industries by Pandit (1985: 60), because they either did not have linkage with the raw material base in the Punjab or were not oriented to the market in Punjab.[9] The footloose nature of these industries indicated the fragility of their location in Punjab. Almost all of these footloose industries were set up by Punjabi refugees who had virtually nothing but their labour power, after they were uprooted from West Punjab at the time of India's partition in 1947. During several of my field trips to Punjab between 1989 and the mid-1990s, I met many of these self-made industrialists. They told me incredible stories of their march from 'humble beginnings' to material success. Particularly striking were the stories told to me by Sunil Munjal, the Managing Director of Hero Cycles, and Gurmukh Singh, of the Bhogal Group of Companies (the major part of their business is in bicycles and sewing machines). Both came from a family of refugees. Brij Mohan Munjal of the Munjal family and Mohinder Singh Bhogal of the Bhogal family were pioneers in setting up the bicycle industry in the town of Ludhiana in Punjab. Common to both the stories was the self-effort and hard work of the pioneers in setting up tiny industrial units to manufacture cycle parts.[10] They received very little state support.

The central government had taken a keen interest in the setting up of the Punjab Agriculture University at Ludhiana, to support research into farming techniques for the purpose of raising food output in Punjab (Randhawa 1974). However, no comparable effort was made to set up a parallel industrial university to support research and development of industrial techniques to raise industrial productivity. These conflicting policies of the centre towards Punjab's agriculture and industry contributed in some way to the emergence of the phenomenon of labour productivity in industry being lower than the labour productivity in agriculture in Punjab. A study based on the data for the mid-1970s showed that in Punjab the average labour productivity in manufacturing was only 77 per cent of the average labour productivity in agriculture, while this figure was 225 per cent for India as a whole (Gill 1983: 292). Normally, the level of technological development in industry is higher than that in agriculture, and that gets reflected through higher labour productivity in industry than in agriculture. The existence of this unusual phenomenon in Punjab of labour productivity in industry being lower than in agriculture pointed very starkly towards the relative backwardness of the industrial sector in Punjab. The cumulative result of the backwardness of the industrial sector in Punjab was that by 1990–91 Punjab had the lowest share of the secondary sector in its SDP in comparison with 16 other major states of India (see Table 6.7). The entrenchment of agriculture in the development process of Punjab gets further highlighted from the data given in Table 6.14.

In 1980–81, seven states out of 17 had a higher share of agriculture in their SDP than Punjab. The share of agriculture in Punjab's SDP was 47.87 per cent in 1980–81. The states with a higher share of agriculture in their SDP than Punjab were Assam (50.11 per cent), Bihar (59.93 per cent), Haryana (58.80 per cent), Madhya Pradesh (50.7 per cent), Orissa (49.7 per cent), Rajasthan (51.9 per cent) and Uttar Pradesh (49.5 per cent). All these states, except Haryana, are economically backward states. *However, by 1990–91, all these states had made significant progress in economic transition from agricultural sector to non-agricultural sectors.* By 1990–91, the share of agriculture in the SDP for all these states had considerably declined. For Assam, the decline was nearly 9 per cent, for Bihar over 13 per cent, Haryana over 16 per cent, Madhya Pradesh nearly 12 per cent, Orissa nearly 7 per cent, Rajasthan nearly 11 per cent and Uttar Pradesh nearly 13 per cent. *Punjab was, however, stuck in its agricultural dependence.* The share of agriculture in Punjab's SDP declined merely by 1.56 per cent, from 47.87 per cent in 1980–81 to 46.31 per cent in 1990–91. In 1990–91, among the 17 major states, Punjab had the highest share of agriculture in SDP. *It had become the most agriculturally dependent state and the least industrialized state by 1990–91.*

Conclusions

Though the constitution formally provides for industry to be a state subject, the over-all centralizing feature of the Indian constitution has converted industry into a central subject. The strategy of planned development further empowered the centre beyond that which was ordained by the constitution.

The central government used public sector investment as a key instrument for the industrialization of India, a process that was seen as the chief means of overcoming the economic backwardness of the newly emerging nation. The political economy of nation building required that inter-state inequalities be reduced. The centre had actively intervened in Punjab's agriculture in order to accelerate the

Table 6.14 Share of agricultural and non-agricultural sectors in the SDP of major Indian states, 1980–81 and 1990–91 (%)

States	*Sectors*	*1980–81*	*1990–91*
Andhra Pradesh	Agricultural	41.21	34.20
	Non-agricultural	58.79	65.80
Assam	Agricultural	50.11	41.48
	Non-agricultural	49.89	58.52
Bihar	Agricultural	59.93	46.52
	Non-agricultural	40.07	53.48
Goa	Agricultural	18.45	14.30
	Non-agricultural	81.55	85.70
Gujarat	Agricultural	46.25	30.95
	Non-agricultural	53.75	69.05
Haryana	Agricultural	58.80	42.60
	Non-agricultural	41.20	57.40
Himachal Pradesh	Agricultural	47.55	35.67
	Non-agricultural	52.45	64.33
Karnataka	Agricultural	46.56	33.10
	Non-agricultural	53.44	66.90
Kerala	Agricultural	42.31	31.26
	Non-agricultural	57.69	68.74
Maharashtra	Agricultural	28.75	21.80
	Non-agricultural	71.25	78.72
Madhya Pradesh	Agricultural	50.71	38.34
	Non-agricultural	49.29	61.66
Orissa	Agricultural	49.79	42.43
	Non-agricultural	50.21	57.57
Punjab	**Agricultural**	**47.87**	**46.31**
	Non-agricultural	52.13	53.69
Rajasthan	Agricultural	51.93	42.72
	Non-agricultural	48.07	57.28
Tamil Nadu	Agricultural	24.64	22.83
	Non-agricultural	75.36	77.17
Uttar Pradesh	Agricultural	49.53	36.74
	Non-agricultural	50.47	63.26
West Bengal	Agricultural	33.15	25.58
	Non-agricultural	66.85	74.42
All India	Agricultural	39.64	32.91
	Non-agricultural	60.36	67.09

Source: Adapted from Bhattacharya and Sakthivel (2004: 1076; Table 5).

Green Revolution and fulfil the national goal of food self-sufficiency. The Green Revolution led to an impressive increase in agricultural production in Punjab. This led to raising the status of Punjab to the top among the Indian states, in terms of per capita income. If the political economy of Indian nationalism in its goal of achieving food self-sufficiency resulted in benefits for Punjab's agriculture, another politico-economic goal of Indian nationalism, namely the reducing of inter-state inequalities, led to a disproportionally low level of central public sector investment in Punjab industry. The lack of adequate public sector investment deprived the historically backward industry in Punjab of the necessary stimulus it needed to overcome its backwardness. The duality of Punjab's agricultural development and industrial backwardness was most dramatically manifested in the relatively low credit-deposit ratio in Punjab. The lack of an adequate demand for credits by industry within the state led to the deposits generated by agricultural development in Punjab being siphoned off to the industrially advanced states. The political instability in Punjab caused by the conflict between the centre and Punjabi Sikh nationalism further harmed the growth of industrialization in Punjab. Punjab's industry remained largely confined to the small-scale sector. The eventual outcome was that the secondary sector remained a relatively weak sector of Punjab's economy. By 1990–91, in comparison with all the major states in India, Punjab had the lowest share of the secondary sector in its SDP. The weakness of the secondary sector was eventually manifested in the relatively slow rate of growth of SDP and per capita SDP in Punjab during the decade 1980–1990 (see Tables 5.5 and 5.6).

During the 25-year period of our study (1966–1991), the centre's economic and political interventions in Punjab have, on the whole, hindered the process of industrialization in Punjab.

7

SUMMARY AND CONCLUSIONS

In a country with multiple and competing nationalisms, federal structures and institutions play a key regulatory role in providing direction to its path of development. Federal mediations are continuously under stress because of competing claims over economic resources, political power and ideological hegemony. Federal success or failure depends on convergence or divergence between competing nationalisms for development and political aspirations. This study has highlighted the role of nationalism and federalism in offering a new understanding of India's path of development.

I have argued that the pattern of economic development in the Indian state of Punjab between 1966 and 1991 was shaped decisively by the strategic developmental perspectives of the Indian nationalist state. My choice of time-period for this study was determined by key geographical and politico-economic considerations, from the historically significant territorial reorganization of Punjab on linguistic grounds in 1966, which gave birth to the present-day Punjabi-speaking state of Punjab, to the historic break in 1991 in the economic policy regime followed by the Indian central state. In July 1991, the Indian central state abandoned its pre-1991 economic policy regime, which was based on giving a key role to central planning in the development strategy, and launched a new economic policy regime based on the IMF–World Bank perspective of privatization, liberalization and structural adjustments.

In this study I have tried to integrate four aspects of the political economy of India and Punjab to present a historical record of the nature of the development process in Punjab between 1966 and 1991. First, I have probed the Indian constitution to throw light on the legal and constitutional dimensions of economic relations between the centre and the states. These dimensions act as a background to the economic policy regimes that the two tiers of the government can follow in fashioning any development path at national and state level. They also highlight the limits under which the two layers of the government have to operate. Second, I have tried to present a critical account of the path of planned economic development that the Indian state followed until 1991. My narrative has been oriented to provide a macro-economic framework for understanding the development process in Punjab up to 1991. Third, I have dealt in some detail with the history of the Punjab and of the Sikhs, the majority religious community of the present Punjab, to indicate specific characteristics of the Punjab state that need to be taken into account in order to understand the specific nature of Punjab's politico-economic relations with the Indian centre. Finally, I have tried to identify the most important dimensions of Punjab's development pattern between 1966 and 1991. This was the main focus and aim of this study, and by dwelling on the three aforementioned aspects I have tried to demonstrate that Punjab's development pattern cannot be understood unless one situates it in the context of Indian federalism, India's development path and the troubled history of relations between the Punjabi Sikhs and the Delhi-based central powers in general and the post-1947 Indian nationalist state in particular.

In the introductory chapter, I located the subject of my study within the broader field of federalism, nationalism and development (especially regional development). Taking a global view of different federal experiences, I identified two diametrically opposite patterns of regional development and conflict. One category of conflicts originated from the relatively more developed regions feeling dissatisfied within a federal arrangement, the other category from the less developed regions feeling dissatisfied with the federal framework. Within this typology of regional developments and federal conflicts, Punjab presents a mixed picture. I alluded to two development criteria to suggest the mixed nature of Punjab's development experience within the Indian federal experience. On the one hand, Punjab became the second richest state of India between 1966 and 1991 in terms of per capita income, but on the other, it was reduced to the lowest rank among the 17 major states of India by 1990–91 in terms of the share of the secondary sector in state domestic product (SDP). I characterized Punjab as rich but not developed on the basis of this seemingly paradoxical status of Punjab in the Indian federation.

It is this paradoxical status of Punjab's development experience in the Indian federal structure that led me to investigate the character of the sectoral composition of Punjab's SDP. In particular, I have proposed that the record of Punjab's agricultural and industrial sectors needs to be probed within the context of the political economy of federal India. I found that a preliminary look at the data suggested that the comparatively better performance of Punjab agriculture vis-à-vis the majority of the other states in India seemed to be a major contributor to raising Punjab's per capita income status, placing it among the richest states. However, this impressive agricultural performance was accompanied by dismal industrial progress, pushing Punjab's industrial ranking among the main Indian states down to the lowest level. Along with the study of Punjab's agriculture and industry, I also included the study of Punjab's state finances because I considered a study of centre–state financial relations under the Indian constitutional framework to be indispensable for an understanding of the functioning of Indian federal arrangements.

Punjab, Sikhs and the centre: an historical view

In order to understand the developmental experience of Punjab within the Indian federation, I considered it essential to bring one characteristic of Punjab which differentiated it from the other Indian states into my analysis. This distinguishing feature is that Punjab is the only state in India where the Sikhs – a small minority in India – were a majority. This aspect of Sikhs' location in Punjab and India provided a particular salience to the study of Punjab's development experience within the Indian federation.

In Chapter 2 I presented an historical account of the key turning points in the history of the evolution of the Sikh community and its role in the shaping of Punjab's history. I emphasized that the birth of Sikhism as a new religion in Punjab in the fifteenth century was a moment of huge historical significance. Out of a complex interaction with Islam and Hinduism, two great religious traditions that have had a profound impact on the culture and way of life of the Punjabi people, arose this new religion which was to play a central role in shaping the subsequent history of Punjab. That the founder of this new faith, Guru Nanak (1469–1539), was imprisoned by the central power of that time (the Mughal ruler Babar) was to set this faith in conflict with the Delhi-based centre literally from the moment of its birth. As the numerical expansion of the egalitarian Sikh faith took place among the peasants and the artisans of Punjab in the sixteenth and seventeenth centuries, the organizational strength and self-confidence of the community grew. Its leaders came to view themselves as the avant-garde articulators and defenders of the interests of all the people of Punjab. Their organizational strength and ideological self-image as leaders of the Punjabi people eventually led the Sikhs to become rulers of Punjab by the end of the eighteenth century. A Sikh chieftain, Ranjit Singh, became the sovereign ruler of Punjab in 1799. Although he was a devout Sikh, he chose to constitute his cabinet from all the communities of Punjab. This multi-community Punjabi state came to an end when, soon after Ranjit Singh's death, the expanding British rule in India annexed Punjab in 1849.

Chapter 2 discussed the politico-economic changes that took place in Punjab during the British rule, and emphasized those aspects of expansion of irrigation networks and advances in agricultural production that were linked to the strategic economic and military objectives of imperial rule. I also pointed out that British agrarian policies contributed to the sharpening of religious identities among the Punjabis. This religious differentiation had contradictory implications: if, on the one hand, this religious differentiation weakened the common Punjabi identity and worked in favour of British rule, it also, on the other hand, led to the sharpening of conflicts between the British rule and some sections of the Punjabi people. In particular, the growth of self-identity among the Sikhs resulted in the Sikh mobilization for democratic self-rule over their religious institutions (the gurdwaras); this, in turn, pitted the Sikhs against British rule.

The end of British rule in India in 1947, accompanied by partition, changed the demographic composition of the new (Indian) Punjab in the post-1947 period. The Sikhs became a majority community in a number of Punjabi-speaking districts of the post-1947 united Punjab, and the territorial reorganization of Punjab linguistically in 1966 led to the birth of the present-day Punjabi-speaking state. The Sikh majority Punjab state soon saw the emergence of the demand for greater autonomy from the Indian central state. The drafting of the Anandpur Sahib Resolution in the early 1970s was a clear example of the most serious exercise of political reflection ever undertaken by the Sikh regional party Akali Dal, whose political and social base was primarily among rural Sikhs dependent on agriculture. I have in some detail explored the social and cultural crisis in Punjab's agrarian society, and analysed the political moves of the Indian central leadership, in order to explain the rise of Sikh militancy. The centralist perspective of the Indian leadership contributed to the growth of Sikh secessionism and the eventual violent confrontation between the Punjabi Sikhs and the centre in the 1980s and early 1990s. The Indian central state had to use its enormous military power to suppress this regional rebellion; I have demonstrated that the ideology of Indian nationalism was used as a justification for suppressing the rebellion. This has brought me to the question of placing Indian nationalism in the context of the evolution of the legal-constitutional structures of the Indian federal state and Indian development strategy.

The ideology of Indian nationalism, centre–state relations in the constitutional framework, and the strategy of development planning

In Chapter 3 I provided an historical overview of the evolution of centre–state relations in India. I argued that the partition of India in 1947 had a decisive influence on shaping Indian nationalist opinion in favour of giving a centralist thrust to the Indian constitution. I demonstrated this by providing evidence that the pre-1947 discussions on the Indian constitution showed an emerging consensus in favour of a decentralizing framework. This decentralizing framework provided for significant powers to reside with the states, including the crucial residuary powers. I pointed out that the decentralizing framework was grudgingly conceded initially by the Indian nationalist leadership because it was seen as a possible way of accommodating the political aspirations of the Muslim minority and thus avoiding the partition of the country. However, when the partition became a reality, the Indian national leadership swung to the centralist perspective. The secular and the Hindu variants of Indian nationalism had converging positions on the need for a strong centre to keep India as 'a strong and united nation'.

This Indian nationalist perspective, in support of a centralizing framework for independent India's constitution, was further boosted by the consensus that had emerged in India on the need to accord a critical role to central planning in India's development strategy. Planning became not only an economic tool for

India's development strategy but also a political tool for Indian nation-building. I have emphasized this dual role of planning in reinforcing the trend towards growing power of the centre vis-à-vis the states.

The political economy of Indian nationalism in the shaping of Punjab's development pattern

I have demonstrated that the political economy of Indian nationalism has played an overarching role in determining the nature of the centre's intervention in different sectors of Punjab's economy. In order to examine centre–state economic relations in the spheres of budgetary finance, agriculture, and industry, I have developed the reconfigured centralization–decentralization (RCD) approach. The RCD approach has enabled me to highlight the over-arching role of centrist Indian nationalism in influencing regional development patterns, with special focus on Punjab.

In Chapter 4 I analysed the trends in central transfers to the states and highlighted the growing share of discretionary transfers over statutory transfers. I have interpreted the growing share of discretionary transfers as a reflection of the growing power of the centre in the mechanism of centre–state financial relations, and have further examined the mechanism of transfer of statutory resources to the states. Being statutory, one would assume that the mechanism of these transfers would be a legally binding neutral operation between the centre and the states. However, on closer examination of the working of the institution of the Finance Commission, which is the vehicle for statutory transfers, I have noted that even in this mode of the transfer of resources to the states, there has been a trend towards growing power of the centre. The most telling outcome of this growing power was the indebtedness of the states to the centre, which I attributed to the gap between the shrinking revenue resources and the expenditure responsibilities of the states. The most elastic sources of revenue were in the hands of the centre, leaving the states with rather inelastic sources of revenue. In contrast with the inelastic sources of revenue to which the states had access, their expenditure responsibilities had also expanded, due to the leading role of the states in the provision of public utilities. This aspect of centre–state relations can be called the vertical imbalance, where the centre on one side and all the states on the other were placed in a relationship in which the states were highly dependent on the centre to meet their constitutional expenditure responsibilities.

The other aspect of centre–state relations that I have analysed relates to the mechanism of apportioning the share of the different states from the total pool of resources available to them. This can be called the horizontal aspect of centre–state relations. My analysis shows that Punjab–centre financial relations are affected by both the vertical and the horizontal aspects of centre–state financial relations. The link between the vertical and the horizontal relations is provided by the political economy of the centre's role as the builder of Indian nationalism. The increase in the financial power of the centre vis-à-vis the states (the vertical aspect) is driven by the need to have a strong centre that can effectively fulfil its historic mission of being the builder of a strong nation state. In deciding the share of different states from the total resource pool (the horizontal aspect), the centre is guided by its strategic role of meeting the needs of different states so that they retain a stake in Indian national unity. I have argued that the relatively low per capita income states can see an economic stake in Indian unity if they can see that the centre is trying to reduce the economic gap between them and the relatively high per capita income states. It is from this angle that we can understand that the centre's perspective of reducing inter-state inequalities is guided by the politics of Indian nationalism. The fact that Punjab, a high per capita income state, received a proportionately low share from the central pool can only be explained by the logic of Indian nationalist needs. I have also used the logic of the political economy of Indian nationalism to explain the special loan granted to Punjab in the 1980s to meet the expenditure on security operations against the Punjabi Sikh militants who were advocating Punjab's autonomy or secession from India.

In Chapter 5 I made an analysis of centre–state relations in agriculture and their implications for Punjab's agriculture. Through a close and detailed analysis of the different provisions of the constitution relating to agriculture, I have shown that while the subject of agriculture is formally a state subject, the overall impact of the structure of the constitution and of many provisions in the constitution is that agriculture has come to be controlled significantly and decisively by the centre. I particularly emphasized the provisions relating to 'national' interest in the constitution, in order to demonstrate how these have contributed to the legal empowerment of the centre in the sphere of agriculture.

After situating agriculture within India's constitutional framework, I moved to locate the pattern of Punjab's agricultural development in the context of the Indian nation state's developmental strategy. In particular, I have focused on the imperative for food self-sufficiency faced by the Indian central state. I demonstrated that the politico-economic significance of the goal of self-sufficiency pursued by the Indian state can only be understood by locating it in the Indian national state's larger strategic politico-economic goal of national sovereignty. I probed the launch of the Green Revolution strategy in India in general and Punjab in particular to emphasize the kernel of this strategy – the attainment of the goal of food self-sufficiency – and discussed in some detail the reasons for which Punjab was especially picked as the key state to launch the Green Revolution. By providing the historical background to the evolution of Punjab's agriculture during British colonial rule, I have emphasized in particular the massive development of irrigation facilities in Punjab, and linked the development of these irrigation facilities to the strategic economic and military goals of the colonial state. With these developed irrigation facilities and the developed farming skills of the Punjab peasantry, I have argued, Punjab was the model state for the Indian central government to launch the Green Revolution.

The Green Revolution fulfilled the expectations of Indian policy-makers.

India achieved food self-sufficiency. The Indian central state was free from the fear that Indian sovereignty could be undermined due to food dependence on any other nation. The consequences for Punjab, however, were mixed. Punjab's agricultural production increased. That pushed Punjab into the position of number-one state in terms of per capita income. But, on the other hand, an agriculturally oriented pattern of development became reinforced and embedded. Furthermore, within agriculture, the priority given to food crops weakened the diversity of crop patterns. Punjab's agriculture basically revolved around two crops: wheat and rice. By 1991, the limits of the Green Revolution strategy seemed to be straining Punjab's agriculture in particular and its economy in general. Very little scope was left for further extensive and intensive cultivation of land. Similarly, Punjab seemed to be overstretching the use of its irrigation resources. The conflicting claims over the use of Punjab's river water resources led to legal and extra-legal conflicts between Punjab and the centre, and also between Punjab and neighbouring states. It appeared that by 1991 the Indian nation state's development strategy in Punjab was turning from its apparent success in the earlier 1960s and 1970s phase into its opposite – a failure. Punjab seemed to be changing from being a beneficiary of the Indian nation state's development strategy to being its victim. My subsequent analysis of centre–Punjab relations in the realm of industry (Chapter 6) further brings to light the flaws in the logic of the development strategy followed by the centre in Punjab.

In this penultimate chapter, starting with an analysis of the constitutional provisions relating to the subject of industry, I have demonstrated that, like agriculture, industry was formally speaking a state concern. I have argued, however, that many other provisions of the constitution allow a very high degree of central government involvement in the field of industry if such involvement is seen to be necessary from the viewpoint of 'national interest'. I have pointed out that between 1966 and 1991 the degree of central intrusion in the field of industry in the name of 'national interest' was, in fact, even higher than it was in the field of agriculture. What constitutes 'national interest' is not, however, an uncontested and uncontroversial terrain. I have examined in detail the criticisms made by several state governments, including that of Punjab, of the centre's use of the provision of 'national interest' to justify central intrusion in the field of industry. I have also noted the support that central government received from several other state governments for its intrusion into the field of industry.

By analysing the contrasting positions of different state governments, I have highlighted the importance of regional nationalism vis-à-vis the centralizing Indian nationalism articulated by the centre. In those states with a more developed sense of regional nationalism (e.g. Tamil Nadu and Punjab), there has been opposition to the centre assuming powers in matters concerning industry in the name of 'national interest'. In contrast, states where regional nationalism is historically weak (e.g. the Hindi-speaking states in central and north India) have generally supported central policies to regulate industrial development in the country. In addition to this ideological dimension of the distance of a state-based regional nationalism from the centre-oriented Indian nationalism, or the affinity of a state-based regional nationalism with the centre-oriented Indian nationalism in determining a state's position regarding the centre's powers of regulation in industry, I have identified the level of industrial development of a state as another determining factor. The industrially more developed states (such as Maharashtra and Gujarat, but also the north Indian state of Haryana) opposed central intervention in industry, while the industrially less developed states (e.g. the states in the Hindi-speaking region as well as the non-Hindi-speaking state of Orissa) favoured greater central intervention in industry. I have explained this spectrum of positions by referring to the central policy of reducing inter-state inequalities. Greater central power in industrial regulation could be used to reduce inter-state inequalities, and was thus obviously beneficial to the industrially less developed states and harmful to the industrially more developed states.

In this spectrum of positions of the different state governments regarding the centre's power in the regulation of industrial development, Punjab stood in a unique situation. It was neither industrially developed like Maharashtra nor was it a poor state such as Bihar. I have argued that it was an industrially backward state but at the same time a high per capita income state, owing its status of high per capita income state to its performance in agricultural production. Examining the nature of industrial development in Punjab, I have pointed out that Punjab was an industrially backward state at the time of the 1947 partition. The destabilization caused by partition gave a further blow to Punjab's industrial sector. In the post-1947 period, and especially in the post-Green Revolution period, central policies on industrial development, instead of facilitating industrial development, contributed to Punjab's industrial backwardness.

During the period of the planned economic development model followed by the central government until 1991, central public sector investment was the most important policy tool in the hands of the central government to encourage industrial development. Even private sector investment was heavily shaped by central government through the policy apparatus of licensing. One of the principal aims guiding the location of public sector enterprises was the reduction of inter-state inequalities. Through an examination of the data on central public sector investment, I have demonstrated that Punjab was allocated a disproportionately low level of this investment. Since Punjab had attained high per capita income status because of the Green Revolution in agriculture, the central government's policy of reducing inter-state inequalities dictated that Punjab did not deserve a generous level of public sector investment. As a result of the inadequacy of central public sector investment in Punjab, the historically backward character of Punjab industry could not be overcome. In order to emphasize the backward character of Punjab's industry, I have highlighted the predominance of the small-scale sector, as well as the most telling evidence: that labour productivity in Punjab's industry was lower than in agriculture. The cumulative impact of this continuing industrial backwardness in Punjab was that, by 1991, Punjab had the lowest share of the secondary sector in the state domestic product of all the 17 major states of India.

By the late 1980s, Punjab's agriculture had reached its critical saturation point. The combination of declining agriculture with backward industry manifested itself in a slowing down of Punjab's SDP growth rate. The Punjab economy needed diversification for sustained development. The possibility of this diversification was thwarted by the path of national development guided by Indian central planning and the federal structure of India. Punjabi nationalist aspirations for a diversified and rounded development of Punjab's economy conflicted with central needs for a food-producing agrarian economy in Punjab. The escalation of this conflict into a violent confrontation between Punjabi Sikh nationalism and Indian nationalism in the 1980s and early 1990s further weakened the Punjab economy.

The new economic policy of liberalization initiated by the central government in 1991 is now gradually unfolding itself. Its full impact on the economies of the various states of India remains to be studied. An initial look at the evidence suggests that the agrarian-oriented structure of the Punjab economy, as constructed prior to 1991, still remains deeply embedded. It remains to be studied whether mere changes in the centre's economic policy can actually lead to adjustments in centre–state relations to any significant degree. Indeed, the thorough restructuring of centre–state relations that is needed to allow the states to significantly shape their own economies may only be possible through a major revision of the constitution of India.

APPENDIX

Ranking of states and union territories according to population 1991 and 2001

Rank according to population 1991	*States/Union territory*	*Population 1991*	*Population 2001*	*Rank according to population 2001*
1	Uttar Pradesh	138,760,417	166,197,921	1
2	Bihar	86,338,853	82,998,509	3
3	Maharashtra	78,706,719	96,878,627	2
4	West Bengal	67,982,732	80,176,197	4
5	Andhra Pradesh	66,304,854	76,210,007	5
6	Madhya Pradesh	66,135,862	60,348,023	7
7	Tamil Nadu	55,638,318	62,405,679	6
8	Karnataka	44,817,398	52,850,562	9
9	Rajasthan	43,880,640	56,507,188	8
10	Gujarat	41,174,060	50,671,017	10
11	Orissa	31,512,070	36,804,660	11
12	Kerala	29,011,237	31,841,374	12
13	Assam	22,294,562	26,655,528	14
14	Punjab	20,190,795	24,358,999	15
15	Haryana	16,317,715	21,144,564	16
16	Delhi	9,370,475	13,850,507	18
17	Jammu and Kashmir	7,718,700	10,143,700	19
18	Himachal Pradesh	5,111,079	6,077,900	21
19	Tripura	2,744,827	3,199,203	22
20	Manipur	1,826,714	2,293,896	23
21	Meghalaya	1,760,626	2,318,822	24
22	Nagaland	1,215,573	1,990,036	25
23	Goa	1,168,622	1,347,668	26
24	Arunachal Pradesh	858,392	1,097,968	27
25	Pondicherry/Puducherry	789,416	974,345	28
26	Mizoram	686,217	888,573	30
27	Chandigarh	640,725	900,635	29
28	Sikkim	403,612	540,851	31
29	A & N islands	277,989	356,152	32
30	Dadra and Nagar Haveli	138,542	220,490	33
31	Daman & Diu	101,439	158,204	34
32	Lakshadweep	51,681	60,650	35
	Uttaranchal	Not applicable	8,489,349	20
	Jharkhand	Not applicable	26,945,829	13
	Chattisgarh	Not applicable	20,833,803	17
Total	**India**	**843,930,861**	**1,028,737,436**	

Source: Adapted from *Census of India* 1991 Series – 20 (Govt of India 1992: 12) and Director, Census Operations Punjab (Govt of Punjab 2005: 100–101); ranking done by me.

Note

1991 Census was not conducted in Jammu and Kashmir. The figures are as the projections prepared by the Standing Committee of Experts. Between 1991 and 2001, three new states were carved: Chattisgarh out of Madhya Pradesh, Jharkhand out of Bihar, and Uttaranchal/Uttarakhand out of Uttar Pradesh. Delhi changed its status from a Union territory to a state.

NOTES

1 INTRODUCTION

1 Instead of following the usual practice of using the initials of the authors cited, I have mentioned the full name of all the scholars with the Singh surname wherever possible. This has been done to avoid confusion resulting from too many Singh entries in the bibliography.

2 '...the Five Rivers – from west to east Jhelum, Chenab, Ravi, Beas and Sutlej – which give the province its name and unite in the southwest to form the Panjnad or Five Streams' (Spate and Learmonth 1972: 516).

3 Ninth Finance Commission Report, in Govt of India 1988a: Appendix V.4.

4 I have ranked the states on the basis of the data on net income generated in the registered factory sector in each state. These data were presented in Table 16.8 of the *Statistical Abstract of Punjab* 1988 (Govt of Punjab 1989). The original source of these data was the *Annual Survey of Industries*, Central Statistical Organisation of the Government of India. I computed the figure for per capita net income generated in the registered factory sector for each state by using the population data for each state from the 1981 census. The 1981 census data were presented in Table 3.21 of the *Statistical Abstract of Punjab 1988* (Govt of Punjab 1989).

5 Govt of India 1984. Three journalists, Giri Lal Jain, Arun Shourie and N. C. Menon, during their periods of editorship of *The Times of India*, *The Indian Express* and *The Hindustan Times*, respectively, articulated this position consistently in the 1980s. A left-wing Indian nationalist perspective is V. D. Chopra *et al.* 1984. Academic writings which argue that inter-state inequalities have increased since Indian national independence tend to give the impression that Punjab has had a favourable treatment from the centre. See Ansari 1987, Gulati and George 1987.

6 An anthology of essays articulating this view is Mali 1989.

7 Some of the journalistic writings are included in Samiuddin 1985.

8 Johar and Khanna 1983, Amrik Singh 1985, Gopal Singh 1987, and Bawa and Raikhy 2000 contain an article each on centre–state economic relations.

9 Kumar *et al.* 1984 and Iqbal Singh 1986 deal with the subject in a few pages.

10 Indian National Congress Memorandum to Sarkaria Commission (Govt of India 1987: 657–677). The central government in India appointed a National Commission on Centre–State Relations in India in 1983 which was headed by Justice R. S. Sarkaria. The Commission came to be popularly known as the Sarkaria Commission and submitted two voluminous reports (Govt of India 1987 and 1988). The two-volume study by the Commission remains the most comprehensive examination of Centre–state relations in India. The details of my interviews with Justice Sarkaria are

mentioned later on in this chapter. The political context of the appointment of the Commission is discussed in the next chapter.

11 Sarkaria Commission Report (Govt of India 1988: 435–446).

12 Memorandum to the Sarkaria Commission by the Government of Punjab (Govt of Punjab 1987: 873) and the Government of Tamil Nadu (Govt of Tamil Nadu 1987: 524–530).

13 This is discussed in detail in Chapter 6, on industry.

14 See also Communist Party of India (West Bengal Unit) Memorandum to the Sarkaria Commission (Govt of India 1987: 479–480).

15 See Goyal (1979) and the Communist Party of India (Marxist) Memorandum to the Sarkaria Commission (Govt of India 1987: 640).

16 See also Govt of India 1988: 407–415.

17 Confidential papers of the Punjab government for restricted circulation to which I was given access.

18 Barnala missed his colleague Sardar Balwant Singh, a finance minister in his government, who, he told me, had knowledge of intricate details of centre–state financial relations. Ironically and tragically, Balwant Singh had been assassinated by Sikh militants for his alleged collaborationist role in dealing with the Indian government.

19 I must mention here the name of Dr Hari Singh, a professor of horticulture at PAU. He was a dear friend who helped to arrange all my interviews at PAU. He died of a heart attack in 1992. His death was not only a severe personal blow; it also deprived me of an irreplaceable academic contact with PAU.

20 Madhav Rao Scindia occupied key ministerial positions in various Congress governments at the centre and died in a plane crash on 29 September 2001. Mr Aiyar is currently a minister in the Congress government at the centre led by Manmohan Singh. Scindia was educated at Oxford and Aiyar at Cambridge. Both of them were known to be leading and articulate members of the Congress Party.

2 THE GEOGRAPHY AND THE POLITICAL ECONOMY OF PUNJAB: AN HISTORICAL OVERVIEW OF PUNJAB–CENTRE RELATIONS

1 The proportion of Sikh population in Punjab in 2001 has gone down from about 63 per cent in 1991 to 59.9 per cent in 2001. The proportion of Hindu, Muslim and Christian population has gone up from 34.5 per cent, 1.2 per cent and 1.1 per cent in 1991 to 36.9 per cent 1.8 per cent and 1.2 per cent in 2001. The share of Punjabi Sikhs in India's total Sikh population has gone down from 78.6 per cent in 1991 to 73.2 per cent in 2001. The share of Sikhs in India's total population has also gone down slightly from 2 per cent in 1991 to 1.9 per cent in 2001 (Govt of Punjab 2005: 98–99). From the anecdotal information that is available, it emerges that the most likely cause of the decline in the proportion of Sikh population in Punjab as well as in India is the migration of Sikhs outside India towards Western and Middle Eastern countries. The rise in the proportion of Hindu and Muslim population in Punjab can be reasonably attributed to a very substantial migration of Hindu and Muslim workers from Uttar Pradesh and Bihar to Punjab for seeking employment in the agricultural and industrial sectors of Punjab. A detailed study of these migration patterns needs reliable data which are not available as yet.

2 The first set of dates refers to birth and death, and the second to the period of guruship. The source of these data is Appendix I 'The Ten Sikh Gurus' in Brown (1999: 197).

3 See Appendix II 'Contributors to the Guru Granth Sahib' in Brown 1999 for full details on these contributors.

4 I have used the spelling 'Harimandar' throughout following the spelling used by Ian

J. Kerr (Kerr 2001) in his entry 'Harimandar' in the *Encyclopaedia of Sikhism* edited by Harbans Singh (2001).

5 Smart (1992: 99) highlights the contribution of Guru Arjan to the evolution of the Sikh community as next in importance to that of Guru Nanak, the first guru, and Guru Gobind Singh, the tenth guru; he writes:

> Of the other Gurus perhaps Arjun is the most important. He led the community from 1581 to 1606. He founded the Golden Temple at Amritsar, collected the scriptures, and came into conflict with the emperor Jehangir – a conflict which led to a clearer self-definition of the Sikhs as a militant and outwardly distinguishable group.

According to Grewal (1998: 42), the peaceful evolutionary phase of Sikhism 'came dramatically to a grave end with the martyrdom of Guru Arjan in the very first year of Jehangir's reign'.

6 Though McLeod makes a probing analysis of the Jat dimension in the evolution of the Sikh community from the period of the third guru to the sixth guru, he unnecessarily succumbs to an element of essentialism in characterizing the Jats as prone to violence:

> The death of Guru Arjan may have persuaded Guru Hargobind of the need for tighter organization, but we find it difficult to envisage a large group of unarmed Jats suddenly becoming commanded to take up weapons. *The Jats will have remained Jats*
>
> (McLeod 1996: 12, italics added)

This essentialist characterization is contrary to McLeod's own general method of historical-evolutionary analysis of the changes in the development of the Sikh community. For a more detailed examination of the dynamics of violence and non-violence in Sikh history and politics, see Pritam Singh (2007: 555–570). After the publication of my 2007 paper, I had a very fruitful and friendly private correspondence with Hew McLeod.

7 For a modern human rights interpretation of Guru Tegh Bahadur's martyrdom, see Pritam Singh (1998: 239). This interpretation was a key input into Amnesty International's decision to declare Guru Tegh Bahadur as one of the five eminent men of the seventeenth century whose ideas and actions were decisive in the struggle for human rights in the seventeenth century. The other four selected by Amnesty International are: John Lilburne (1617–1657), John Locke (1632–1704), William Pen (1644–1718) and Voltaire (1694–1778). Amnesty International brought out a publication on this subject to mark the fiftieth anniversary of the Universal Declaration of Human Rights (Amnesty International 1998).

8 Rabindranath Tagore, the Indian Noble laureate, wrote a Bengali poem *Bandi Bir* (Warrior Bound) in 1899 celebrating the heroism of Banda Singh Bahadur (Banerjee 1992: 275–276), an indication of the impact Banda's martyrdom left on the historical memory of the Indian literati during the early phase of the Indian struggle for independence from the British rule. 'The poem was a source of inspiration to several other Bengali writers as well as to Bengali militant youth engaged in the struggle for India's independence' (ibid.: 275–276).

9 The first massacre is remembered by the Sikhs in their collective memory as *chhota ghallughara* (the small holocaust) and the second one as *wadda ghallughara* (the big holocaust). Khushwant Singh (1999: 154) notes that the estimates of the Sikhs killed in the second massacre vary from 12,000–30,000 (by Muslim and English historians) to 5,000–7,000 (by a Marathi newsletter record). Khushwant Singh (1999: 129) and Ganda Singh (1956: 33) agree a figure of 10,000 Sikh deaths for the first massacre.

The second massacre must have led to more than 10,000 deaths to be remembered as a 'big holocaust' in comparison with the 'small holocaust'.

10 Khushwant Singh provides the details of high offices held by Muslims and Hindus (1999: 294) and by several Europeans in his chapter 'Europeanization of the Army' (ibid.: 258–267).

11 Tahir, analysing the work of a Punjabi Muslim poet, Qadiryar (b. 1802) 'who ranks amongst the foremost Punjabi poets' (1999: 55), argues that in one of his works, the *Var* (Ballad), the poet celebrated the military victories of Hari Singh Nalwa over the Pathans and Afghans. Hari Singh Nalwa was one of the most distinguished Sikh generals in Ranjit Singh's army. Tahir states that

> [if] the *Var* is examined, nowhere does the poet mention the Muslim or Islam. It is the Pathan and the Afghan against the Punjabi. He composed the *Var* neither as a Muslim nor as a Sikh, but as a Punjabi. Hari Singh is written of as a Punjabi battling against the Afghans and the Pathans. *The provincial feeling may have been prompted by the political situation prevailing in Ranjit Singh's Punjab.*
>
> (ibid.: 64, italics added)

Darshan Singh analyses the work of another eminent Punjabi Muslim poet, Shah Muhammad, who in his war-ballad written in 1849 bemoans the defeat of the Sikh army in the first Anglo-Sikh war as a defeat of the Punjabi kingdom of Ranjit Singh and refers to the war as 'a war between Punjab and Hind (Hindustan)' (1999: 73). Hindustan is one of the Hindi words used for India.

12 'The growth of the Christian community in the Punjab is borne out by census figures: 1881 – 3,796; 1891 – 19,547; 1901 – 37,980; 1911 – 163,994; 1921 – 315,931; 1931 – 414,788' (Khushwant Singh, 1999a: 137).

13 A Sikh scholar, Bhai Kahn Singh Nabha, wrote a booklet *Hum Hindu Nahin Hain* (We Are Not Hindus) as a rebuttal against the claims made by the Hindu reformist movement that Sikhism was a branch of Hinduism. 'This action and reaction broke up the close social relationship which had existed between the two sister communities' (Khushwant Singh 1999a: 147). This booklet has acquired the character of a classic among the Sikhs. There is a translation by a Canada-based Sikh, Jarnail Singh (1984).

14 Oberoi (1994) focuses on the internal contest within the Sikh community for explaining the hegemonic victory of Khalsa Sikh identity while Fox (1985) focuses on the external influence (colonial rule) in explaining the rise of militant Khalsa identity. Ballantyne (1999) attempts a bold synthesis as well as a critique of the internalist versus externalist interpretations of the evolution of Sikh identity by transcending the limitations of the nineteenth century focus of these interpretations. See also Kerr (1988).

15 Kapur gives a vivid description of the situation at Janam Asthan gurdwara at Nankana Sahib, the birthplace of Guru Nanak:

> The management of the Janam Asthan gurdwara had been the subject of considerable controversy for some years. The *mahant* [Udasi priest] of the *gurdwara*, Narain Das, had a reputation for immorality and licentiousness, and in 1918 his conduct had elicited sharp condemnation from the local congregation. Narain Das was accused of scandalous behaviour, of sacrilege and of misuse of *gurdwara* funds with little effect. The considerable revenue derived from estates associated with the *gurdwara*, amounting to some Rs.500,000 annually, made the *mahant* relatively immune from censure.
>
> (1986: 107).

16 Kapur interprets the change in government policy as not from one that was pro-*mahant* management and anti-Sikh to one that became pro-Sikh, but as one from neutrality or 'non-involvement' between the contending parties to one that was more sympathetic to Sikh control. However, he emphasizes that 'the hideous massacre at Nankana compelled the Punjab government to reassess its stance' (1986: 110).

17 Quoted by Mohinder Singh (1988: 50). Gandhi's message is also a celebration of his philosophy of non-violence. By following the non-violent forms of struggle to regain democratic control of the gurdwaras and succeeding in their struggle, the Sikhs can be seen, from a Gandhian perspective, to have demonstrated the moral strength and the practical-political use of Gandhi's philosophy of *ahimsa* (non-violence). Uberoi (1996: 112–123) examines the ideological interface between Gandhism and Sikhism, especially in the context of this specific Sikh struggle. See also Mukherji (1984, 1985). Banerjee (2000) demonstrates that the Pathan leader Abdul Gaffar Khan, who is credited with adapting the Gandhian methods to the Pathan territory of North West Frontier in 1930–1947, was deeply impressed by the Sikh leaders like Baba Kharak Singh whom he had met in jail. For a critical review of Banerjee, see Birinder Pal Singh (2002: 316–318). For a Sikh nationalist interpretation of Gandhi's telegraphic message as an ideological weapon to keep Sikhs within the Hindu and Indian nationalist fold, see Ajmer Singh (2003: 81).

18 The Sikh Gurdwaras Act of 1925, enacted by the British government, laid down that the SGPC should consist of 120 members elected by practising religious (Kesadhari) Sikhs in quinquennial elections, the five heads of the main Sikh religious centres (*takhts*), 12 appointees of Punjab's princely states which had remained under British control during the period of Ranjit Singh's rule and 14 co-opted members (cited by Robinson 1987: 102).

19 Heeger (1971) shows that the Congress Party in Punjab was predominantly a Hindu-based party and had a strong pro-Hindu bias in its political programmes and activities. Robinson (1987: 129 and 139) and Nayar (1968: 463–464) also highlight the Hindu-bias in the Punjab Congress Party.

20 According to Spate, the Sikhs were the largest single community in only one district, Ludhiana, 'while they formed over 10 percent of the population in eight Districts west of the Beas-Sutlej, six of these were over 60 percent Muslim' (1947: 205). Robinson, quoting the report of the Indian Statutory Commission published in 1930, shows that the Sikhs constituted 11.1 per cent of Punjab's population in 1921 (1987: 113).

21 In a visit to Punjab in 1942, Jinnah made a public appeal to the Sikhs:

> Since I am on Punjab soil I should like to say that the question between the Hindus and Muslims is an all-India question and the question between the Sikhs and the Muslims is that of Pakistan; ... we have no designs on our Sikh friends. I only appeal to them to free themselves from external influences and meet us, and I am confident that we shall come to a settlement which shall reasonably satisfy our Sikh friends.
>
> (*Indian Annual Register*, 1942, Vol. II, quoted by Robinson 1987: 148)

By 'external influences', Jinnah meant the Hindu Congress leaders because the British rulers were considered neutral between the three competing communities – Hindus, Muslims and the Sikhs.

22 Jawaharlal Nehru, in a move to win over the Sikhs to the Indian side, declared in a press conference in July 1946 that 'the brave Sikhs of the Punjab were entitled to special consideration. I see nothing wrong in an area and a set-up in the North, where the Sikhs can also freely experience the glow of freedom' (*The Statesman*, 7 July 1946, quoted by Narang 1983: 70).

23 The concerns of the Sikhs regarding the gurdwaras were expressed in a memorandum given to the Cabinet Mission in 1946 by the Sikh leaders:

> out of the existing province of the Punjab a new province may be formed as an additional unit in the United India of the future in such a way that all the important Sikh *gurdwaras* and shrines may be included in it as also a substantial majority of the Sikh population in the existing province of the Punjab.
>
> (*Indian Annual Register*, 1946, Vol. I, quoted by Robinson 1987: 162)

Spate (1947: 209) also highlights the Sikh concerns about Nankana Sahib in the negotiations leading to partition. The Sikhs' fears about their religious shrines have one similarity and one huge dissimilarity with the Serbs' fears in the 1990s about their shrines. The similarity is that the Serbs feared that if the Muslim-majority Kosovo region became independent, some of the most sacred Serbian Christian shrines would be left in Kosovo and the dissimilarity is that the Serbs are a majority religious group in Serbia in 'occupation' of the Muslim-majority Kosovo region. Sikhs, on the other hand, were a minority both in the pre-1947 and the immediate post-1947 Punjab. The Sikhs' pain about the loss of Nankana Sahib gurdwara is reflected in the daily Sikh prayer in which the Sikhs pray, among other things, for unhindered access to Nankana Sahib.

24 Had the Sikhs opted for Pakistan, they would have been about 15 per cent of Pakistan Punjab's population (Spate 1947: 210). Spate was hired as a technical adviser by a Muslim group, the Ahmaddiya community of Qadian in Gurdaspur district, to present their case before the Radcliffe Boundary Commission. He unconvincingly argues that 'to an outsider they [the Sikhs] would seem to have better prospects as such a sizeable minority in Pakistan than as a drop in the ocean of India'. He repeats the point: 'During the political crisis in the Punjab in March and April 1947 the Sikhs finally threw in their lot with Congress. I cannot help feeling that they have lacked long term vision and leadership.'

25 A better description of the linguistic reality of these areas would be to characterize them as Harayanavi speaking areas. Saxena (1996) argues that a large number of languages in North India have been denied recognition and subsumed under Hindi because of the overwhelming power of the Hindi speaking elites in India's state structure. Harayanavi is one such language that has been denied recognition. I am thankful to Prof. Satya Pal Gautam of Jawaharlal Nehru University, New Delhi, for drawing my attention to the aspect of Harayanavi language in this context. For a case study of the failure of a movement for due recognition of one North Indian language, Maithili, see Brass (1974, Part II). Brass shows that the Hindi movement has successfully 'swallowed' Maithili.

26 For a study of Sikh politics as a minority community in the pre-1966 Punjab, see Nayar (1966).

27 Pritam Singh, a retired civil servant of the Punjab government, comments: 'A number of states had been reorganized on [a] linguistic basis but Punjab was the only parent state which was deprived of its capital and control over river waters. All this gave rise to a "Deprivation Syndrome"' (P. Singh 1997: 25). 'In order to avoid confusion between those works written by this retired civil servant Pritam Singh and those written by me, I refer to this Pritam Singh as P. Singh henceforth and in the bibliography.

28 A part of the post-1947 Punjab, which covered the area under the Sikh princely states and was called Patiala and East Punjab States Union (PEPSU), had the status of a state in the Indian Union. PEPSU had a non-Congress government come into power after the first general elections in 1952. This non-Congress United Front government

was a coalition of Akalis, Communists, other small parties and independents. It came into power on 21 April 1952. It was the first instance of a non-Congress government in any state of post-1947 India. It fell in March 1953 when the chief minister Gian Singh Rarewala was unseated through an election petition. Despite his request for continuing for a period of six months before getting re-elected and a request from the United Front party for continuing the government with another leader, President's Rule was proclaimed on 4 March 1953 and the Assembly was dissolved (Govt of India 1988: 184 and 187). PEPSU was merged into Punjab in 1956 (Narang 1983: 129). The dismissal of the PEPSU ministry by the centre was the first instance of dismissal of a non-Congress government in any state in post-independent India. Grewal (1998: 185) makes a factual error when he refers this to be the first instance of the President's Rule in the country. The first instance of the President's Rule in the country was in Punjab on 20 June 1951 when the central Congress leaders wanted a change in the leadership of the Punjab Congress party and used the President's Rule to facilitate this change (Govt of India 1988: 184 and 186).

29 Two studies of the pre-Naxalite communist movement in Punjab are Josh (1979) and Gurharpal Singh (1994).

30 Ajmer Singh (1992) is an example of a former Naxalite turned supporter of Sikh militancy.

31 The account of the water dispute given here is taken from Grewal (1998: 220–221).

32 One acre foot is equal to one foot of water standing over one acre of land (Dhillon 1983: 7). Dhillon was a retired Chief Engineer (Irrigation Works) of the Punjab government.

33 Grewal comments: 'In Amritsar, however, it was generally believed that this was the work of a Congress legislator' (1998: 224). This comment suggests that the Congress party was working behind the scenes to sharpen Hindu–Sikh polarization. This polarization was intended to benefit the Congress in winning over the majority Hindu vote in the rest of the country, especially north India.

34 According to Malhotra (1989: 344), Mrs Gandhi had indicated to the army chief General A. S. Vaidya on 15 January 1984 her intention regarding the army action at the Golden Temple. For further discussion on this, see Ajmer Singh (2003: 457).

35 The text of her radio broadcast is reproduced in Govt of India 1984: 105–109. Her broadcast used the emotive language of Indian nationalism: 'the unity and integrity of our motherhood is being challenged by a few who find refuge in holy shrines' (ibid.: 107). Tapan Raychaudhuri, a retired professor of Indian history at Oxford, told me and Iftikhar Malik, a South Asian studies scholar, in Oxford on 18 January 2003, that Arjun Sen Gupta, a close adviser of Mrs Gandhi, told him (Raychaudhuri) that Indira Gandhi had talked to Sen Gupta and a group of other key advisors immediately after signing the order to send the army into the Golden Temple. She is reported to have said: 'By ordering the army into the Golden Temple, I have signed my death warrant because I know that religion is a very powerful force in moving Indian people to action.' It appears that though the electoral considerations of gaining Hindu vote by this action might have been a factor in her decision, the fact that she was aware of the risk to her life indicates that more powerful historical forces were at play in making her choose a path of military confrontation with the Sikhs. Perhaps, she saw herself as a historical victim of the confrontation between Indian nationalism and Sikh nationalism. It seems that she chose to act in the interests of asserting Indian nationalism as a historical necessity. It is debatable, however, whether the interests of Indian nationalism could have been better served by seeking a negotiated settlement with the moderate Akali Sikh leadership.

36 Chopra (1985) has provided a very candid description of the anti-Sikh sentiments among North Indian Hindus around this time.

37 In an interview with Harminder Kaur (1990: 17), Lieutenant-General Krishnaswamy Sundarji, who was in overall charge of the operation (subsequently promoted to the chief of the army staff), told her that a total of ten brigades were moved into Punjab. Mary Anne Weaver in her report to the *Sunday Times* (London, 17 June 1984) observed:

> Not since independence has the army been used in such numbers – about 15,000 troops took part in the assault, with another 35,000 standing by – to put down an internal rebellion. Not even in the more ruthless days of the empire had the army been used to storm such an important religious shrine.
>
> (quoted in Dhillon 1992: 222)

38 Preface to Harminder Kaur (1990: x).

39 Two well-known journalistic accounts of the operation, which appeared soon after it, are: Mark Tully and Satish Jacob (1985), and Kuldip Nayar and Khushwant Singh (1984). Lieutenant General K. S. Brar (1993), who led the operation as a major general, has given his own version of the confrontation, basically aimed at justifying his own role. Though no scholarly study has emerged so far, two of the best accounts are by Harminder Kaur (1990) and Amiya Rao *et al.* (1985).

40 Though Nayar claims that, 'Chauhan publicly called for the murder of Mrs Gandhi on the BBC programme, *World at One*' (Nayar and Singh 1984: 106), Chauhan in an interview with me in August 1988 in London stated that he had merely predicted, on the basis of his knowledge of Sikh history, that Mrs Gandhi would be killed.

41 This remark was made by a leading BJP activist of Chandigarh during a conversation there with me in December 1984 just a few days after the election verdict. He confided in me that he was echoing the judgement of the BJP ideologue Nanaji Deshmukh. In comparison with this long-term view of the election verdict taken by the perceptive Hindu nationalists, Jaffrelot interprets this election result in a rather narrow manner: 'The election of 1984 marked a serious reverse for the BJP.' He does, however, acknowledge that the political context of 1984 proved favourable to the rise of Hindu nationalism. The BJP scored 85 seats in the 1989 elections (1996: 369). Deshmukh had already endorsed the leadership of Rajiv Gandhi even before the elections. In a document entitled 'Moments of Soul Searching' circulated on 8 November 1984 in which he articulated Hindu sentiments, he had called for 'full cooperation and sympathy' for Rajiv Gandhi. This document has been reproduced in full by Islam (2002).

42 Arjan Singh came from a wealthy landowning and politically influential Hindu Rajput family that had been close to the Nehru-led Congress party since the 1950s. He had joined Congress party in 1960 after having been granted a personal meeting with Jawaharlal Nehru where Nehru had given him 'his blessing' (Jeffrelot 2003: 80).

43 Dhillon (1992), whose account is critical of Longowal, devotes a whole chapter to the Accord called 'A Deed of Surrender'.

44 I attended his funeral, which attracted an unprecedented gathering of the Sikh population in Punjab.

45 Soon after the elections, I spoke to several members of well-established Hindu business families of Ludhiana, the most industrialized town of Punjab, about their voting pattern. Many of them said that they had voted for the Akali Dal because they believed that it was essential for political stability in Punjab that Akali government came to power. A few of them had voted for the Akali Dal candidates only once earlier in the parliamentary elections of 1977 as a protest against Indira Gandhi's emergency rule. Dhami, in a detailed study of an assembly constituency – Dhuri in

Sangrur district – gives two different explanations for the small Hindu vote in favour of the Akali candidate. One centred on the local networks:

> [A] small minority of Hindu vote has gone in favour of the Akali candidate. It has been reported that a couple of Hindu local influentials, having links with the top Akali leaders, canvassed for the Akali candidate. They represent a nucleus of small aspiring Hindu faction that wanted to be near the new power centre. And it is likely that 2 to 5 percent Hindu voters supported Akali Dal.
> (1987: 299)

The other explanation was in terms of the support of some Hindus for the moderate Longowal tendency in Akali politics: '...probably the "Sant Longowal" factor worked in the case of a few Hindu voters' (ibid.: 300) who voted for the Akali candidate. Narang (1987: 307) also noted the phenomenon of some Hindus voting for Akali candidates.

46 The sentiment among the erstwhile Sikh supporters of the Congress had also changed because of the traumatic events of 1984. One Congress candidate for an assembly constituency whom I knew personally confided to me during the election campaign that he had asked some of his close supporters to vote for the Akali candidate because he, as a Sikh, felt that the issue in the 1985 elections was not 'one of Akali versus Congress but that of Sikh *izzat* [honour] versus central government arrogance'. He obviously lost the election and the Akali candidate won with a big margin.

47 For a unique photographic presentation of this massive gathering see Patwant Singh 1989: 86–87. This photo, spread over two A3-sized pages, is an invaluable record of the gathering.

48 This was disclosed to me by a number of Punjab journalists in 1986. Dalbir Singh and Ajmer Singh had the most authentic and detailed knowledge on this subject. I am especially indebted to Ajmer Singh for sharing with me his in-depth and extensive knowledge about the Sikh militant movement.

49 This is my translation of the original from Punjabi. I have made a more detailed analysis of the Sikh militant viewpoint elsewhere and these paragraphs have been taken from there (Pritam Singh 1987: 173).

50 Sen Gupta (1985) highlights the political and security concerns of the Indian state regarding Punjab being a border state adjoining Pakistan, and Sharma (1996) provides more details regarding the support the Sikh militants received from Pakistan. Sharma, as an Indian army officer, was involved in several intelligence assignments.

51 Pettigrew (1995: 109) points out the very high degree of centralization that took place during that period:

> Law and order is normally an individual state matter but in the Punjab law and order issues were controlled by Delhi. Elimination lists were drawn up not by the Director General of Police (DGP – the highest police official in the Punjab Government) but by the Director General of Intelligence who took his orders from the Intelligence Bureau (IB). Law and order became further controlled by New Delhi with the large army presence that was despatched to the province in December 1991. At that time 38 divisions were deployed in the state.

52 A British Punjabi weekly, *Des Pardes* (31 January 2003: 9), reported Badal's statement that he had refused the Akali Dal ticket to Amarinder Singh in 1997 for the Rampura Phool constituency that Singh had asked for and that Amarinder Singh had rejected the alternative offer for Akali nomination from Bathinda constituency.

53 The annexations that took place after the annexation of Punjab were Jhansi, Nagpur and Hyderabad in 1853 and Awadh in 1856 (Fisher 1999: xvi).

3 FEDERALISM, NATIONAISM AND INDIA'S DEVELOPMENT STRATEGY: AN HISTORICAL OVERVIEW

1 Jadunath Sarkar, quoted in Govt of India 1988: 5.
2 On the annexation of Punjab see Khushwant Singh 1999a and Grewal 1998. On the annexation of Jhansi, Nagpur, Hyderabad and Awadh, see Fisher 1999. On the 'Sepoy Mutiny', see Omissi 1994 and Pritam Singh 2007d.
3 The discussion that follows on various developments regarding centre–state relations during the British rule in India is based on the evidence provided by Govt of India 1988. Any additional supporting evidence is mentioned specifically at the relevant points.
4 The Montagu-Chelmsford Report led to the enactment of this act (Govt of India 1988: 6).
5 There is a popular and widespread misconception in India and Pakistan that after the 1947 partition India founded a secular republic while Pakistan was created as an Islamic theocratic state. My view is that a closer examination of this misconception generates a more complex view of both states. I have argued in detail elsewhere that the secularism of India's constitution is severely tainted by Hindu bias in many clauses of the constitution. It is also important to remember in this context that it is only in 1976 during Indira Gandhi's Emergency rule (1975–1977) that the word 'secular' as a characterization of the Indian republic was inserted into the constitution through an amendment – the 42nd Amendment – of the constitution (Pritam Singh 2005). Regarding Pakistan, it is important to highlight that Jinnah, the founder of Pakistan, declared in his first speech after the formation of Pakistan that his vision for its future was that of a secular state. See Ali 1983 and Jalal 1985.
6 M. C. Setalvad, who later became an Attorney-General of India, observes that: 'the founding fathers were painfully conscious that the feeling of Indian/nationhood was still in the making and required to be carefully nurtured. They therefore built a constitutional structure with a powerful central Government envisaging the emergence of an indivisible and integrated India' M. C. Setalvad, 'Union and State Relations under the Indian Constitution' (Tagore Law Lectures), quoted in Govt of India 1988: 7.
7 For pioneering work that explicates the application of the concept of a state capitalist path of development to India's strategy of planned development within the framework of a mixed capitalist economy, see Bettelheim 1968, Chattopadhyay 1970 and 1992, and Desai 1959 and 1984. The Sarkaria Commission on Centre-State Relations has highlighted that the centre assumed high economic importance because governmental intervention was seen at the time of independence as vital for overcoming industrial backwardness: 'Not much had been done for economic development of the country in the pre-independence era. To catch up with the industrially developed nations, the progress that took them centuries, had to be compressed in decades' (Govt of India 1988: 8).
8 'The Constitution framers were aware that several provinces, regions or areas of India were economically and industrially far behind relatively to others. There were great economic disparities. The problem of economic integration had many facets' (Govt of India 1988: 8).

> Two questions, however, stood out: one question was how to achieve a federal, economic and fiscal integration, so that the economic policies affecting the interests of India as a whole could be carried out without putting an ever-increasing strain on the unity of India, particularly in the context of a developing economy. The second question was how to foster the development of areas which were underdeveloped without creating too many preferential or discriminative barriers.
>
> (*Automobile Transport Ltd* v. *State of Rajasthan*, AIR 1962 SC 1406, quoted in Govt of India 1988: 8)

9
> The nation was committed to a socio-economic revolution designed not only to secure the basic needs of the common man and economic unity of the country, but further to bring about a fundamental change in the structure of the Indian society in accordance with egalitarian principles. It was felt by the Constitution framers that such a transformation could be brought about only by a strong Central Government.
>
> (Govt of India 1988: 8)

10 Article 1 (Constitution 1989: 1).

11 See Appendix for a complete list of the states and Union territories. The Union territories are ruled directly by the centre – see articles 239 to 241 of the constitution.

12 The view that the country was divided into 'different states for convenience of administration' was later abandoned when the principle of organizing states by language was accepted.

13 Basu, a retired judge of the Calcutta High Court and a former member of India's Law Commission, compares the American dual citizenship system with India's single citizenship as follows:

> As a radical solution of the problem of reconciling national unity with 'state rights', the framers of the *American* Constitution made a logical division of everything essential to sovereignty and created a dual polity, with a dual citizenship, a double set of officials and a double system of Courts. [...] An *American* is a citizen not only of the state in which he resides but also of the United states, i.e., of the federation, under different conditions; and both the federal and state Governments, each independent of the other, operate, *directly* on the citizen who is thus *subject to two Governments, and owes allegiance to both*. But the *Indian* Constitution, like the Canadian, does not introduce any double citizenship, but one citizenship, viz. the citizenship of India, and birth or residence in a particular state does not confer any separate status as a citizen of that State.
>
> (Basu 1993: 56, italics original)

14 Ambedkar was the chairman of the drafting committee of the Constituent Assembly and had done a doctorate on American federalism at Columbia University (Austin 2004, Saez 2002: 30–31).

15 See Appendix for rankings of states according to population in 1991 and 2001. Uttar Pradesh (Rank 1), Bihar (Rank 2), Madhya Pradesh (Rank 6), Rajasthan (Rank 9), Haryana (Rank 15), Delhi (Rank 16), Jammu Region of Jammu and Kashmir (Rank 17) and Himachal Pradesh (Rank 18) constitute the Hindi speaking heartland of India. The ranking, based on the 1991 census, has marginally changed in 2001 as a result of the creation of three new states after 1991. The proportion of the Hindi-speaking population in India according to the 1981 Census was 39.9 per cent. The proportion of the population in other linguistic groups in India varied between 0.3 per cent (Kashmiri) to 8.2 per cent (Bengali) (Census of India 1981, quoted in Govt of Punjab 1992: 86). The proportion of the Hindi-speaking population had further increased to 41.7 per cent in the 1991 Census (Govt of Punjab 2005: 106).

16 Out of the total number of nine prime ministers in India until 1991, seven were from Uttar Pradesh, the most populous state in India. For the names and tenures of different prime ministers of India until 1991, see Basu (1993: Table X.C).

17 Article 249 of the constitution.

18 Articles 251 and 254.

19 Article 253 (my emphasis).

20 Article 248.

21 Articles 200 and 201.

22 First Proviso to Article 31 A(1), Proviso to Article 31C, Article 254(2) and 288(2) and Proviso to Article 304(b) read with Article 255 are examples of such provisions.
23 Article 249.
24 Article 252.
25 Article 74.
26 Article 352.
27 Article 353(a) for executive powers and Article 353(b) for legislative powers.
28

> A Proclamation of Emergency has the effect of converting the State List into Concurrent List; and therefore, if Parliament legislates on any subject in the state List, the State laws, to the extent of repugnancy, shall be null and void and the law made by Parliament shall prevail. The executive powers of the States also become subject to the Directions of the Union as to the manner in which these powers are to be exercised.
>
> (Govt of India 1988: 11)

29 Article 356.
30 Article 124 stipulates this procedure.
31 'The need for a strong united India which was the prime objective before the Constitution framers appears to have been the silent premise dominating the process of adjudication of Union–State disputes' (Govt of India 1988: 12).

4 FEDERAL FINANCIAL RELATIONS IN INDIA AND THEIR IMPLICATIONS FOR CENTRE–PUNJAB FINANCIAL RELATIONS

1 The constitution of India is available at the website http://indiacode.nic.in/coiweb/welcome.html. I have also used a text of the constitution published by the Eastern Book Company of Lucknow in 1989; the merit of this publication is that it provides the text of the constitution without any commentary. For a text of the constitution with a good commentary, see Bakshi (2002). All three sources have the same wording.
2 See Appendix for the list of the states and the Union territories. The administration in the states is normally run through the elected assemblies and the Union territories directly by the central government through its nominees.
3 Article 248.
4 Article 249 and Article 250.
5 Articles 251 and 254.
6 Article 253.
7 Article 280.
8 Article 281.
9 That the Planning Commission is an unconstitutional body is widely recognized in the literature on centre–state relations. In contrast with the provision for setting up of a Finance Commission, there is no provision in the constitution for setting up a Planning Commission. The Planning Commission was set up by an executive decision of the Cabinet of the central government. See Mitra (1983, 1987), Govt of India (1987), Gulati (1987) and Qureshi (1989: 49).
10 Discretionary transfers are 'transfers that are largely in the discretion of the centre ... they are very much like gifts of the centre and, therefore, the considerations which govern their dispensation can be much more political than economic or objective' (George 1987: 247). See also: Gulati (1987: 17); Lakdawala (1989: 191).
11 'Both statutory and at least a major part of Plan transfers ... are supposed to be governed by clearly stated criteria, whatever they be, as spelt out from time to time, departures from which are not easily defensible' (George 1987: 247).
12 Justice Qureshi's interpretation of Article 282 is that 'the power to give grants under

Article 282 is an 'emergency power' to be used in exceptional circumstances only' (Qureshi 1989: 50).

13 Gulati's estimates of these transfers as reported in the introduction to his book (Gulati 1987: 17) are the same as George's (George 1987: 248) though Gulati does not give the amounts of the different transfers. West Bengal government estimates differ from the estimates of George and Gulati for the period 1979–84 and therefore for the whole period 1951–84. West Bengal estimates for 1951–84 are: statutory = 40.4 per cent, plan = 30.2 per cent and discretionary = 29.4 per cent. See Govt of West Bengal (1987: 603).

14 Article 282 on 'Expenditure defrayable by the Union or a State out of its revenue' states: 'The Union or a State may make any grants for any public purpose, notwithstanding that the purpose is one with respect to which Parliament or the Legislature of the State, as the case may be, may make laws.' There are two diametrically opposite ways in which this Article has been interpreted. One interpretation sees it as containing a justification for the free hand that the centre or a state may use in the transfer of funds. The other interpretation sees it as merely providing an exception to the general rule whereby transfer of funds must have a direct constitutional legitimacy provided by Parliamentary sanction of the recommendations of the Finance Commission (Article 275). In other words, on the second interpretation, Article 282 must not be used to justify the abrogation of law in the matters of transfer of funds. The fact that defenders of discretionary transfers can and *do* make successful use of Article 282, illustrates how interpretations can be made to suit political expediency.

15 Punjab government memorandum to the Commission on Centre–State Relations (Sarkaria Commission) (Govt of Punjab 1987: 936–937). Hanson (1966: 321) notes that 'the principle on which Central assistance to State plans is allocated has never been made clear'. See also Khatkhate and Bhatt (1987: 48), who observe that 'no definite criteria are laid down by the Planning Commission with regard to Central assistance to the states' and that:

> [t]he States have adhered to the pattern of expenditure as proposed by the Planning Commission even when it is not suited to their needs [...] The Central Government has got an instrument in the Plan and Plan assistance to introduce a national bias in State policies.

16 Views expressed by Prof. K. S. Gill, who was Chairman, Perspective Planning Division, Planning Division, Government of India, for many years during Nehru's and Indira Gandhi's prime ministership, in a recorded interview with me in New Delhi on 29 December 1989. Prof Gill was also Vice-Chairman, Punjab Planning Board in the late 1970s, and Chairman, of the Punjab Government Committee, which prepared its memorandum to the Commission on Centre-State Relations.

17 I am very thankful to the following IAS officers for sharing with me their views regarding the inner culture of the IAS: Pawan Chopra and Chitra Chopra (both from the Rajasthan Cadre), Jivtesh Singh Maini (Punjab Cadre), Sarat Nanda and Umesh Nanda (both from the Haryana Cadre) and Surjit Mitra (from the Orissa Cadre). All these officers have worked at the centre also.

18 For example, see West Bengal (Govt of West Bengal 1987: 603), Punjab (Govt of Punjab 1987: 939), Karnataka (Govt of Karnataka 1987: 234) and Tamil Nadu (Govt of Tamil Nadu 1987: 498–499) for strong criticisms of the functioning of the Finance Commissions. Most state governments neither criticized nor appreciated the Finance Commissions though almost all the state governments were critical of the Planning Commission transfers and that of discretionary transfers through central government ministries. Haryana is perhaps the only state government which considered that 'the

agency of the Finance Commission and Planning Commission are adequate' (Govt of Haryana 1987: 183).

19 Punjab government memorandum (Govt of India 1987: 907).

20 Ibid.

21 Punjab government memorandum (Govt of India 1987: 908–909).

22 Ibid.

23 Ibid.

24 The total outstanding central loan to all the 25 states on 31 March 1989 was Rs.56,051.92 crores – Rs.560.5192 billions (for 1990–95) (Govt of India 1989: Annexure IX.1 and Annexure IX.2, 89–90). This amount constitutes about 63 per cent of the total debt of all the state governments, estimated to be Rs.89,461 crores (Govt of India 1989: 35). The exchange rate in 1989 was £1 = Rs.35 approx. and it is £1 = Rs.82 approx. at present (January 2008).

25 States invest not only in:

> government sector investments (school, roads, bridges, etc.) but also in ... departmental and non-departmental enterprises (irrigation works, State Electricity Boards, State Road Transport Corporations and a large number of other enterprises) ... in most cases, (there) is extremely poor performance of the enterprises.
>
> (Qureshi 1989: 35–36)

26 This view is articulated in the Punjab Government Memorandum (see Govt of India 1987: 910). The word 'state' in 'state-interventionist path of development' connotes an abstract notion of state.

27 Punjab government memorandum (Govt of India 1987: 912).

28 Ibid.

29 Tamil Nadu government memorandum (Govt of India 1987: 516).

30 Tamil Nadu government memorandum (Govt of India 1987: 516).

31 For Punjab, the Ninth Finance Commission observed that: 'Special loans to the tune of Rs.2,300 crores were given to Punjab during 1984–89'. One of the factors necessitating these loans was identified as 'the high cost of combating terrorism'. 'The special circumstances prevailing in the state' are located as a factor in explaining that 'the state certainly has had to bear a high burden in terms of expenditure on law and order'. The various terms used – 'special circumstances', 'special case', 'special loan', 'combating terrorism' and 'expenditure on law and order' – are various euphemisms used by the Commission to evade mentioning the conflict between the Punjabi nationalist movement and the Indian state representing Indian nationalism. See Qureshi (1989: 39) for the data cited here. The political economy of the nationalist conflicts has been discussed in Pritam Singh (1999a).

32 A leading human rights activist has observed a split in the Indian nationalist elites' self-consciousness regarding the police repression in nationalist and other forms of conflict. An analysis of 'editorials in newspapers, letters to the editors, political commentaries, speeches by politicians at public meetings and statements by sundry others' reported double standards in their response to violation of human rights committed by the Indian security forces in repressing nationalist and other forms of conflict:

> The partisan behaviour of these forces during communal riots, or the repression on the rural poor can perhaps be more easily discussed in newspaper columns and political platforms since they do not carry overtones of 'treason', even though they are stained with the same bloody trail of tortures and massacres. Punjab and Kashmir, however, are different.
>
> (Banerjee 1990: 1193)

33 Punjab government memorandum (Govt of India 1987: 913).
34 Justice Qureshi's note of dissent (Qureshi 1989: 52).
35 These conclusions are the same, except for minor changes, as made in the Punjab government memorandum (Govt of India 1987: 918).
36 Chapter III, 'Assessment of States' Revenue Receipts and Expenditure' (Qureshi 1989). Barbara Harriss-White has drawn my attention to low returns also from the commercial activities of the states' trading corporations. See also Harriss (1983, 1991).
37 The source of statistical information on these instruments discussed below is Punjab government memorandum (Govt of India 1987), unless otherwise stated. I am thankful to Professor K. S. Gill who clarified and elaborated many points discussed in this section. Prof. Gill was the author of the Punjab government memorandum submitted to the Commission on Centre–State Relations (Govt of India 1987).
38 Even if a public sector undertaking is run by a state government, any foreign assistance to it is channelled through the central government. See Cassen (1994), Cassen and Joshi (1995). I am thankful to Professor Robert Cassen, the former Director of Queen Elizabeth House, University of Oxford, for a very fruitful discussion on this subject.
39 Punjab government memorandum (Govt of India 1987: 921).
40 Punjab government memorandum (Govt of India 1987: 922).
41 Punjab government memorandum (Govt of India 1987: 923).
42 For details, see Tamil Nadu government memorandum (Govt of India 1987: 509–515).
43 This point is highlighted in the Tamil Nadu government memorandum (Govt of India 1987: 508–509).
44 The four macro level studies of Punjab economy published during the 1980s were Johar and Khanna (1983), Mehra (1983), P. Singh (1983) and Lekhi and Singh (1986). Only one book, Johar and Khanna (1983), carries an article, the only one, on this subject: 'centre–State Financial Relations in India with special reference to Punjab'. Six prominent books with a focus on Punjab politics published in the 1980s were Dalip Singh (1981); Kumar *et al.* (1984); Amrik Singh (1985); Samiuddin (1985); Deol (1986); and Gopal Singh (1987). In all of them, the issue of centre–Punjab financial relations is either not taken up at all or relegated to marginality. None of the well-known books on Punjab published outside India during the 1980s carries even a sub-chapter on centre–Punjab financial relations. See Bains (1985); Jarnail Singh (1985); Mirza *et al.* (1985); Iqbal Singh (1986); Bains (1988); Masood and Stockdale (1988); Sims (1988). The most influential academic journal in India, *Economic and Political Weekly*, has not had a single paper on centre–Punjab financial relations though it has otherwise carried a number of excellent papers on other aspects of Punjab's political economy. The academic journals in the West (*Asia Survey*, *Pacific Affairs* and *Journal of Commonwealth and Comparative Politics*), which otherwise have published excellent papers on Punjab, have not carried a single paper on centre–Punjab financial relations. The only serious work which initiated the analysis on this subject is Punjab government memorandum to the Commission on Centre–State Relations, which published its report in 1987. But even this document focused more on centre–state financial relations in general than on Punjab. Of the 39 tables of statistical data, only two tables related to Punjab specifically.
45 Some articles articulating this view are included in an anthology of essays brought out by a Maoist Punjabi nationalist group (see Mali 1989).
46 This view was articulated during the troubled decade of the 1980s, more than by anyone else, by three journalists, Giri Lal Jain, Arun Shourie and N. C. Menon (who represent a complex amalgam of Indian and Hindu nationalism) in the editorials of

The Times of India, *The Indian Express* and *The Hindustan Times*, respectively. Though there is not even a single scholarly paper endorsing this view about centre–Punjab financial relations, there are a few papers which by their argument that inter-state inequalities have increased since Indian national independence, tend to give the impression that Punjab has had a favourable treatment from the centre. See Ansari 1987; Gulati and George 1987.

47 The data on per capita income of Indian states between 1949 and 1987 are presented in Table 5.3 of the next chapter.

48 Though the papers did not give the year to which this figure related, but from the context of the discussion it appeared to be 1988.

49 When the report of the Eleventh Finance Commission came out in 2000, there was a concerted effort by the high income states against its recommendations, which favoured the poorer states. The richer states (Maharashtra, Gujarat, Punjab, Haryana, Andhra Pradesh and Tamil Nadu) got together under the leadership of Andhra Pradesh chief minister N. Chandrababu Naidu to argue that the rich states 'can no longer pay for the cause of regional equality' (Saran 2000: 19) while the central government felt that it was its 'federal duty to strive for even development across India' (Gardner 2000). See also Tavleen Singh (2000) and Gardner (2001) for this new politico-economic development in India which symbolized a critique of the dominant central ideology of reducing inter-state inequalities for the cause of 'national unity'.

50 See Kudaisya (2006) for a good politico-historical account and useful deployment of the concept of Hindustani and Hindi heartland.

51 Punjab government memorandum to the Commission on Centre–State Relations (Govt of India 1987: 909).

5 CENTRE–STATE RELATIONS IN AGRICULTURE AND THEIR IMPLICATIONS FOR PUNJAB AGRICULTURE

1 For a discussion of the centre's power in the financing of state projects on water management, see Bhargava 1976: 228–230.

2 I have elsewhere examined in greater depth the link between the Hindu bias and the centralization bias in India's constitution; see Pritam Singh 2005.

3 Kessinger (1974) is a very fascinating long range historical micro-level study of rural change in Punjab. The strength of this study is its time-scale, which covers both the regime types (colonial and national), but its weakness is that by focusing on only one village, it is unable to address the issues concerning the macro-level development trends in Punjab economy and society.

4 The limitations of space here do not allow me to elaborate fully on all the components of this formulation. Some useful references for further study are: B. Chandra (1966) on historical background; Bettelheim (1968), Johnson (1979) and Chakravarty (1989) on self-reliance; Prasad (1989), especially Chapter 11, and Bagchi (1988) on regional development; and Bhagwati (1992) on poverty reduction. Bardhan (1989) and Khilnani (1999) also take up some of these themes. Khilnani's account highlights the importance of the goals of self-reliance and political sovereignty in the Nehruvian strategy of development. For a recent discussion on this issue in the context of the importance of the public sector versus the private sector in alternative paradigms of development in India, see Ram Mohan (2005).

5 According to Professor S. S. Johl (2005), 'In the mid-1960s, the country was importing huge quantities of foodgrains. In 1964–65, India imported around 13 million tons of foodgrains.' Johl is the Deputy Chairman of the State Planning Board, Govern-

ment of Punjab. I am grateful to him for giving me two extended interviews during one of his visits to the UK.

6 M. L. Dantwala was a leading Indian government economic policy planner. See also Dantwala (1976). Prasad, an Indian Economic Service officer who worked in the Planning Commission and the various key central government economic ministries, captures the gravity of the situation:

> The need to increase foodgrains production was so urgent that the HYV [High Yielding Varieties] Programme was implemented in suitable areas with the help of farmers who could afford the package deal. According to M. L. Dantwala, the Government had to grow more food as quickly as possible, irrespective of where it was grown and by whom.
>
> (2005: 53)

7 C. Subramaniam, when questioned about why the Green Revolution policies were adopted when they were, replied, 'Our political survival was dependent on food production' (Kohli's interview with C. Subramaniam, Madras, 11 March 1979, quoted in Kohli 1989: 78). Similarly, Indira Gandhi, who was the prime minister at that time, later commenting on the adoption of the Green Revolution strategy, noted: 'When it [the Green Revolution strategy] had been evolved, it was a question of sheer survival: It was hardly time to think of anything except increasing production' (*Hindustan Times*, 19 April 1968 quoted by Kohli 1989). I. Ali points out that political survival was also the main motivating force behind the British colonial state's intervention in Punjab agriculture:

> Ultimately it depended on the state structure whether it wished to utilize the potential of colonization for economic development or distort it for purposes of its own survival. One of the roots of underdevelopment in the Punjab lay in the fact that the latter option was adopted.
>
> (1989: 23)

8 Subramaniam was awarded India's highest civilian honour, the Bharat Ratna (Jewel of India), in 1998 in recognition of his historic contribution to the country's success in achieving the goal of food self-sufficiency. When he died on 7 November 2000 at the age of 90, he was widely hailed as the 'father' of the Green Revolution (*The Economist*, 2000).

9 On the policy shift, see Chakravarty (1989) and P. N. Dhar (1989); on details of the politico-economic pressures on the Indian state, see Sims (1988) and Frankel (1978). It is interesting and instructive to note that if self-sufficiency and the quick rise in food production dictated Indian nationalist state's intervention in Punjab agriculture, self-sufficiency and the quick rise in horse and camel production for militaristic imperial needs was one of the key objectives that dictated the colonial state's intervention in Punjab agriculture. I. Ali writes:

> The central Government stressed the need to make India independent of overseas supplies of horses, and to create a readily available reserve of country-bred animals for an emergency. It pointed out that Jhelum colony had become the most important area for imperial horse breeding in India, but the numbers produced were still inadequate to meet the annual requirements of British cavalry regiments stationed there. It therefore wanted as large an area as possible to be devoted to horse and mule breeding in the new [Lower Bari Doab] colony.
>
> (I. Ali 1989: 30–31)

Ali points out that in its communications with the provincial Punjab government, 'The Government of India expressed concern over the increasingly insecure foreign sources of cavalry remounts. In Argentina, Australia, Canada and the United States the production of riding horses was said to be rapidly declining' (ibid.: 31). Ali further points out that in the 'two large colonisation projects, Jhelum and Lower Bari Doab' where horse-breeding operations dominated '...*the aim was to make India a self-sufficient producer of cavalry horses*' (ibid.: 135, italics added). He shows that the needs of the colonial state led to distortions in the developmental pattern of Punjab's agriculture. 'In a period when the horse was being rapidly displaced as a military animal by technological change, the British in South Asia began diverting extensive agricultural resources for its production and upkeep' (ibid.: 135). Ali also describes the preferential treatment given by the colonial state to the Bilochis, the camel-owning tribe, over the Janglis, the cattle-owning tribe in order to encourage breeding and upkeep of camels which was 'an animal of much importance to military transport' (ibid.: 123–129).

10 Large sections of the Punjabi peasantry, from the districts that constitute the present Indian Punjab, had been induced during the colonial period to migrate to the canal colony districts. I. Ali points out that 'In terms of population densities ... the canal colonies had a profound impact on demographic levels in the Western Punjab' (1989: 61). Percentage rises well above the provincial average for 1891–1941 were recorded in the districts of Jhang, Lahore, Layallpur, Montgomery, Multan, Shahpur and Skeikhupura. Migration took place from high population density districts, such as Amritsar, Jullundur and Ludhiana to the low density canal colony districts. By 1941, the canal colony districts could no longer be regarded as the sparsely populated districts that they were in the nineteenth century.

11 In an interview with me Professor S. S. Johl reiterated this observation.

12 Though Ajit Singh (1983: 46–48) also emphasizes the slower growth of industry in Punjab in comparison with its agriculture, he provides a slightly favourable view of the role of the Punjab state government in its effort to develop Punjab's industrial sector. I discuss this aspect in greater detail in the next chapter on industry.

13 This anti-industry ruralization pressure has also been observed in the Punjab–centre conflict in Pakistani Punjab. Farhan Bokhari in his report 'Punjabi Farmers Seek New Deal' (1991) wrote that:

> [the] Pakistani Federal government may find it increasingly difficult to sell its agricultural policy to Punjab. [...] Mr. Mohammad Azad Cheema, a provincial legislator and secretary-general of the Chamber of Agriculture in Lahore, says that the government must provide new incentives to agriculture, under the same terms as to the industrial sector.

14 Govt of Punjab (1992: 116), and Economic and Political Weekly Research Foundation (1995: 3,323).

15 These observations for the 1979–84 period are based on my interpretation of the data provided in Table 5 of Prasad 1989: 114.

16 See also Johar and Parminder Singh (1983: 11–12) and Dhillon (1990: 5) for observations regarding area under cultivation.

17 Even of this 'forest' area, most of it was manmade plantations of eucalyptus. See D. S. Kang 1982: 198.

18 See Gill and Singhal (1984), Hardip Singh (1987: 32), Sarkaria Commission Report (Govt of India 1988: 442–444).

19 RCPI *Punjab Da Kisani Masla* (in Punjabi) [The Question of the Peasantry in Punjab], 13 March 1984, quoted by Hardip Singh (1987: 33).

20 Computed from the data provided in Table 6.16 and Table 6.18 in the *Statistical Abstract of Punjab 1991* (Govt of Punjab 1992: 175–177).

21 Computed from the data in Table 6.3 in the *Statistical Abstract of Punjab 1991* (Govt of Punjab 1992: 141).

22 *Financial Times*, 4 September 1992, report on developments in international wheat trade in the USA, Australia, the EC, Canada, Argentina and Egypt. See also D. S. Sidhu (1979).
23 Also see papers on Punjab agriculture by Gill (1983), Johar and Parminder Singh (1983), Johar and Raikhy (1983), Grewal and Rangi (1983) in Johar and Khanna (1983); for the views of a senior Punjabi administrator with special interest in Punjab agriculture, see Gill (1987).
24 Prof Harjinder Singh Shergill, of the Department of Economics, Punjab University, Chandigarh, has in personal correspondence with me argued that, while the present cropping pattern in Punjab (especially the growing of rice, which requires intensive water use) might have serious environmental consequences in the long run, the shift away from these food crops would economically ruin the Punjab peasantry. His argument against growing non-food crops is that there is no price incentive and marketing facility for non-food crops. Prof B. P. Singh, of the Department of Sociology, Punjabi University, Patiala, has in correspondence with me disagreed with Prof Shergill's views. Prof Singh believes that, in the interests of sustainability, Punjabi farmers should move away from food crops (especially rice) even if this results in short-term economic losses. Despite serious differences in the approaches of these two serious and well-meaning scholars, about the feasibility and desirability of the diversification of Punjab's crops, both remain trapped in ways of thinking that do not see a non-agrarian and industrial future for Punjab.

6 CENTRE–STATE RELATIONS IN INDUSTRY AND THEIR IMPLICATIONS FOR THE PATTERN OF INDUSTRIAL DEVELOPMENT IN PUNJAB

1 Dhar's paper was first published as a three-part article titled 'The Logic of Development' in the Indian daily *The Times of India* on 29 November, 2 and 3 December 1968. This paper, with a slightly different title 'centre–state Relations in the Field of Industrial Development' is included in the volume edited by Jain *et al.* (1972).
2 According to the Sarkaria Commission, this act has been amended ten times (Govt of India 1988: 408).
3 The Industrial Policy Resolutions of 1970, 1973, 1980 and 1981 were merely variants of the 1956 Resolution (Govt of Orissa 1987: 918–919).
4 The data source was Government of Punjab report on the Factories Act 1950, which was quoted by Khanna (1983). According to the Factory Act, all factories employing more than ten workers and using mechanical power were covered in the study.
5 The data for 1966 and 1992 are presented in Table 6.8. The figure for 1990 is calculated from *Statistical Abstract of Punjab 1993* (Govt of Punjab 1994: 379).
6 B. Sarkar, then economic adviser to the Government of Punjab, mentioned in the preface to the *Statistical Abstract of Punjab 1992* (Govt of Punjab 1993) that the provision of the comparative data on the small-scale sector and the medium- and large-scale sector in Punjab industry was a new feature being added to the *Statistical Abstract of Punjab 1992*.
7 In all federations, the issue of outflow of bank savings from one federal unit to another generates discontentment against the federal institutions facilitating such outflow. Before the break-up of the Soviet Union, Lithuania had demanded compensation from Moscow for all the bank deposits of Lithuanian citizens which 'have not been entirely invested within the regional boundaries and thus have been responsible for development elsewhere' (Bookman 1991: 55). At the height of the violent confrontation between the Sikh militants and the centre, the militants had threatened 'action' against the banks participating in the transfer of Punjabi bank savings to

other states in India. See article in *The Times of India* (Anon 1991). The Government of Punjab has also consistently pointed towards this drain of resources from Punjab. For example, 'Low credit-deposit ratio indicates that deposits mobilized in Punjab are being increasingly invested outside the State' (Govt of Punjab 1993–94: 72).

8 No federation can be free from the problem of differential impact of a federally determined monetary policy on different units in a federation. For example, Robert Bourassa, premier of the Quebec province in Canada, protested against the high interest rate policy pursued by the Canadian federal government. According to Bourassa, high interest rates adversely affected the Quebec province's plans to increase investment, production and exports. Furthermore, high interest rates caused an 'artificial' rise in the Canadian dollar with respect to other currencies, further reducing Quebec's ability to compete in the global economy (interview conducted by *The Wall Street Journal* and published on 17 August 1990, cited in Bookman 1991: 42).

9 Pandit made one error in making this classification. He included 'agricultural implements' also in the category of footloose industries in Punjab (Pandit 1985: 60). Agricultural implements were clearly oriented to the rural market in Punjab and cannot therefore be included in the category of footloose industrial products in Punjab.

10 I was presented a book by the Bhogal family on the life of Mohinder Singh Bhogal (see Phul 1989) which described vividly the enterprising efforts of Mr Bhogal in setting up his business without much help from the state. The book concludes very aptly with an advice from Mr Bhogal that young men wanting to succeed in industry must follow a philosophy of self-help: '...develop the habit of hard work right from the beginning ... every individual must learn to work with his own hands and acquire some practical skill. This saves him from dependence on others...' (ibid.: 231).

BIBLIOGRAPHY

Ahluwalia, I. S., 1985. *Industrial Growth in India*. Delhi: Oxford University Press.

Ali, I., 1989. *The Punjab under Imperialism, 1885–1947*. Delhi: Oxford University Press.

Ali, I., 1999. 'Sikh Settlers in the Western Punjab during British Rule'. In: Pritam Singh and S. S. Thandi, eds *Punjabi Identity in a Global Context*. New Delhi: Oxford University Press, 1999, pp. 139–151.

Ali, S., 1989. 'Delhi's Diktat: States Grow Restless as the Centre's Grip Tightens'. *Far Eastern Economic Review*, Vol. 144, 6 April, 19–21.

Ali, T., 1983. *Can Pakistan Survive?: The Death of a State*. New York: Penguin.

Amnesty International, 1998. *The Long March to Freedom: Some of the People Whose Ideas, Writings and Actions Have Played a Part in the Struggle for Human Rights and Justice Around the World Across the Centuries*. London: Amnesty International.

Anderson, M. R. and Guha, S., eds, 1998. *Changing Concepts of Rights and Justice in South Asia*. Delhi: Oxford University Press.

Anon., 1991. 'Militants Impose Code on Banks', *The Times of India*, 11 August.

Anon., 2005. 'Iraq: A Nearly Final Constitution'. *The Economist*, 3–9 September, 55–56.

Anon., 2005a. 'Russia and its Regions: Beyond Siberia'. *The Economist*, 3–9 September, 39–40.

Ansari, M. M., 1987. 'Financing of the States Plan: A Perspective for Regional Development'. In: I. S. Gulati. *Centre-State Budgetary Transfers*. Delhi: Oxford University Press, 1987, pp. 211–223.

Austin, G., 2004. *The Indian Constitution: Cornerstone of a Nation*. 8th impression. New Delhi: Oxford University Press. First published in 1966.

Azad, N., ed., 1983. *Punjab Di Arthikita* [The Economy of Punjab]. Patiala: Punjabi University.

Azad, N. S., 1980. *Small Peasantry in Punjab: An Analysis of Production Conditions*. PhD thesis, Punjabi University, Patiala.

Bagchi, A. K., ed., 1988. *Economy, Society and Polity: Essays in the Political Economy of Indian Planning*. Calcutta: Oxford University Press.

Bains, A. S., 1988. *Siege of the Sikhs* [orig. Punjabi title: *Sikhan di Gherabandi*]. Toronto: New Magazine Publishing Company.

Bains, A. S., 1996. 'Punjab Situation'. In: P. V. Rao, ed. *Symphony of Freedom: Papers on Nationality Question*. Hyderabad: All India Peoples Resistance Forum, 1996.

Bains, H., 1985. *The Call of the Martyrs: On the Crises in India and the Punjab Situation in the Punjab*. London: Workers Publishing House.

Bakshi, P. M., 2002. *The Constitution of India: with Selective Comments*. 5th edition. Delhi: Universal Law Publishing Co.

Bal, S. S., ed., 1979. *Proceedings of the Punjab History Conference Twelfth Session, March 17–19, 1978*. Patiala: Punjabi University.

Bal, S. S., 1986. *British Administration in the Punjab and Its Aftermath*. Amritsar: Guru Nanak Dev University.

Ballantyne, T., 1999. 'Resisting the "Boa Constrictor" of Hinduism: the Khalsa and the Raj'. *International Journal of Punjab Studies*, 6(2), July–December, 195–215.

Ballard, R., 1999. 'Panth, Kismet, Dharam te Qaum: Continuity and Change in Four Dimensions of Punjabi Religion'. In: Pritam Singh and S. S. Thandi, eds *Punjabi Identity in a Global Context*. New Delhi: Oxford University Press, 1999, pp. 7–37.

Banerjee, D. and Ghosh, A., 1988. 'Indian Planning and Regional Disparity in Growth'. In: A. K. Bagchi, ed. *Economy, Society and Polity: Essays in the Political Economy of Indian Planning*. Calcutta: Oxford University Press, 1988, pp. 104–165.

Banerjee, H., 1992. 'Bandi Bir'. In: Harbans Singh, ed. *The Encyclopaedia of Sikhism Vol. 1*. Patiala: Punjabi University, 1992, pp. 275–276.

Banerjee, M., 2000. *The Pathan Unarmed: Opposition and Memory in the North West Frontier*. Santa Fe: School of American Research Press.

Banerjee, S., 1990. 'Mid-Summer Madness Over "Human Rights"'. *Economic and Political Weekly*, 2 June, pp. 1,193–1,196.

Bardhan, P., 1989. *The Political Economy of Development in India*. Oxford: Basil Blackwell.

Barratt, R. N., ed., 1982. *International Dimensions of the Environmental Crisis*. Colorado, Boulder: Westview Press.

Barrier, N. G. and Dusenbery, V. A., eds, 1989. *The Sikh Diaspora: Migration and The Experience Beyond Punjab*. Delhi: Chanakya Publications.

Basu, D. D., 1965. *Commentary on the Constitution of India*, Vol. 4. 5th edition. Calcutta: S. C. Sarkar & Sons.

Basu, D. D., 1993. *Introduction to the Constitution of India*. 15th edition. New Delhi; Prentice Hall of India.

Bawa, R. S. and Raikhy, P. S., eds, 2000. *Punjab Economy: Emerging Issues*. Amritsar: Guru Nanak Dev University.

Bettelheim, C., 1968. *India Independent*. London: MacGibbon & Kee.

Bhagwati, J., 1992. *India's Economy: The Shackled Giant*. Unpublished version of the Radhakrishnan Lectures, Oxford.

Bhagwati, J. and Desai, P., 1972. *India: Planning for Industrialisation*. Delhi: Oxford University Press.

Bhalla, G. S. and Chadha, G. K., 1982. 'Green Revolution and Small Peasant: A Study of Income Distribution'. *Economic and Political Weekly*, 22 May.

Bhalla, G. S., Chadha, G. K., Kashyap, S. P. and Sharma, R. K., 1990. *Agricultural Growth and Structural Changes in the Punjab Economy: An Input–Output Analysis*, Washington, D.C.: International Food Policy Research Institute.

Bhambri, C. P., 1985. 'The Failure to Accommodate'. In: Amrik Singh, ed. *Punjab in Indian Politics: Issues and Trends*. Delhi: Ajanta, 1985, pp. 203–212.

Bharadwaj, K., 1982. Regional Differentiation in India: A Note. *Economic and Political Weekly*, XVII (14, 15, 16), April, 605–614.

Bhargava, M., 1976. *Inter-Governmental Financial Relations in India Since Independence*. Allahabad: Chaitanya Publishing House.

Bhattacharya, B. B. and Sakthivel, S., 2004. 'Regional Growth and Disparity in India: Comparison of Pre- and Post-Reform Decades'. *Economic and Political Weekly*, 6 March, 1,071–1,077.

Bhattacharya, M., 1992. The Mind of the Founding Fathers. In: N. Mukarji and B. Arora, eds, 1992. *Federalism in India: Origins and Development*. New Delhi: Vikas Publishing House, pp. 87–104.

Birch, A. H., 1989. *Nationalism and National Integration*. London: Unwin Hyman.

Blaut, J. M., 1987. *The National Question: Decolonising the Theory of Nationalism*. London and New Jersey: Zed Books.

Blough, R., 1962. 'Fiscal Aspects of Federalism'. In: A. W. MacMahon. *Federalism: Mature and Emergent*. New York: Russell & Russell, 1962, pp. 384–405.

Bokhari, F., 1991. 'Punjabi Farmers Seek New Deal'. *Financial Times*, 5 November.

Bookman, M. Z., 1991. *The Political Economy of Discontinuous Development: Regional Disparities and Inter-regional Conflict*. New York: Praeger Publishers.

Bose, S., 1998. 'Hindu Nationalism and the Crisis of the Indian State: A Theoretical Perspective'. In: S. Bose and A. Jalal, eds *Nationalism, Democracy and Development*. Delhi: Oxford University Press, 1998, pp. 104–164.

Brar, K. S., 1993. *Operation Blue Star: The True Story*. Delhi: UBS Publishers.

Brass, P., 1974. *Language, Religion and Politics in North India*. London: Cambridge University Press.

Brown, K., ed., 1999. *Sikh Art and Literature*. London: Routledge.

Byres, T., 1994. *State and Development Planning in India*. Delhi: Oxford University Press.

Cassen, R. and Associates. 1994. *Does Aid Work?* Oxford: Clarendon Press.

Cassen, R. and Joshi, V., eds, 1995. *India: The Future of Economic Reforms*. Delhi: Oxford University Press.

Centre for Monitoring Indian Economy, 1990. *Basic Statistics Relating to the Indian Economy*, Vol. 2: States, Bombay: Centre for Monitoring Indian Economy, September.

Chadha, G. K., 1986. *The State and Rural Economic Transformation: The Case of Punjab 1950–85*. Delhi: Sage Publications.

Chakravarty, S., 1989. *Development Planning: The Indian Experience*. Delhi: Oxford University Press.

Chandra, B., 1966. *Rise and Growth of Economic Nationalism in India: Economic Policies of Indian National Leadership, 1880–1905*. New Delhi: Peoples Publishing House.

Chattopadhyay, P., 1970. 'State Capitalism in India', *Monthly Review*, 21(10), March, 14–39. Also included in: S. A. Shah, ed. *Towards National Liberation: Essays on political economy of India*. Montreal: np, 1973, pp. 56–76.

Chattopadhyay, P., 1992. 'India's Capitalist Industrialisation: An Introductory Outline'. In: B. Berberoglu, ed. *Class, State and Development in India*. Delhi: Sage, 1992, pp. 141–156.

Chaudhry, D. R., 1994. 'Punjab–Haryana Disputes'. In: Gopal Singh, ed. *Punjab: Past, Present and Future*. Delhi: Ajanta, 1994, pp. 400–411.

Chaudhuri, P., 1971. 'India: Objectives, Achievements and Constraints'. In: P. Chaudhuri, ed. *Aspects of Indian Economic Development*. London: George Allen and Unwin, 1971, pp. 17–91.

Chopra, P., 1985. 'A Turning Point for Sikhs'. In: Amrik Singh, ed. *Punjab in Indian Politics: Issues and Trends*. Delhi: Ajanta, 1995, pp. 331–352.

Chopra, V. D., Mishra, R. K. and Singh, N., 1984. *Agony of Punjab*. Delhi: Patriot Publishers.

Constituent Assembly Debates, 1949. Vol. XI, 21 November, 1949. Delhi.

Constitution, 1989. *The Constitution of India*, 7th (October) edition, incorporating Bills of 63rd to 65th Amendments. Delhi/Lucknow: Eastern Book Company.

Dantwala, M. L., 1976. 'Agricultural Policy Since Independence'. *Indian Journal of Agricultural Economics*, 31(4), October–December 1976.

Dantwala, M. L., 1985. 'Technology, Growth and Equity in Agriculture'. In: J. Mellor and G. Desai, eds *Agricultural Change and Rural Poverty*. Baltimore: John Hopkins University, 1985, pp. 110–123.

Darling, M. L., 1947. *The Punjab Peasant in Prosperity and Debt*. 4th edition. Bombay, New York: India Branch, Oxford University Press. First published in 1925.

Datta, B., 1987. 'An Evaluation of the Seventh Award'. In: I. S. Gulati, ed. *Centre–State Budgetary Transfers*. Delhi: Oxford University Press, 1987, pp. 154–176.

Davey, K., 1983. *Financing Regional Government: International Practices and their Relevance to the Third World*. New York: John Wiley & Sons.

Deol, H., 2000. *Religion and Nationalism in India: The Case of the Punjab*. London: Routledge.

Deol, J. S., 1986. *State Politics in India (with special reference to Punjab)*. Jalandhar: New Academic Publishing Co.

Desai, A. R., 1959. *Social Background of Indian Nationalism*. Bombay: Popular Prakashan.

Desai, A. R., 1984. *India's Path of Development: A Marxist Approach*. Bombay: Popular Prakashan.

Desai, M., 1975. 'India: Emerging Contradictions of Slow Capitalist Development'. In: Robin Blackburn, ed. *Explosions in a Subcontinent*. London: Penguin, 1975, pp. 11–50. Included also in Desai 2005.

Desai, M., 2005. *Development and Nationhood: Essays in the Political Economy of India*. New Delhi: Oxford University Press.

Dhami, M. S., 1987. 'Shift in the Party Support Base in 1985 Punjab Assembly Elections: A Preliminary Analysis'. In: Gopal Singh, ed. *Punjab Today*. Delhi: Intellectual Publishing House, 1987, pp. 286–304.

Dhar, P. N., 1989. 'The Indian Economy: Past Performance and Current Issues'. In: R. Lucas and G. Papanek, eds *The Indian Economy: Recent Developments and Future Prospects*. Delhi: Oxford University Press, 1989, pp. 3–22.

Dhar, P. N., 2003. 'Centre-State Relations and Industrial Development'. In: P. N. Dhar, *The Evolution of Economic Policy in India: Selected Essays*. Delhi: Oxford University Press, pp. 76–88.

Dhillon, B. S., 2006. 'Personality and Mission of Guru Nanak in Guru Granth Sahib'. *Journal of Perspectives on Guru Granth Sahib*, Vol. IV, pp. 15–27.

Dhillon, B. S., 2007. 'The Sikh–Rajput Relations During the Eighteenth Century'. *Journal of Sikh Studies*, Vol. XXXI, pp. 15–37.

Dhillon, G. S., 1992. *India Commits Suicide*. Chandigarh: Singh and Singh Publishers.

Dhillon, K. S., 1998. 'A Decade of Violence'. In: J. S. Grewal and I. Banga, eds *Punjab in Prosperity and Violence*. Delhi: K. K. Publishers and Chandigarh: Institute of Punjab Studies, 1998, pp. 104–122.

Dhillon, P. S., 1983. *A Tale of Two Rivers: Ravi-Beas Water Dispute*. Chandigarh: Dhillon Publications.

Dhillon, S. S., 1990. 'Economic Aspect of Punjab Problem', *Bulletin of the Christian Institute for Religious Studies, Batala*, 19(1), January.
Dikshit, R. D., 1975. *The Political Geography of Federalism*. Delhi: Macmillan.
Dutt, S., 1984. *India and the Third World*. London: Zed Books.
Economic and Political Weekly Research Foundation, 1995. National Accounts Statistics of India, 6: Net State Domestic Product. *Economic and Political Weekly*, 30(50), 23 December, 3321–3328.
The Economist, 2000. Chidambaram Subramaniam: Obituary, 18 November.
Fadia, B. L. and Menaria, R. K., 1990. *Sarkaria Commission Report and Centre–State Relations*. Agra: Sahitya Bhawan.
Fisher M. H., ed., 1999. *The Politics of the British Annexation of India 1757–1857*. Delhi: Oxford University Press.
Forster, G., 1798. *A Journey from Bengal to England through North India, Kashmir, Afghanistan and Persia into Russia, 1783–1784*. 2 vols. London: np.
Fox, R. G., 1985. *Lions of the Punjab: Culture in the Making*. Berkeley: University of California Press and Delhi: Archives Publishers.
Frankel, F., 1978. *India's Political Economy, 1947–77*. Princeton: Princeton University Press.
Gardner, G., 2000. 'Reforming States Attack Vajpayee Over Federal Revenue Share-out'. *Financial Times*, 22 August.
Gardner, G., 2001. 'Disparities of Region and Sex Arise to Haunt India's Future'. *Financial Times*, 29 March.
George, K. K., 1986. 'Discretionary Budgetary Transfers: A Review'. *Economic and Political Weekly*, 15 November. Reprinted as GEORGE 1987.
George, K. K., 1987. 'Discretionary Budgetary Transfers: A Review'. In: I. S. Gulati, ed. *Centre-State Budgetary Transfers*. Delhi: Oxford University Press, 1987.
Gill, K. S., 1983. 'Agricultural Development in Punjab'. In: R. S. Johar and J. S. Khanna, eds *Studies in Punjab Economy*. Amritsar: Guru Nanak Dev University, 1983, pp. 1–10.
Gill, K. S., 1993. *A Growing Agricultural Economy: Technological Change, Constraints and Sustainability*. New Delhi: Oxford & IBH Publishing Co.
Gill, M. S., 1987. 'Needs of Punjab Economy'. *The Tribune*, 10 June.
Gill, S. S. and Singhal, K. C., 1984. 'Farmers' Agitation: Response to Development Crisis of Agriculture'. *Economic and Political Weekly*, 19(40), 6 October, pp. 1,728–1,732.
Gill, T. S., 1998. 'Nehru, Indira Gandhi and Punjab'. In: J. S. Grewal and I. Banga, eds *Punjab in Prosperity and Violence*. Delhi: K. K. Publishers and Chandigarh: Institute of Punjab Studies, 1998, pp. 34–46.
Gill, T. S., 1999. 'Jawaharlal Nehru and the Punjab'. In: Pritam Singh and S. S. Thandi, eds *Punjabi Identity in a Global Context*. New Delhi: Oxford University Press, 1999, pp. 333–340.
Government of Andhra Pradesh, 1987. *Memorandum* (to the Sarkaria Commission). In: Government of India 1987.
Government of Assam, 1987. Replies to the Questionnaire (of Sarkaria Commission). In: Government of India 1987.
Government of Bihar, 1987. Replies to the Questionnaire (of Sarkaria Commission). In: Government of India 1987.
Government of Gujarat, 1987. Replies to the Questionnaire (of Sarkaria Commission). In: Government of India 1987.

Government of Haryana, 1987. Replies to the Questionnaire (of Sarkaria Commission). In: Government of India 1987.

Government of Himachal Pradesh, 1987. Replies to the Questionnaire (of Sarkaria Commission). In: Government of India 1987.

Government of India, 1967. *Report of the Study Team on Centre–State Relationships*, Vol. 1. Delhi: The Administrative Reforms Committee.

Government of India, 1984. *White Paper on the Punjab Agitation*, New Delhi: Government of India Press.

Government of India, 1987. *Commission on Centre–State Relations Report, Part II*. Nasik: Government of India Press.

Government of India, 1988. *Commission on Centre–State Relations Report, Part I*. Nasik: Government of India Press.

Government of India, 1988a. *First Report of the Ninth Finance Commission (for 1989–90)*. Delhi: Government of India Press.

Government of India, 1989. *Second Report of the Ninth Finance Commission (for 1990–1995)*. Delhi: Government of India Press.

Government of India, 1990. *Economic Survey 1989–90*. New Delhi: Ministry of Finance.

Government of India, 1991. Census of India Series 20, Punjab Paper 1 of 1991 Provisional Population Tables, New Delhi: Government of India.

Government of India, 1992. Census of India 1991, Provisional Totals, Series 20, Punjab Paper 1 of 1991 Supplement. New Delhi: Government of India.

Government of India, 1994. *The Statistical Abstract 1992*. New Delhi: Central Statistical Organisation, Department of Statistics, Ministry of Planning and Programme Implementation.

Government of Jammu and Kashmir, 1987. Replies to the Questionnaire (of Sarkaria Commission). In: Government of India 1987.

Government of Karnataka, 1987. Replies to the Questionnaire (of Sarkaria Commission). In: Government of India 1987.

Government of Kerala, 1987. Replies to the Questionnaire (of Sarkaria Commission). In: Government of India 1987.

Government of Madhya Pradesh, 1987. Replies to the Questionnaire (of Sarkaria Commission). In: Government of India 1987.

Government of Maharashtra, 1987. Replies to the Questionnaire (of Sarkaria Commission). In: Government of India 1987.

Government of Manipur, 1987. Replies to the Questionnaire (of Sarkaria Commission). In: Government of India 1987.

Government of Meghalaya, 1987. Replies to the Questionnaire (of Sarkaria Commission). In: Government of India 1987.

Government of Meghalaya, 1987a. Welcome Address of the Chief Minister (to the Sarkaria Commission). In: Government of India 1987.

Government of Nagaland, 1987. Replies to the Questionnaire and Additional Points, and Memorandum, (to Sarkaria Commission). In: Government of India 1987.

Government of Orissa, 1987. Replies to the Questionnaire (of Sarkaria Commission). In Government of India 1987.

Government of Punjab, 1975. *Statistical Abstract of Punjab 1974*. Chandigarh: Economic Advisor to the Government of Punjab.

Government of Punjab, 1976. *Statistical Abstract of Punjab 1975*. Chandigarh: Economic Advisor to the Government of Punjab.

Government of Punjab, 1979. *Statistical Abstract of Punjab 1978*. Chandigarh: Economic Advisor to the Government of Punjab.

Government of Punjab, 1987. Memorandum (to the Sarkaria Commission). In Government of India 1987.

Government of Punjab, 1987a. *Statistical Abstract of Punjab 1986*. Chandigarh: Economic Advisor to the Government of Punjab.

Government of Punjab, 1988. *Statistical Abstract of Punjab 1987*. Chandigarh: Economic Advisor to the Government of Punjab.

Government of Punjab, 1989. *Statistical Abstract of Punjab 1988*. Chandigarh: Economic Advisor to the Government of Punjab.

Government of Punjab, 1990–91. *Economic Survey of Punjab 1990–91*. Chandigarh: Economic Advisor to the Government of Punjab.

Government of Punjab, 1992. *Statistical Abstract of Punjab 1991*. Chandigarh: Economic Advisor to the Government of Punjab.

Government of Punjab, 1993. *Statistical Abstract of Punjab 1992*. Chandigarh: Economic Advisor to the Government of Punjab.

Government of Punjab, 1993–94. *Economic Survey of Punjab 1993–94*. Chandigarh: Economic Advisor to the Government of Punjab.

Government of Punjab, 1994. *Statistical Abstract of Punjab 1993*. Chandigarh: Economic Advisor to the Government of Punjab.

Government of Punjab, 1998. *Statistical Abstract of Punjab 1997*. Chandigarh: Economic Advisor to the Government of Punjab.

Government of Punjab, 1999. *Statistical Abstract of Punjab 1998*. Chandigarh: Economic Advisor to the Government of Punjab.

Government of Punjab, 2003. *Statistical Abstract of Punjab 2002*. Chandigarh: Economic Advisor to the Government of Punjab.

Government of Punjab, 2005. *Statistical Abstract of Punjab 2004*. Chandigarh: Economic Advisor to the Government of Punjab.

Government of Rajasthan, 1987. Replies to the Questionnaire (of Sarkaria Commission). In: Government of India 1987.

Government of Sikkim, 1987. Replies to the Questionnaire (of Sarkaria Commission). In: Government of India 1987.

Government of Tamil Nadu, 1987. Replies to the Questionnaire (of Sarkaria Commission). In: Government of India 1987.

Government of Tripura, 1987. Memorandum (to the Sarkaria Commission). In: Government of India 1987.

Government of Uttar Pradesh, 1987. Replies to the Questionnaire (of Sarkaria Commission). In: Government of India 1987.

Government of West Bengal, 1987. Replies to the Questionnaire (of Sarkaria Commission). In: Government of India 1987.

Goyal, S. K., 1979. *Monopoly Capital and Public Policy: Business and Economic Power*. New Delhi: Allied Publishers.

Grewal, B. S., 1975. *Centre–State Financial Relations in India*. Patiala: Punjabi University.

Grewal, B. S., 1986. 'Locational Surplus and the Redistributive Role of National and Sub-national Governments'. *Environment and Planning C: Government and Policy*, Vol. 4. London: Pion, pp. 317–324.

Grewal, J. S., 1996. *The Akalis: A Short History*. Chandigarh: Punjab Studies Publications.

Grewal, J. S., 1998. *The Sikhs of the Punjab*. Cambridge: Cambridge University Press.

Grewal, J. S. and Banga, I., eds, 1998. *Punjab in Prosperity and Violence*. Delhi: K. K. Publishers and Chandigarh: Institute of Punjab Studies.

Grewal, S. S. and Rangi, P. S., 1983. 'Imbalances in Growth of Punjab Agriculture'. In: R. S. Johar and J. S. Khanna, eds *Studies in Punjab Economy*. Amritsar: Guru Nanak Dev University, 1983, pp. 47–64.

Griffiths, A. and Wall, S., 1997. *Applied Economics*. 7th edition. London: Addison Wesley Longman.

Gulati, I. S., ed., 1987. *Centre–State Budgetary Transfers*. Delhi: Oxford University Press.

Gulati, I. S., 1987a. 'Approach of the Finance Commissions'. In: I. S. Gulati, ed. *Centre-State Budgetary Transfers*. Delhi: Oxford University Press, 1987, pp. 63–85.

Gulati, I. S. and George, K. K., 1987. 'Interstate Redistribution through the Budget'. In: I. S. Gulati, ed. *Centre–State Budgetary Transfers*. Delhi: Oxford University Press, 1987, pp. 267–282.

Gupta, H. R., 1992. 'Dal Khalsa'. In: Harbans Singh, ed. *The Encyclopaedia of Sikhism*, Vol. 1. Patiala: Punjabi University, 1992, pp. 494–496.

Gupta, J. R. and Kalra, M., 2005. *Federal Transfers and Inter-state Disparities in India*. New Delhi: Atlantic Publishers.

Habib, I., 1976. 'Jatts of the Punjab and Sind'. In: Harbans Singh and N. G. Barrier, eds *Punjab: Past and Present: Essays in Honour of Dr. Ganda Singh*. Patiala: Punjabi University, 1976, pp. 92–103.

Hannah, D. H. W., 1957. 'The Indian Constitution and Agriculture'. Delhi: Indian Council of Agricultural Research, (unpublished).

Hansen, A. B., 2002. 'The Punjab 1937–47 – A Case of Genocide?'. *International Journal of Punjab Studies*, 9(1), January–June, 1–28.

Hanson, A. H., 1966. *The Process of Planning – A Study of India's Five Year Plans: 1950–64*. London: Oxford University Press.

Hardy, D. and Mihaljek, D., 1992. 'Economic Policymaking in a Federation'. *Finance and Development*, June, 14–17.

Harriss, B., 1983. *Agricultural Change and the Mercantile State: A Study of Public Policy in Tamil Nadu*. Development Studies Occasional Paper No. 22, School of Development Studies, University of East Anglia, June.

Harriss, B., 1991. *Markets, Society and the State: Problems of Marketing Under Conditions of Small Holder Agriculture in West Bengal*. Report to the World Institute for Development Economics Research (WIDER), Helsinki, Finland for the Project SSA W90/91 Rural Development and Poverty in Eastern India.

Harriss, J., 1989. 'Indian Industrialisation and the State'. In: H. Alavi and J. Harris, eds *Sociology of 'Developing Societies': South Asia*. London: MacMillan, 1989, pp. 70–90.

Hasrat, B. J., 1992. 'Anglo-Sikh War I, 1845–46'. In: Harbans Singh, ed. *The Encyclopaedia of Sikhism*, Vol. 1. Patiala: Punjabi University, 1992, pp. 164–169.

Hasrat, B. J., 1992a. 'Anglo-Sikh War II, 1848–49'. In: Harbans Singh, ed. *The Encyclopaedia of Sikhism*, Vol. 1. Patiala: Punjabi University, 1992, pp. 169–175.

Heeger, G. A., 1971. 'The Politics of Integration: Community, Party and Integration in Punjab'. Unpublished PhD thesis, University of Chicago.

Helweg, A., 1989. 'Sikh Politics in India: The Emigrant Factor'. In: N. G. Barrier and V. A. Dusenbery, eds *The Sikh Diaspora: Migration and The Experience Beyond Punjab*. Delhi: Chanakya Publications, 1989, pp. 305–336.

Hicks, U., 1978. *Federalism Failure and Success: A Comparative Study*. New York: Oxford University Press.

Holland, S., 1976. *The Regional Problem*. London: Macmillan.

Islam, M., 1994. 'Punjab Agriculture during the Great Depression'. *International Journal of Punjab Studies*, 1(1), January–June, 31–48.

Islam, S., 2002. *Undoing India: The RSS Way*. Delhi: Media House.

Jaffrelot, C., 1994. 'The Genesis and Development of Hindu Nationalism in the Punjab: from the Arya Samaj to the Hindu Sabha (1875–1910)'. *Indo-British Review*, XXI(1), 3–39.

Jaffrelot, C., 1996. *The Hindu Nationalist Movement and Indian Politics, 1925 to the 1990s*. London: Hurst.

Jaffrelot, C., 2003. *India's Silent Revolution: The Rise of the Lower Castes in North India*. London: Hurst.

Jain, S. N., Kashyap, S. C. and Srinivasan, N., eds, 1972. *The Union and the States*. Delhi: National Publishing House.

Jalal, A., 1985. *The Sole Spokesman: Jinnah, the Muslim League and the Demand for Pakistan*. Cambridge: Cambridge University Press.

Jeffrey, R., 1994. *What's Happening To India? Punjab, Ethnic Conflict and the Test for Federalism*. 2nd edition. London: Macmillan.

Jennings, I., 1953. *Some Characteristics of the Indian Constitution*. London: Oxford University Press.

Jhaveri, N. J., 1987. 'Distribution of Non-Plan Transfers: Needed an Alternative Approach'. In: I. S. Gulati, ed. *Centre-State Budgetary Transfers*. Delhi: Oxford University Press, 1987, pp. 111–120.

Johar, K. L. and Rana, S. P., 1990. *Centre-State Tensions: A Study*. Delhi: Harman Publishing House.

Johar, R. S. and Khanna, J. S., eds, 1983. *Studies in Punjab Economy*. Amritsar: Guru Nanak Dev University.

Johar, R. S. and Raikhy, P. S., 1983. Agricultural Productivity in Punjab – An Analysis of Inter-District Variations. In: R. S. Johar and J. S. Khanna, eds *Studies in Punjab Economy*. Amritsar: Guru Nanak Dev University, 1983, pp. 36–46.

Johar, R. S. and Singh, Parminder, 1983. 'Agricultural Development in Punjab'. In: R. S. Johar and J. S. Khanna, eds *Studies in Punjab Economy*. Amritsar: Guru Nanak Dev University, 1983, pp. 11–35.

Johar, R. S., Khanna, J. S. and Raikhy, P. S., 1983. 'Industrial Development of Punjab – A Study in Characterisation, Case For, and Constraints'. In: R. S. Johar and J. S. Khanna, eds *Studies in Punjab Economy*. Amritsar: Guru Nanak Dev University, 1983, pp. 150–177.

Johl, S. S., 1986. Report of the Expert Committee on Diversification of Agriculture in Punjab. Unpublished Government of Punjab document.

Johl, S. S., 2005. 'Food and Agriculture: Sow Right for a Rich Harvest'. In: India: The Tasks Ahead, Special Supplement, *The Tribune*. Chandigarh, 24 September.

Johnson, B. L. C., 1979. *India: Resources and Development*. London: Heinemann Educational Books.

Johnston, R. J., Knight, D. and Kofman, E., 1988. *National Self-Determination and Political Geography*. London: Croom Helm.

Josh, B., 1979. *Communist Movement in Punjab 1926–1947*. Delhi: Anupama Publication.

Joshi, L. M., ed., 1980. *Sikhism*. 2nd edition. Patiala: Punjabi University.

Judge, P. S., 1992. *Insurrection to Agitation: The Naxalite Movement in Punjab*. Bombay: Popular Prakashan.

Kang, D. S., 1982. 'Environmental Problems of the Green Revolution with a Focus on Punjab, India'. In: R. Barratt, ed. *International Dimensions of the Environmental Crisis*. Colorado: Westview Press, 1982.

Kapur, R. A., 1986. *Sikh Separatism: The Politics of Faith*. London: Allen and Unwin.

Kaur, H., 1990. *Blue Star Over Amritsar*. Delhi: Ajanta.

Keating, M., 1988. *State and Regional Nationalism: Territorial Politics and the European State*. London: Harvester Wheatsheaf.

Kerr, I. J., 1988. 'Fox and the Lions: The Akali Movement Revisited'. In: J. O'Connell *et al.*, eds *Sikh History and Religion in the Twentieth Century*. Toronto: University of Toronto, 1988, pp. 211–225.

Kerr, I. J., 2001. 'Harimandar'. In: Harbans Singh, ed. *The Encyclopaedia of Sikhism*, Vol. 2. Patiala: Punjabi University, 2001, pp. 239–248.

Kessinger, T., 1974. *Vilyatpur 1848–1968*. Berkeley: University of California Press.

Khanna, J. S., 1973. 'A Study on Regional Imbalances in the Indian Economy'. Unpublished report submitted to the Planning Commission, Government of India, August 1973.

Khanna, J. S., 1983. 'Lagging Industrial Development in Punjab: An Analysis'. In: R. S. Johar and J. S. Khanna, eds *Studies in Punjab Economy*. Amritsar: Guru Nanak Dev University, 1983, pp. 84–132.

Khatkhate, D. R. and Bhatt, V. V., 1987. 'Accommodating the Planning Dimension'. In: I. S. Gulati, ed. *Centre–State Budgetary Transfers*. Delhi: Oxford University Press, 1987, pp. 41–59.

Khilnani, S., 1999. *The Idea of India*. London and New Delhi: Penguin.

Kohli, A., 1989. *The State and Poverty in India*. Cambridge and New York: Cambridge University Press.

Krishnaswamy, K. S., Gulati, I. S. and Vaidyanathan, A., 1992. 'Economic Aspects of Federalism in India'. In: N. Mukarji and B. Arora, eds *Federalism in India: Origins and Development*. New Delhi: Vikas Publishing House, 1992, pp. 180–212.

Kudaisya, G., 2006. *Region, Nation, Heartland: Uttar Pradesh in India's Body Politic*. Delhi: Sage.

Kumar, A. and Kumar, S., 2002. 'The Recent Assembly Elections in Punjab: Some Reflections on Results and Changing Voter Preferences'. *International Journal of Punjab Studies*, 9(1), January–June, 113–135.

Kumar, D., 1991. 'Industrialists Flee Ludhiana'. *The Times of India*, 28 November.

Kumar, P., 1998. 'Violence in Retrospect'. In: J. S. Grewal and I. Banga, eds *Punjab in Prosperity and Violence*. Delhi: K. K. Publishers and Chandigarh: Institute of Punjab Studies, 1998, pp. 123–137.

Kumar, P., Sharma, M., Sood, A. and Handa, A., 1984. *Punjab Crisis: Context and Trends*. Chandigarh: Centre for Research in Rural and Industrial Development.

Kumar, R. N., 2000. *The Sikhs and the State in 20th Century India: Historical Introduction from a human rights perspective*. Reuter Foundation Paper 128, Green College, Oxford.

Kumar, R. N., 2002. 'Human Rights in Punjab: Constitutional Guarantees and Institutional Practice'. *International Journal of Punjab Studies*, 9(1), January–June, 29–56.

Kumar, R. N., Singh, A., Agrwaal, A. and Kaur, J., 2003. *Reduced to Ashes: The Insur-*

gency and Human Rights in Punjab Final Report, Vol. 1. Kathmandu: South Asia Forum for Human Rights (for Committee for Coordination on Disappearances in Punjab).

Kundu, A., Misra, G. K. and Meher, R. K., 1986. *Location of Public Enterprises and Regional Development*. New Delhi: Concept Publishing Company.

Lakdawala, D. T., 1967. *Union–State Financial Relations*. Bombay: Lalvani Publishing House.

Lakdawala, D. T., 1987. *Lessons of Planning*. Delhi: Oxford University Press.

Lakdawala, D. T., 1989. 'Federal Financial Transfers: How Much Progression?' *Economic and Political Weekly*, XXIV(4), 28 January, pp. 191–194.

Leff, C. S., 1999. 'Democratisation and Disintegration in Multinational States: The Breakup of the Communist Federations'. *World Politics*, 51(2), January 1999, 205–235.

Lekhi, R. K. and Singh, Joginder, 1986. *Punjab Economy*. Delhi and Ludhiana: Kalyani Publishers.

Leslie, P., 1988. *Ethnonationalism in a Federal State: The Case of Canada*. (Research Paper 24). Kingston: Queen's University Institute of Intergovernmental Relations.

Lucas, R. and Papanek, G., eds, 1989. *The Indian Economy: Recent Developments and Future Prospects*. Delhi: Oxford University Press.

McLeod, W. H., 1996. *The Evolution of the Sikh Community*. Delhi: Oxford University Press.

MacMahon, A. W., ed., 1962. *Federalism: Mature and Emergent*. New York: Russell & Russell.

Maini, G., 2004. *The Giant Awakens: Punjab Industry and Growth*. New Delhi: India Research Press.

Malhotra, I., 1989. *Indira Gandhi: A Personal and Political Biography*. London: Hodder and Stoughton.

Mali, M. S., ed., 1989. *The National Question in Punjab: Views of Left Wing Intellectuals* [orig. Punjabi title: *Punjab da Quami Masla: Khabe Pakhi Chintakan di Nazar Vich*]. Sirhind: Lok Geet Parkashan.

Malik, I., 1995. 'Identity Formation and Muslim Party Politics in the Punjab, 1897–1936: A Retrospective Analysis'. *Modern Asian Studies*, 29(2), 293–323.

Malik, I., 1998. 'Pluralism, Partition and Punjabisation: Politics of Muslim Identity in the British Punjab'. *International Journal of Punjab Studies*, 5(1), January–June, 1–27.

Malik, I., 1999. 'Muslim Nationalism and Ethno-regional Postulations: Sir Fazl-I-Husain and the Party Politics in the Punjab'. In: Pritam Singh and S. S. Thandi, eds *Punjabi Identity in a Global Context*. New Delhi: Oxford University Press, 1999, pp. 201–232.

Marathe, S. S., 1986. *Regulation and Development: The India Policy Experience of Controls over Industry*. New Delhi: Sage Publications.

Masood, M. A. and Stockdale, Peter, 1988. *The Khalistan Riddle*. Islamabad: Modern Book Depot.

Mazumdar, R. K., 2003. *The Indian Army and the Making of Punjab*. Delhi: Permanent Black.

Meher, R., 1999. 'Inter-State Disparities in Levels of Development and the Implications of Economic Liberalisation on Regional Economies of India'. *Review of Development and Change*, IV(2), 198–224.

Mehra, S. P., 1983. *Punjab Today (An Economic Overview)*. Jalandhar: New Academic Publishing Co.

Mellor, J. and Desai, G., eds, 1985. *Agricultural Change and Rural Poverty*. Baltimore: John Hopkins University Press.

Merkl, P. H., 1975. *Political Continuity and Change*. Delhi: Allied.

Mirza, S., Hasnat, S. and Mahmood, S., 1985. *The Sikh Question*. Lahore: Panjab University.

Mishra, S. C., 1983. *The State and the Agrarian Economy of Punjab and Bombay before and after Independence*. Development Studies Occasional Paper No. 22, School of Development Studies, University of East Anglia, June.

Mitra, A., 1983. 'The Centre'. *Seminar*, 281, January, 40–43.

Mitra, A., 1987. 'Will Growth and Centralized Fiscal Arrangements Do?' In: I. S. Gulati, ed. *Centre-State Budgetary Transfers*. Bombay: Oxford University Press, 1987, pp. 23–40.

Mooij, J., 1989. 'Food Policy and State Form: A Comparative Research in Two South Indian States'. Unpublished paper.

Mukarji, N. and Arora, B., eds, 1992. *Federalism in India: Origins and Development*. New Delhi: Vikas Publishing House.

Mukherji, P. N., 1984. 'Gandhi, Akalis and Non-Violence'. *Man and Development*, IV(3), September, 58–77.

Mukherji, P. N., 1985. 'Akalis and Non-Violence: An Inquiry into the Theory and Practice of Non-Violence'. In: Amrik Singh, ed. *Punjab in Indian Politics: Issues and Trends*. Delhi: Ajanta, 1985, pp. 71–118.

Munshi, M. C., 1973. 'Location of Industry: Evolution of a Policy'. In: C. N. Vakil, ed. *Industrial Development of India: Policy and Problems*. New Delhi: Orient Longman, 1973, pp. 248–263.

Nair, K., 1961. *Blossoms in the Dust: the human dimension in Indian development*. London: Gerald Duckworth.

Nanjundappa, D. M. and Rao, G. V. K., 1987. 'Reexamining the Bases of Plan Assistance'. In: I. S. Gulati, ed. *Centre–State Budgetary Transfers*. Delhi: Oxford University Press, 1987, pp. 236–243.

Narain, I. and Mathur, P. C., 1964. 'Union–State Relations in India: A Case Study of Rajasthan'. *Journal of Commonwealth Political Studies*, 2(2), 120–140.

Narang, A. S., 1983. *Storm Over the Sutlej: The Akali Politics*. New Delhi: Gitanjali Publishing House.

Narang, A. S., 1987. 'Elections in Punjab: Emerging Paradoxes'. In: Gopal Singh, ed. *Punjab Today*. Delhi: Intellectual Publishing House, 1987, pp. 305–313.

Nayar, B. R., 1966. *Minority Politics in Punjab*. New Jersey: Princeton University Press.

Nayar, B. R., 1968. 'Punjab'. In: M. Weiner, ed. *State Politics in India*. New Jersey: Princeton University Press, 1968, pp. 434–502.

Nayar, B. R., 1989. *India's Mixed Economy*. Bombay: Popular Prakashan.

Nayar, K. and Singh, Khushwant, 1984. *Tragedy of Punjab: Operation Blue Star and After*. New Delhi: Vision Books.

Nayar, K., 1985. 'After the Accord'. In: Amrik Singh, ed. *Punjab in Indian Politics: Issues and Trends*. Delhi: Ajanta, 1985, pp. 390–398.

Noorani, A. G., 1985. 'Probing the Delhi Pogroms'. In: Amrik Singh, ed. *Punjab in Indian Politics: Issues and Trends*. Delhi: Ajanta, 1985, pp. 273–289.

Noorani, A. G., 1985a. 'The Punjab Accord: The Balance Sheet'. In: Amrik Singh, ed. *Punjab in Indian Politics: Issues and Trends*. Delhi: Ajanta, 1985, pp. 383–389.

Oberoi, H., 1994. *The Construction of Religious Boundaries: Culture, Identity and Diversity in the Sikh Tradition*. Delhi: Oxford University Press.

O'Connell, J. T., Israel, M., Oxtoby, W. G., McLeod, W. H. and Grewal, J. S. eds, 1988, *Sikh History and Religion in the Twentieth Century*. Toronto: University of Toronto.

Omissi, D., 1994. *The Sepoy and the Raj*. London: Macmillan.

Pandit, M. L., 1978. 'Some Less Known Factors Behind the Industrial Change in Punjab and Haryana'. *Economic and Political Weekly*, XIII(47), 25 November, pp. 1,935–1,940.

Pandit, M. L., 1985. *Industrial Development in the Punjab and Haryana (Domination of footloose industries)*. Delhi: BR Publishing Corporation.

Paranjape, H. K., 1964. *The Planning Commission: A Descriptive Account*. New Delhi: The Indian Institute of Public Administration.

Paranjape, H. K., 1970. *Centre–State Relations in Planning*. New Delhi: The Indian Institute of Public Administration.

Parkash, O., 1983. *The Finances of Punjab State*. Amritsar: Guru Nanak Dev University.

Patnaik, P., 1975. 'Imperialism and the Growth of Indian Capitalism'. In: Robin Blackburn ed. *Explosions in a Subcontinent*. London: Penguin, 1975, pp. 51–78.

Pettigrew, J., 1995. *The Sikhs of the Punjab: Unheard Voices of State and Guerrilla Violence*. London: Zed.

Phandis, U., 1989. *Ethnicity and Nation-building in South Asia*. Delhi: Sage Publications.

Phul, G. S., 1989. *Dream to Reality: A Biography of S. Mohinder Singh Bhogal*. Ludhiana: Bhogal Sons.

Prasad, C. S., 2005. *India: Economic Policies and Performance, 1947–48 to 2004–05: Year-wise Economic Review of the Indian Economy since Independence*. New Delhi: New Century Publications.

Prasad, K. N., 1983. *Problems of Indian Economic Development: National and Regional Dimension*. Delhi: Sterling Publisher.

Prasad, P., 1989. *Lopsided Growth: Political Economy of Indian Development*. Bombay: Oxford University Press.

Puri, H., Judge, P. S. and Sekhon, J. S., 1999. *Terrorism in Punjab: Understanding Grassroots Reality*. Delhi: Har-Anand.

Puri, S. S., 1970. 'Union-State Relationships in Agricultural Administration'. *Indian Journal of Public Administration*, XVI(3), July–September.

Qureshi, Justice A. S., 1989. 'A Note of Dissent'. In: Government of India, 1989. *Second Report of the Ninth Finance Commission (for 1990–1995)*. Delhi: Government of India Press.

Ram Mohan, T. T., 2005. *Privatisation in India: Challenging Economic Orthodoxy*. London and New York: RoutledgeCurzon.

Randhawa, M. S., 1974. *Green Revolution*. Delhi: Vikas Publishing House.

Rao, A., Ghosh, A., Bhattacharya, S., Ahuja, T. and Pancholi, N. D., 1985. *Oppression in Punjab: A Citizens for Democracy (CFD) Report to the Nation*. Delhi: Hind Mazdoor Kisan Panchayat Publications.

Rao, H., 1987. 'Income Tax Proceeds: Are the States Getting Their Due Share?'. In: I. S. Gulati *Centre-State Budgetary Transfers*. Delhi: Oxford University Press, 1987, pp. 185–194.

Rao, M. G. and Singh, N., 2005. *Political Economy of Federalism in India*. Delhi: Oxford University Press.

Rao, P. V., ed., 1996. *Symphony of Freedom: Papers on Nationality Question*. Hyderabad: All India Peoples Resistance Forum.

Rath, S., 1984. *Federalism Today: Approaches, Issues and Trends*. Delhi: Sterling.

Ray, A., 1966. *Inter-Governmental Relations in India, A Study of Indian Federalism.* Bombay: Asia Publishing House.

Riar, S., 1999. 'Khalistan: The Origins of the Demand and its Pursuit Prior to Independence, 1940–1945'. In: Pritam Singh and S. S. Thandi, eds *Punjabi Identity in a Global Context.* New Delhi: Oxford University Press, 1999, pp. 233–244.

Robinson, M., 1987. 'Religion, Class And Faction: The Politics Of Communalism In: Twentieth Century Punjab'. DPhil Thesis, University of Sussex.

Rudolph, L. I. and Rudolph, S. H., 1987. In: *Pursuit of Lakshmi: The Political Economy of the Indian State.* Chicago: The University of Chicago Press.

Saez, L., 2002. *Federalism Without a Centre.* New Delhi: Sage Publications.

Samiuddin, A., ed., 1985. *The Punjab Crisis: Challenge and Response.* Delhi: Mittal Publications.

Sandhu, J. S. and Singh, Ajit, 1983. 'Industrial Development in Punjab – Some Features'. In: R. S. Johar and J. S. Khanna, eds *Studies in Punjab Economy.* Amritsar: Guru Nanak Dev University, 1983, pp. 133–149.

Sandhu, R. S., 1999. *Struggle for Justice: Speeches and Conversations of Sant Jarnail Singh Khalsa Bhindranwale.* Dublin, Ohio: Sikh Educational & Religious Foundation.

Santhanam, K., 1960. *Union–State Relations in India.* Bombay: Asia Publishers.

Saran, R., 2000. 'Reform or Perish: Rich States Protest Against the Precedence to Poverty Over Performance in Allocation of Funds', *India Today*, XXV(36), 29 August–4 September, pp. 18–21.

Sastri, K. A. N., 1987. 'Minor States of the North, Monarchical and Non-Monarchical'. In: K. A. N. Sastri, ed. *A Comprehensive History of India, Vol 2: The Mauryas and Satavahanas 325 B.C.–A.D. 300.* 2nd reprint. New Delhi: Peoples Publishing House, 1987, pp. 116–137.

Saxena, S., 1996. 'Language and the Nationality Question'. In: P.V. Rao, ed. *Symphony of Freedom: Papers on Nationality Question.* Hyderabad: All India Peoples Resistance Forum, 1996, pp. 288–297.

Schoenfeld, B., 1960. *Federalism in India.* Washington: Public Affairs Press.

Sen, A., 1982. *The State, Industrialisation and Class Formation in India; A Neo-Marxist Perspective on Colonialism, Underdevelopment and Development.* London: Routledge.

Sen Gupta, B., 1985. 'The Geopolitical Dimension'. In: Amrik Singh, ed. *Punjab in Indian Politics: Issues and Trends.* Delhi: Ajanta, 1985, pp. 353–365.

Shah, S. A., ed., 1973. *Towards National Liberation: Essays on political economy of India.* Montreal: np.

Sharma, D. P., 1996. *The Punjab Story: Decade of Turmoil.* Delhi: APH Publishing.

Sharma, S., 2004. 'Water Wars and the Real Message'. *Hindu Business line*, www.blonnet.com/2004/07/21/stories/2004072100011000.htm.

Shenoy, B. R., 1974. *PL-480 and India's Food Problem.* Delhi: East West Press.

Sheth, D. L. and Narang, A. S., 1985. 'The Electoral Angle'. In: Amrik Singh, ed. *Punjab in Indian Politics: Issues and Trends.* Delhi: Ajanta, 1985, pp. 123–134.

Sidhu, D. S., 1979. *Price Policy for Wheat in India.* Delhi: S Chand and Co.

Sidhu, H. S., 1996. 'Agricultural Development and Agro-Industries in the Process of Industrialisation: A Case Study of Punjab (India)'. *International Journal of Punjab Studies*, 3(2), July–December, 109–150.

Sims, H., 1988. *Political Regimes, Public Policy and Economic Development: Agricultural Performance and Rural Change in Two Punjabs.* Delhi: Sage Publications.

Singh, Ajit, 1983. *Industrialisation, Employment and Basic Needs in a Fast-Growing Agrarian State: A Study of the Indian Punjab*. World Employment Program Research Working Paper, International Labour Organisation.

Singh, Ajmer, 1992. *Militant Sikh Struggle* [orig. Punjabi title: *Kharku Sikh Sangharash*]. Sangrur: Vichar Prakashan.

Singh, Ajmer, 2003. *Twentieth Century Sikh Politics: From One Slavery to Another* [orig. Punjabi title: *Vihvin Sadi Di Sikh Rajniti: Iq Ghulami Ton Dooji Ghulami Tak*]. Chandigarh: Narinder Singh.

Singh, Amarinder, 1992. 'Anandpur Sahib Resolution'. In: Harbans Singh, ed. *The Encyclopaedia of Sikhism*, Vol. 1. Patiala: Punjabi University, 1992, pp. 133–141.

Singh, Amrik, ed., 1985. *Punjab in Indian Politics: Issues and Trends*. Delhi: Ajanta.

Singh, Birinder Pal, 1998. 'The Logic of Sikh Militancy'. In: J. S. Grewal and I. Banga, eds *Punjab in Prosperity and Violence*. Delhi: K. K. Publishers and Chandigarh: Institute of Punjab Studies, 1998, pp. 138–155.

Singh, Birinder Pal, 2002. 'Review of M. Banerjee (2000) The Pathan Unarmed: Opposition and Memory in the North West Frontier'. *International Journal of Punjab Studies*, 9(2), July–December, 316–318.

Singh, Birinder Pal, 2002a. *Violence As Political Discourse: Sikh Militancy Confronts the Indian State*. Shimla: Indian Institute of Advanced Study.

Singh, Dalip, 1981. *Dynamics of Punjab Politics*. Delhi: Macmillan.

Singh, Darshan, 1999. 'Shah Mohammad on Punjabi Identity'. In: Pritam Singh and S. S. Thandi, eds *Punjabi Identity in a Global Context*. New Delhi: Oxford University Press, 1999, pp. 69–77.

Singh, Ganda, 1935. *Banda Singh Bahadur*. Amritsar: Khalsa College.

Singh, Ganda, 1956. *A Brief Account of the Sikhs*. Amritsar: SGPC.

Singh, Ganda, 1992. 'Banda Singh Bahadur'. In: Harbans Singh, ed. *The Encyclopaedia of Sikhism*, Vol. 1. Patiala: Punjabi University, 1992, pp. 273–275.

Singh, Giani Ajmer, 1977. *The Draft of the New Policy Programme of the Shiromani Akali Dal*. Amritsar: Shiromani Akali Dal.

Singh, Gobinder, 1987. 'Punjab Accord and Punjab Problem: A Study in Relevance'. In: Gopal Singh, ed. *Punjab Today*. Delhi: Intellectual Publishing House, 1987, pp. 327–342.

Singh, Gopal, ed., 1987. *Punjab Today*. Delhi: Intellectual Publishing House.

Singh, Gopal, ed., 1994. *Punjab: Past, Present and Future*. Delhi: Ajanta.

Singh, Gurharpal, 1991. Review of H. Sims, 'Political Regimes, Public Policy and Economic Development'. *Journal of Commonwealth and Comparative Politics*, XXIX(1), March, 102–103.

Singh, Gurharpal, 1994. *Communism in Punjab: A Study of the Movement up to 1967*. Delhi: Ajanta.

Singh, Harbans, ed., 1992. *The Encyclopaedia of Sikhism*, Vol. 1. Patiala: Punjabi University.

Singh, Harbans, 1994. *The Heritage of the Sikhs*. 2nd edition. Delhi: Manohar.

Singh, Harbans, ed., 1997. *The Encyclopaedia of Sikhism*, Vol. 3. Patiala: Punjabi University.

Singh, Harbans, ed., 2001. *The Encyclopaedia of Sikhism*, Vol. 2. 2nd edition. Patiala: Punjabi University.

Singh, Harbans, and Barrier, N. G., eds, 1976. *Punjab: Past and Present: Essays in Honour of Dr. Ganda Singh*. Patiala: Punjabi University.

Singh, Hardip, 1987. *Emergence and Growth of Bhartiya Kisan Union in Punjab.* MPhil thesis, New Delhi: Jawaharlal Nehru University.

Singh, Iqbal, 1986. *Punjab Under Siege: A Critical Analysis*. New York and London: Allen-Macmillan.

Singh, Jarnail, 1984. *Sikhs – We are not Hindus, by Bhai Kahan Singhji Nabha*. Ontario: The Sikh Social and Educational Society.

Singh, Jarnail, 1985. *Sikh Symposium*. Toronto: The Sikh Social and Educational Society.

Singh, Khushwant, 1997. 'Ranjit Singh'. In: Harbans Singh, ed. *The Encyclopaedia of Sikhism Vol. 3.* Patiala: Punjabi University, 1997, pp. 479–487.

Singh, Khushwant, 1999. *A History of the Sikhs*, Vol. 1: 1469–1839. Reprint with corrections (1st edition 1963). New Delhi: Oxford University Press.

Singh, Khushwant, 1999a. *A History of the Sikhs*, Vol. 2: 1839–1988. (1st edition 1966). New Delhi: Oxford University Press.

Singh, Mohinder, 1978. *The Akali Movement*. Delhi: Macmillan.

Singh, Mohinder, 1988. *The Akali Struggle: A Retrospect.* New Delhi: Atlantic Publishers.

Singh, Nikky-Guninder Kaur, 1993. *The Feminine Principle in the Sikh Vision of the Transcendent*. London: Cambridge University Press.

Singh, P., 1983. *Emerging Pattern in Punjab Economy*. Delhi: Sterling Publishers.

Singh, P., 1997. *Political Economy of the Punjab: An Insider's Account*. New Delhi: MD Publications.

Singh, Pashaura, 2005. 'Understanding the Martyrdom of Guru Arjan'. *Journal of Punjab Studies.* 12(1), Spring, 29–62.

Singh, Pashaura, 2006. *Life and Work of Guru Arjan*. Delhi: Oxford University Press.

Singh, Patwant, 1989. *The Golden Temple*. Delhi: Time Books International.

Singh, Pritam, 1982. 'Current Akali Politics: Some Trends'. *Secular Democracy*, October, Special Punjab Issue, 46–52.

Singh, Pritam, 1983. 'Imperialism, Indian Capitalism and Punjab Economy' (original title in Punjabi: *Samrajwad, Bharati Punjiwad ate Punjab di Arthikta*.) In: N. Azad, ed. *Punjab Di Arthikta.* Patiala: Punjabi University, 1983, pp. 3–22.

Singh, Pritam, 1984. 'AIR and Doordarshan Coverage of Punjab after the Army Action'. *Economic and Political Weekly*, 8 September.

Singh, Pritam, 1984a. 'Akali Agitation: Growing Separatist Trend'. *Economic and Political Weekly*, 4 February.

Singh, Pritam, 1985. 'Government Media and Punjab'. *Economic and Political Weekly*, 12 January.

Singh, Pritam, 1985a. 'Role of Media'. In: Amrik Singh, ed. *Punjab in Indian Politics: Issues and Trends*. Delhi: Ajanta, 1985, pp. 155–184.

Singh, Pritam, 1987. 'Two Facets of Revivalism'. In: Gopal Singh, ed. *Punjab Today.* Delhi: Intellectual Publishing House, 1987, pp. 167–179.

Singh, Pritam, 1990. Review of Blaut (1987) 'The National Question'. *Journal of Development Studies*, 26(3), April, 550–552.

Singh, Pritam, 1992. 'Economic Interests and Human Rights in Indo-British Relations: House of Commons' Debate on Punjab'. *Economic and Political Weekly*, 28 March.

Singh, Pritam, 1993. 'Punjab's Economic Development and the Current Crisis'. *Seminar* Annual No. 401: India 1992, January, 1993, 60–65.

Singh, Pritam, 1994. 'Political Economy of the British Colonial State and the Indian

Nationalist State and the agrarian-oriental development pattern in Punjab'. *Indo-British Review*, XXI(1), 97–110.

Singh, Pritam, 1998. 'Sectarianism and Human Rights Discourse: The Politics of Human Rights in the Post-Colonial Punjab'. In: M.R. Anderson and S. Guha, eds *Changing Concepts of Rights and Justice in South Asia*. Delhi: Oxford University Press, 1998, pp. 239–274.

Singh, Pritam, 1999. 'Punjabi Nationalism: "The Third Way" between Sikh Secessionism and Indian Nationalism'. Paper presented at the British Association for South Asian Studies Annual Conference, 23–24 September, 1999, London School of Economics. Abstract of the paper available at www.staff.brad.ac.uk/akundu/basas/basasc 99.html.

Singh, Pritam, 1999a. 'Capital, State & Nation'. *International Journal of Punjab Studies*. (6)1, 85–99.

Singh, Pritam, 2001. 'Punjab Terrorism: Truth Still Uncovered'. *Economic and Political Weekly*, 6 October, 3829–3831.

Singh, Pritam, 2005. 'Hindu bias in India's "Secular" Constitution: Probing Flaws in the Instruments of Governance'. *Third World Quarterly*. 26(6), 909–926.

Singh, Pritam, 2007. 'The Political Economy of the Cycles of Violence and Non-Violence in the Sikh Struggle for Identity and Political Power: Implications for Indian Federalism'. *Third World Quarterly*. 28(3), 555–570.

Singh, Pritam, 2007a. 'Punjab's Electoral Competition'. *Economic and Political Weekly*, 10 February.

Singh, Pritam, 2007b. *Vidhan Sabha chonna wich congress ate akalian vichkar mukable di daur* (translation: Electoral Race between the Congress and the Akalis). *Des Pardes* (translation: Home and Away), Southall (UK), 16 February.

Singh, Pritam, 2007c. *Punjab di Siasit de Badlade Rang* (translation: Changing Scenarios of Punjab Politics). *Des Pardes* (translation: Home and Away), Southall (UK), 23 March.

Singh, Pritam, 2007d. 'Competing Nationalisms in the Contestation over Sikh Role in 1857', paper presented at the conference Mutiny at the Margins: New Perspectives on the Indian Uprising of 1857 at Edinburgh University, 23–26 July 2007.

Singh, Pritam, and Thandi, S. S., eds, 1999. *Punjabi Identity in a Global Context*. New Delhi: Oxford University Press.

Singh, S. P., 1973. *Centre–State Relations in Agricultural Development*. Delhi: Vikas Publishing House.

Singh, Saran (no date). *The Formation of Sikhism and The Coins of the Sikhs 1469–1849*. Kuala Lumpur: Sikh Naujawan Sabha Malaysia.

Singh, Sukhpal, 1999. 'Green Revolution and Agro-Industrialisation: A Case Study of Primary Food Processing Industries in the Indian Punjab'. *International Journal of Punjab Studies*, 6(1), January–June, 55–83.

Singh, Sukhwant, 1980. 'Agricultural Development in the Punjab (1849–1947)'. *Journal of Regional History*, I, 88–106.

Singh, Sukhwant, 1982. 'Emergence of Capitalistic Tendencies in the Punjab Agriculture Under British Rule'. *Journal of Regional History*, III, 47–56.

Singh, Sukhwant, 1983. 'Composition and Distribution of Peasant-Proprietors in the Punjab (Late 19th Century)'. *Journal of Regional History*, IV, 99–114.

Singh, Sulakhan, 1980. 'Udasi Establishment Under Sikh Rule'. *Journal of Regional History*, I, 70–88.

Singh, Sulakhan, 1983. ‘Udasi Beliefs and Practices’. *Journal of Regional History*, IV, 73–98.

Singh, Tavleen, 2000. ‘Rewarding the Brats. The 11th Finance Commission has a Message for States: Good Governance Does Not Pay’. *India Today*. XXV(36), 29 August–4 September, 17.

Sinha, A., 2005. *The Regional Roots of Development Politics in India*. Bloomington: Indiana University Press.

Smart, N., 1992. *The World's Religions*. Cambridge: Cambridge University Press.

Sohal, S. S., 1983. ‘British Policies and Moneylenders in the Agrarian Economy of the Punjab’. *Journal of Regional History*, IV, 115–27.

Sohal, S. S., 1987. ‘Political Economy of Communalism: Late Nineteenth Century Colonial Punjab’. *Man and Development*, 9(2), 12–20.

Spate, O. H. K., 1947. ‘The Partition of the Punjab and of Bengal’. *Geographical Journal*, 110(4–6), December, 201–222.

Spate, O. H. K. and Learmonth, A. T. A., 1972. *India and Pakistan: A General and Regional Geography*. Reprint of 3rd edition. London: Methuen & Co Ltd. First published in 1954.

Srinivasan, N., 1972. ‘Centre–State Relations in the Field of Agricultural Development’. In: S. N. Jain, S.C. Kashyap, and N. Srinivasan, eds *The Union and the States*. Delhi: National Publishing House, 1972, pp. 110–129.

Srivastva, R., 1989. ‘Planning and Regional Disparities in India’. Paper submitted to the conference on The State and Development Planning in India, School of Oriental and African Studies, London, 21–24 April.

Subramaniam, C., 1979. *The New Strategy in Indian Agriculture: The First Decade and After*. New Delhi: Vikas.

Subramaniam, C., 1982. ‘A Blueprint for Indian Agriculture’. *The Indian Express*, 11 April.

Svennilson, I., 1962. ‘Problems of Economic Integration’. In: A. W. MacMahon, ed. *Federalism: Mature and Emergent*. New York: Russell and Russell, 1962, pp. 458–470.

Tahir, M. A., 1999. ‘A Coat of Many Colours: The Problematics in Qadiryar’. In: Pritam Singh and S. S. Thandi, eds *Punjabi Identity in a Global Context*. New Delhi: Oxford University Press, 1999, pp. 55–68.

Talbot, I., 1988. *Punjab and the Raj, 1849–1947*. Delhi: Manohar.

Talbot, I., 1991. ‘British Rule in the Punjab, 1849–1947’. *Journal of Imperial and Commonwealth History*, XIX(2), May, 203–221.

Talbot, I., 1994. ‘Khizr, the Unionist Party and the Struggle for a United Punjab: 1943–1947’. *Indo-British Review*, XXI(1), 73–88.

Tatla, D. S., 1999. *The Sikh Diaspora: The Search for Statehood*. London: University of London Press.

Tiwana, N., 1999. ‘Unionism in the British Punjab: A Personal Memoir’. In: Pritam Singh and S. S. Thandi, eds *Punjabi Identity in a Global Context*. New Delhi: Oxford University Press, 1999, pp. 253–256.

Todaro, M. P. and Smith, S. C., 2003. ‘The Economy of Nigeria: Case Study’. In: M. P. Todaro and S. C. Smith, *Economic Development*. 8th edition. London: Addison Wesley and Pearson.

Tully, M. and Jacob, S., 1985. *Amritsar: Mrs. Gandhi's last battle*. London: Pan Books.

Uberoi, J. P. S., 1980. ‘The Five Symbols of Sikhism’. In: L. M. Joshi, ed. *Sikhism*. Patiala: Punjabi University, 1980, pp. 131–146.

Uberoi, J. P. S., 1996. *Religion, Civil Society and the State: A Study of Sikhism*. Delhi: Oxford University Press.

Vakil, C. N., ed., 1973. *Industrial Development of India: Policy and Problems*. New Delhi: Orient Longman.

Verma, P. S., 1994. 'Power Elites and 1992 Punjab Vidhan Sabha Elections'. In: Gopal Singh, ed. *Punjab: Past, Present and Future*. Delhi: Ajanta, 1994, pp. 381–399.

Vithal, B. P. R., 1987. 'States' Plan Outlays and Resource Mobilisation: Criterion for Central Assistance'. In: I. S. Gulati, ed. *Centre-State Budgetary Transfers*. Delhi: Oxford University Press, 1987, pp. 224–235.

Vohra, R. N., 1978. 'Martyrdom of Guru Arjan Dev'. In: S. S. Bal, ed. *Proceedings of the Punjab History Conference Twelfth Session, March 17–19, 1978*. Patiala: Punjabi University, 1979, pp. 80–82.

Webster, John C. B., 1976. *The Christian Community and Change in Nineteenth Century North India*. Delhi: Macmillan.

Weiner, M., ed., 1968. *State Politics in India*. New Jersey: Princeton University Press.

Wheare, K. C., 1962. 'Federalism and the Making of Nations'. In: A. W. MacMahon, ed. *Federalism: Mature and Emergent*. New York: Russell & Russell, 1962, pp. 28–43.

Williamson, H. W., 2005. 'Coalition Agreement: Germany to Revamp Federal System'. *Financial Times*, 9 November.

Williamson, J. G., 1965. 'Regional Inequality and the Process of National Development: A Description of the Patterns'. *Economic Development and Cultural Change*, XIII(4), Part II, July, pp. 3–84.

Wylam, P. M., 1992. 'Duleep Singh Maharaja'. In: Harbans Singh, ed. *The Encyclopaedia of Sikhism*, Vol. 1. Patiala: Punjabi University, 1992, pp. 599–602.

Yong, T. T., 1994. 'Prelude to Partition: Sikh Responses to the Demand for Pakistan, 1940–1947'. *International Journal of Punjab Studies*, 1(2), 167–195.

INDEX